FORGOTTEN HEROES

GALWAY SOLDIERS
OF THE
GREAT WAR 1914–1918

FORGOTTEN HEROES

GALWAY SOLDIERS
OF THE
GREAT WAR 1914–1918

WILLIAM HENRY

MERCIER PRESS

WHAT YOU NEED TO READ

MERCIER PRESS
Douglas Village, Cork
www.mercierpress.ie

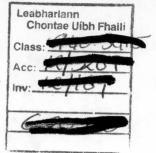

Trade enquiries to CMD Distribution
55A Spruce Avenue, Stillorgan Industrial Park, Blackrock County Dublin

© William Henry, 2007

ISBN: 978 1 85635 556 8

10 9 8 7 6 5 4 3 2 1

A CIP record for this title is available from the British Library

Mercier Press receives financial assistance from the Arts Council/
An Chomhairle Ealaíon

Printed and bound by J.H. Haynes & Co. Ltd, Sparkford.

IN MEMORY OF
ALL
GALWAYMEN WHO FOUGHT
IN THE
GREAT WAR

CONTENTS

ACKNOWLEDGEMENTS   9

FOREWORD   11

INTRODUCTION   13

WAR IN EUROPE   17

    BATTLELINES DEFINED   18
    ANSWER THE CALL   20
    CHRISTMAS 1914   23
    FIGHT TO A FINISH   25
    BROTHERS IN ARMS   27
    PEACE AND REMEMBRANCE   32

ARMY AND NAVY PROFILES   36

GALWAY ROLL OF HONOUR   69

GALWAY MEN'S S & B ASSOCIATION
NEW YORK AMERICAN ARMY BANNER LIST   229

NOTES   231

REFERENCES   238

BIBLIOGRAPHY   245

INDEX   247

ACKNOWLEDGEMENTS

Thanks to my wife Noreen, sons Patrick and David, and daughter Lisa. I wish to thank the following people for their generous support, providing very important information and photographs: Brian Walsh, Michael Conneely, Michael Lynskey, Francis Keaney, Helen Spelman, Gerry Carthy, Eamonn McNally, Heather & the late Stephen Smyth, Joe Loughnane, Padraic McCormack, Gerald Comber, John Jordan, Mary Walsh, Patsy and Rita O'Connor, Linda Finnerty, Maureen Annetts, Julie Somay, Tom Small, Frank Lally, Billy Lally, Tony & Margaret Carolan, Sales Langan, Thomas Lynch, Cathriona Conneely, Fr Michael O'Flaherty, Mary O'Shea, Nuala Nolan, John Lawless, P.J. O'Reilly, Tom McDonagh, Michael McDonagh, Doughlas Rafter, Pádraig Maloney, Oliver Maloney, Michael Joseph Gardiner, Mary McLoughlin, Bernard McLoughlin, Anne Everiss, Mike Everiss, Michael Coughlan, Mike Clancy, Frank Carney, Brian Fahy, Geraldine Raftery, Vincent Griffin, Mary Lambe, Mike Flynn, P.J. Summerly, Christopher O'Byrne, Seán Malone, Richard Connolly, Collette Heaney, the late Patrick Heaney, Valera Raftery, Martin Flaherty, Chris Costello, Mary Raftery, Edward Caulfield, Gabriel Fogerty, Richard Conneely, Paddy Monaghan, Pádraig Mannion, Dennis Kearney, Mary O'Connor, Paul O'Halloran, Jimmy Gillespie, Brian Ruffley, Maurice Lahlen, Joe Burgess, Seán McSweeney, Donal Quinn, Christy Craughwell, Maureen Parslow, Margaret 'Dillie' Thornton, Anne Campbell, John Connolly, Ultan Macken, Cathal Devlin, the late Bunny Devlin, Martin Devlin, Colman Shaughnessy, Pat Barrett, Frank Costello, Martin Lynskey, Michael Gannon, Paddy Curran, Anne Curran, Stephen Curran, Tom Riddle, Simon McKiernan, Mary Deely, Michael Deely, Peadar Houlighan, Gerard Kennedy, Heather Gardiner, Eugene Duggan, Marcella Jordan, Kathleen Berry, Colm McDonogh, Val Folan, Gerry Aagent, Paddy 'Moore' Flaherty, Mary Smith, Anne Walsh, Tom O'Donnell, Raymond Scully, Noel Carney, Pat Ward, Mary Molloy, Bridget O'Breen, Seán Ashe, Jimmy McElroy, Vivienne O'Connor, Leo

Larkin, Pat Sweeney, Edward 'Chick' Sweeney, Anna Cronin, Finbarr O'Shea, Thomas Feeney, Frank Feeney, Aidan O'Malley, Tony Finnerty, Dominick Kearney, Lieutenant Colonel R.J.S. Bullock-Webster, Bill & Alice Scanlan, Colm & Valerie Noonan, Paddy & Anne O'Flaherty, Damian Burke, Ronnie & Barbara Ward, Eamonn Carr, Cathy Rabbitt, Mary McGrath, Mary O'Sullivan, Pat Hughes, John Hughes, Mary Connelly, Olive Organ, Raymond Skully, Mary Molloy, Kathleen Villers-Tuthill, P.J. Fallon, Tommy Holohan, Tom Leonard, Johnny Murphy, Mickey & Marie Fitzgerald, John Kelly, John Farrell, Carmel King, Mary Duane, Patrick Howley, Treasa King, Ambrose Joyce. I am also very grateful for the generous support received from the Commonwealth Graves Commission and the Naval and Military Press Ltd.

A special thanks to the following; the staff of the James Hardiman Library, NUIG; Galway County Library, Island House; The National Library of Ireland, Dublin; Michael Faherty, Marie Boran, Michael O'Connor, Geraldine Curtain, Liam Frehan, Anne Mitchell, Maureen Moran. To all in the media who gave excellent publicity to this project: Brendan Carroll, Dave Hickey, Stan Shields, Joe O'Shaughnessy, Ronnie O'Gorman, Dickie Byrne, Eamonn Howley, Tom Kenny, Keith Finnegan, Jimmy Norman, Tom Gilmore, Jim Carney, Mary Conroy, Peadar O'Dowd and Des Kelly. Special thanks also to Kieran Hoare, Noreen Henry, James Casserly, Liam Curley, Marita Silke, Tim Collins, Colm Walsh, for proofreading my work and making many valuable suggestions. Bob Waller for his excellent work in reproducing photographs. Mary McDonnell for repairing photographs. Again I am deeply indebted to a very special friend, Jacqueline O'Brien, who has, as always, given so generously of her time, researching, proofreading and for her expert advice, encouragement and support throughout this project: *Mon plus grand accomplissment en litterature fut de trouver l'amitié, un support en toute occasion et une totale confiance d'une merveilleuse et sincére personne, Jackie.*

Permission to use the cover photograph was given by Mary McGrath.

FOREWORD

The Great War, etched as it is on the consciousness of many nations, was first and foremost a huge blood-letting. No other conflict has been so closely identified with loss of life among soldiers as the First World War. Thrown into unspeakable conditions in many arenas of conflict, into situations where all the trappings of martial glory which might sustain men-at-arms were stripped away, all that men were left with was personal courage and an unbreakable comradeship with their colleagues.

In his companion volume to this book, *Galway and the Great War*, William Henry has captured the public mood in Galway towards the Great War, as well as showing the changing attitudes towards the conflict as it dragged on. The unrelenting publicity juggernaut unleashed on Galway by the authorities to recruit as many men as possible into the armed forces is clearly outlined, and without doubt this had an effect on many people. Similarly, the sea-change caused – in the first instance – by the Dublin Insurrection of 1916 and later the highly politicised anti-conscription campaign of 1918 on Galway people's attitude towards the conflict are outlined in detail.

An understanding of the reasons why these men went to war when they did is important. There are a variety of reasons; the call of duty, the search for adventure, political idealism and economic necessity all played their part. The promise of devolved government through home rule, a promise later reneged on by the British government, should not be overlooked as an important factor. The revolution that occurred between 1913 and 1923 in a European context had an impact on the Galway area, mainly through the struggle for independence. This meant that many of these soldiers found themselves in a very different political climate when they returned from the front. Furthermore, the public commemoration of their sacrifice became highly politicised and identified with a unionist perspective. In the twenty-six counties in particular, their memory was maintained by their families and surviving comrades rather than through public commemoration as was done elsewhere. In a sense this book can be seen as a tribute to those family and comrades who kept their memory alive.

Drawing together a variety of printed and electronic sources, newspaper articles and archival material, as well as the input of many of the families and comrades of those who fell in the Great War, this work highlights the meticulous research of the author in drawing together the most comprehensive listing of war dead from the city and county of Galway. Almost every Galway family name can be found in this listing, and the numbers who enlisted abroad attest to the impact of emigration at the time. It is also sobering to see the names of those who are buried in Baghdad and Basra, places where soldiers are still dying today. Each profile, with the regiment, place of death, age, supplementary notes and place of remembrance, will be an invaluable record to genealogists and historians of the future. Furthermore, it is appropriate that the names of these brave soldiers and sailors be remembered in their home county.

After the vicissitudes and political wrangling over this conflict and its commemoration in the twentieth century, and the recent welcome moves by the Irish state to commemorate all Irish men and Irish women who fell in armed conflict, it is the courage and bravery of these men who fought for the freedom of small nations in the most horrendous of conditions which shows through in the end.

Kieran Hoare
2007

INTRODUCTION

This is my second book on the subject of the Great War of 1914–1918. The first book, *Galway and the Great War*, explained in detail the effects that the war had on Galway. It also explored the origins, and recorded the main battles of the war. Letters and interviews by Galway soldiers at the front were also included so these subjects will not be dealt with in any great detail in this book, but there is a brief outline of them to accompany the photographic profiles. This book, *Forgotten Heroes, Galway Soldiers of the Great War 1914-1918*, now completes a very important record of Galwaymen who fought and died in the war. However, the photographs and documents included are only a fraction of what has been lost or discarded over the years. The book also includes a roll of honour, i.e., a list of the Galway soldiers and sailors who were killed, or died from various causes while fighting during the Great War. The importance of recording such a list can be judged by the following letter to the *Galway Advertiser* by the late Margaret O'Sullivan some twenty years ago. It was published under the heading 'Not Only Two':

> Dear Editor – In reply to the letter in your Advertiser this week Still Older Galway, the gentleman referred to his two brothers going off to the Battlefields of France, to fight for the Freedom of small nations. He stated that they were the only two from the city that never returned. My brother John Walsh, The Tramyard, Forster Street, never returned either. I have in my family the King George medal, rewarded posthumously, to my mother, also three other medals for bravery. He was blown to bits on the field and never laid to rest. R.I.P. – Sincerely, Mrs. Margaret O'Sullivan, 3 Corrib Park, Newcastle.

This was in reply to a previous letter, indicating that only two Galwaymen had been killed in the Great War. Margaret's brother was killed at the third battle of Ypres (Passchendaele). This, along with additional information uncovered, suggested that other Galwaymen must have been killed and overlooked. When contact was made with the Commonwealth

War Graves Commission, it became obvious that hundreds of men from Galway city and county had lost their lives in the Great War. This immediately triggered an investigation of other official military records. The next area of investigation was the contemporary newspapers, and so, *The Connacht Tribune, The Galway Express, The Tuam Herald* and the *East Galway Democrat* were then explored for the years between 1914 and 1918. This painstaking research was carried out with the immense support and help of Jacqueline O'Brien, and took some three years to complete. Appeals were also made through the media for members of the public to come forward with any personal documents and uniformed photographs of family members who had fought in the war.

It is important at this stage to explain how the roll of honour was compiled. Four main sources were explored when compiling this list of Great War dead: the records of the Commonwealth War Graves Commission; *Soldiers Died in the Great War* CD by the Naval and Military Press Ltd; *Ireland's Memorial Records 1914–1918* and, as already mentioned, the contemporary newspapers. Additional sources included personal family documents, interviews, attestation papers and personal lists of soldiers and sailors killed donated by other sources of research. In a number of cases, there are differences recorded between the main sources, such as the ages of soldiers killed, dates they were killed, battalions to which they were attached, how they died, and home addresses. Even the spelling of some names and addresses are recorded differently. I have used the Commonwealth War Graves Commission records as the base on which to build the roll of honour as they contain the most comprehensive information regarding the soldiers' personal details. To overcome the differences between the records and to try and ensure that none of the records was ignored, all the information that was available is included as follows: there the age of a soldier is recorded differently, then both ages are recorded, such as: Age 21 or 28; where battalions differ, both are recorded as: First & Third; Killed in Action or Died of Wounds are recorded where these differ, and Death is recorded where it is unknown how a person died; where the address differs, one is recorded in brackets. The term

Co. Galway is not included in the address for soldiers who were from around the county; the address is given, i.e. Born Kilclooney, Ballinasloe. However, in the city the full address is recorded, i.e. Born Bohermore, Galway. Where France or Flanders is recorded, it simply means the theatres of war in which they fought, because the actual location of their death was not recorded in the documents explored. Where the regiment is unknown, British Expeditionary Force is recorded. Where no actual date was available, 1914–1918 is recorded. There are obvious mis-spellings of names and addresses recorded, but these are taken directly from the military records and therefore cannot be altered. There were some civilians recorded by the Commonwealth War Graves Commission, and they are also included in this list. From the dates recorded, soldiers continued to die from wounds after the war and it is also obvious that others were victims of the influenza pandemic, which broke out in 1918. It has been estimated that it caused the deaths of some twenty to forty million people worldwide; some put the figure even higher. It is often referred to as Spanish Flu, and sometimes 'trench fever', because it was believed to have originated among the soldiers in hospital camps on the western front.

Because the list is in alphabetical order, the names and addresses of those killed are not included in the index. The same applies to the photographic profiles as they also follow an alphabetical sequence. The information included with some of the photographic profiles is very sketchy and is based mainly on personal family documents and interviews. The rank held by an individual upon discharge is the one recorded for these profiles. Although the age recorded for some recruits may seem young, this is not unusual as it was quite common for young men to falsify their age to enlist in the military. The list of soldiers who died is not definitive as the complete death toll for Galway, and indeed Ireland, during the Great War may never be accurately known.

One major problem that surfaced during the research was that the nationality of many soldiers was recorded as United Kingdom. Because of this I had to rely on definite information from family members to identify some of these men as Galway soldiers. Another problem arose because

Ireland's Memorial Records 1914–1918 does not record the cemeteries or memorials associated with each soldier. Nevertheless, I was able to identify many of these cemeteries and memorials using the military numbers of the soldiers and sailors when exploring the Commonwealth War Graves Commission records. This situation poses the question: how many more Irish soldiers are simply recorded as United Kingdom? Another area explored were two rolls of honour in Ballinasloe, a short one in St John's church and a rather long one held in a local hall near St Grennan's Terrace. Veterans of the war compiled the second one sometime during the 1920s or 1930s to commemorate their fallen comrades from Ballinasloe. This list only recorded the rank and names of the soldiers killed. It became clear during the research that some of these men were not born in Co. Galway, and therefore they are not included in the list of dead.

This is the most complete record of Great War dead compiled for Galway to date, and because of time constraints with this publication it was deemed necessary to draw it to a close. Nevertheless, any additional information and photographs would be extremely welcome and will be included in an ongoing roll of honour and any future publication. The roll of honour concludes with a separate list of American soldiers, who were of Galway origin, and who lost their lives in the Great War. They were recorded on a banner that was later presented to the Renmore barracks museum by the Galway Men's S & B Association New York.

William Henry
2007

WAR IN EUROPE

Following the assassination of Archduke Franz Ferdinand and his wife Sophie on 28 June 1914 in Sarajevo, a wave of anticipation swept across Europe. Although many expected serious repercussions, even the most exaggerated cynical 'scare mongering' could not have foretold the catastrophe that was about to befall the continent. Old alliances and treaties were immediately reinforced by the opposing powers. Although sparked by this assassination, the origins of the Great War had its roots deep in an arms race and feelings of distrust, which had engulfed Europe for over twenty years. The central powers consisted of Austria–Hungary and Germany, and because of their geographic location they could mobilise troops and supplies quickly to the frontlines. This was vital to protect themselves against the triple alliance of the major powers of Great Britain, France and Russia. Belgium and Serbia were also involved from the beginning. The allies' largest army, Russia, was cut off by geography from Britain and France, which meant that the royal navy would have to supply Russia by sea. Once the armies mobilised, Europe was plunged into the most horrific conflict that the world had ever witnessed, causing the deaths of over 8,300,000 servicemen.[1]

Although the Russian army was poorly equipped, and all of its land supply routes were cut off, it was nonetheless quick to mobilise and committed to having 800,000 troops poised on the German border should war break out with France. This did not deter Germany, who had its 'Schlieffen Plan' already formulated, and it committed seven-eighths of its troops to the western front. The idea was to defeat France in six weeks, and then turn their attention on Russia and defeat them at their ease. With this in mind the German armies swept across Belgium and into France. The French plan for war was essentially a defensive one, as they did not believe that the Anglo-French-Prussia treaty of 1839 would be broken. This treaty guaranteed Belgian neutrality, and would oblige the British to send an expeditionary force to support France if this agreement was broken.[2]

On 4 August 1914, Britain declared war on Germany, and thus, Ireland was drawn into the conflict. Although most Irish people supported Britain, Ireland was nonetheless struggling to achieve home rule, which would give it some degree of independence. The leader of the Irish Nationalist Party, John Redmond, pledged the support of the Irish Volunteers, which was at the time an extremely large nationalist military organisation. Home rule was deferred until the war was over. This was acceptable to the vast majority of nationalists, and most of them were quite prepared to fight the Germans in Europe on the understanding that this would be Ireland's 'ticket' to home rule. The suspension of home rule caused a split among the Irish Volunteers, as there was growing concern and suspicion among many Irishmen that the bill might never be implemented because of strong opposition by Ulster unionists. However, the vast majority of Irishmen enlisted following Redmond's appeal for troops to go to France. On 12 August 1914, the British Expeditionary Force began embarking for mainland Europe; thousands of troops, animals and equipment were on the way to the front. The troops were under the command of Field-Marshal Sir John French, a veteran of the second South African War 1899–1902. Many on both sides believed that the war would be over by Christmas 1914. However, it would prove a long and bitter conflict, with the slaughter of men on a scale the likes of which had never been witnessed before. Turkey and Bulgaria allied themselves with Germany, and as the war progressed other countries joined on the side of the allies.[3]

BATTLELINES DEFINED

The German armies marched into Belgium on 4 August 1914 and moved quickly across the country until they reached Mons, where they met with strong opposition from the British Expeditionary Force. The British took up positions between the Belgian towns of Mons and Conde where they hoped to stop the Germans from sweeping into northern France. On the morning of 23 August, German field guns began to pound the British lines and the allies got their first taste of exploding shrapnel, while German bullets were trained on all allied positions. The attack forced the French, who were supporting the British flank, to withdraw. The German commander, Alexander von Kluck, had about 160,000 troops engaged in the attack, but the British held their ground, assuming that the French would regroup and rejoin the action. However, by the following day, it was clear that the British were alone, and so a retreat was ordered. The Connaught Rangers took up the rearguard action and suffered many casualties during the initial retreat. By that afternoon, the First Irish Guards and First Grenadier Guards took over the responsibility of covering the retreat. During the rearguard action, Irish Guards officer, Lieutenant Colonel George Morris from Spiddal was killed in the Villers Cotteret area while giving encouragement to his men.

Time was not on their side and in blazing sunshine the retreating troops made their way along the dusty road towards Paris, continually harassed by the enemy. Some fourteen miles from Paris the German advance halted; they were now far from their homeland and because of their swift progress, their supply lines were fully stretched. This gave sufficient time for the British and the Fifth French Army to regroup and exploit a gap, which had appeared between the German forces. On 5 September the two sides tested each other again at the River Marne, resulting in a German retreat. The retreat continued until 12 September when the Germans halted behind the River Aisne, and there they utilised their already prepared line of entrenched positions.[4]

It was at the River Aisne that the first of three battles took place for control of this area. The German entrenchments located north of the river were supported by artillery. With the Germans firmly dug in, and not prepared to relinquish any more ground, the allies had little choice but to attack. They crossed the river in the Soissons area, but came under heavy artillery fire as they advanced up the wooded slopes on the far side. The allied commanders began to realise that this was more than a rearguard action, and that the Germans were well prepared to meet any attack. The Germans had constructed a series of elaborate trench systems, capable of housing men and equipment. The British also dug in and, like the enemy, built second and third line trenches connected by communication trenches. For the troops, Christmas and home now seemed very far away as both sides settled down to trench warfare.

Life in the trenches was often miserable for the men as rain sometimes filled the dugouts with water, creating terrible muddy conditions. Swarming rats added to the problems. Most of the fighting took place along the western front, which ran for about 600 miles, from the English Channel to the border of Switzerland. This front had been established by Christmas 1914, because both sides had become embroiled in what became known as the 'race to the sea' in an attempt to out-flank each other. Along this front soldiers faced each other across treacherous barbed wire fences and the almost certain death of 'no-mans-land'. The eastern front extended from Riga on the Baltic Sea to the shores of the Black Sea, and a line from Switzerland along the Italian frontier to Trieste signified the southern battlefront. Other theatres of war included the Balkans, Mesopotamia, Egypt, Palestine, Africa, Asia, the Pacific Ocean and, of course, the infamous Gallipoli.[5]

ANSWER THE CALL

On 4 August 1914, Lieutenant Colonel Henry Francis Jourdain, commander of the Connaught Rangers in Renmore barracks, Galway received his mobilisation orders. These orders changed the lives of thousands of families throughout the province, as urgent appeals for recruits were sent out. This call to arms was answered most generously, as young men began arriving at Renmore barracks from all over Connacht. Temporary military camps were set up outside the barracks to cater for the young soldiers as they prepared to set off on this 'great adventure'. By Christmas 1914, many homes in Galway were affected by the loss of young family members. The early months of 1915 showed no sign of an end to the conflict, rather the opposite, and major recruiting drives were required to feed the blood-letting taking place across the battlefronts.[6]

The young male population of the city, particularly the Claddagh, was devastated in the early stages, with over 700 men going off to war. Because many of the Claddagh men were already experienced seamen, most of them joined the navy. Members of Galway Urban Council took an active part in encouraging men to join the army and set up the Galway Recruiting Committee in June 1915. It concentrated much of its efforts throughout the county: local authorities and councillors from the various population centres, such as Loughrea, Ballinasloe, Moylough, Mountbellew, Tuam, Clifden, Oughterard, Moycullen, Williamstown and many other areas were contacted and encouraged to form their own sub-committees to support the recruiting drives. As the war progressed, the methods used to encourage young men to join the colours became more and more cunning. There was great enthusiasm for war in the initial stages, and the idea of going overseas to defend the unfortunate people of Belgium certainly appealed to many, particularly when they were told of the atrocities being committed by the German 'beasts'.

Many more joined believing that home rule for Ireland would be achieved on the battlegrounds of Europe, and the authorities made many idle promises regarding this issue. Employment was also a major factor, and assurances of families being 'looked after' if soldiers were killed or wounded also increased numbers. Newspaper advertisements, articles and letters glorifying, exploiting and embellishing heroic deeds of valour were published regularly. The recruiting meetings introduced various groups, both military and civilian, who used every method at their disposal to reach the audience, arriving as they did accompanied by colourful military bands. People were warned that they would lose their homes and all financial stability. Worse still was the threat of family members being raped and killed once the German armies arrived on Irish shores. In some cases bishops and priests preached from the pulpits in favour of the 'just war' for civilisation. The pressure on young men was tremendous, and even girlfriends and wives were requested to use their influence to encourage their men to join the army. Groups of young men were also targeted through sporting clubs, choirs, etc. and were encouraged to join on the guarantee that they would serve together. The threat of conscription loomed continually, and was used to intimidate people throughout the war years. If all of this failed, then 'white feather' tactics were always an option, as those who remained at home were often subjected to being called a coward.[7]

While at home, most young men were joining Irish regiments, such as the Connaught Rangers, Royal Dublin Fusiliers, Royal Munster Fusiliers, Leinster Regiment, South Irish Horse, Royal Irish Rifles and Fusiliers, Irishmen abroad, and those of Irish parents, were enlisting in regiments such as the London Irish, Manchester Irish, Liverpool Irish, Tyneside Irish and the Irish Guards. They were also enlisting in Scottish regiments, and many Irish names turn up in the records of the Black Watch and Seaforth Highlanders. Irishmen were also well represented in the Canadian, Australian and New Zealand armies, and later the US army.[8]

Meanwhile, at home various fundraising and support organisations sprang up to support the troops in the field and of course their families. They included the Connaught Rangers Comfort Fund; the Connaught War Relief Fund; County Galway War Fund Association; Soldiers and Sailors Comfort Fund and the County of Galway Naval and Military War Fund. The aim of these associations was to raise the much-needed finance to supply various articles of clothing, books, games, cigarettes, etc., to the troops. Finance was raised through fundraising events and sponsorship of one type or another and support continued for the duration of the war. This work was mainly carried out by the women of Galway, who were also taking up positions in the workplace because of the reduced male population of the city. The war industry in Galway grew with large orders for uniforms placed at the Galway Woollen Mills at Newtownsmith. The Galway Munitions Factory also gave employment when it opened on Earl's Island in 1917.[9]

CHRISTMAS 1914

The first Battle of Ypres began on 20 October 1914, and over the following four years this much fought over Belgian town witnessed all the horrors of war. Because of its strategic location, it was vital to both sides. By the time the war ended, the battlegrounds of Ypres were saturated with the blood of hundreds of thousands of soldiers. German shelling reduced the town to rubble and appalling weather conditions added to the misery for the troops. The first battle ended in late November, by which time both sides had suffered some 150,000 casualties each, among them many Irishmen. The Second Connaught Rangers had lost so many men that it could no longer be considered a unit and the survivors had to be amalgamated with the first battalion. Over the following years, the bodily remains of thousands of men were never found, having been blown into oblivion. The only testament to their existence are their names recorded on the Menin Gate Memorial, Ypres, Tyne Cot Cemetery and many other war memorials.[10]

As Christmas 1914 loomed, the men were fully aware that they would not be home for the festive season, and letters and parcels from home were a welcome addition to the repetitive daily rations. Even in the trenches the spirit of goodwill shone through as darkness fell on Christmas Eve. That night, a unique event unfolded along various sections of the western front. It seems that the Germans lit up some of their trenches and the British began calling out greetings to them. In one sector, someone shouted 'no shooting' and a number of British troops sat up on the parapet of their trench. Soon the Germans did the same and both sides began speaking to each other, those who could manage to communicate. One British officer asked the Germans to sing the folksong *Volkslied*, which they did. He then asked them to sing something from Schumann and one of them sang *The Two Grenadiers*. With trust building on both sides, two British soldiers walked across 'no-mans-land' and greeted the German troops. The British and German officers in this section agreed that there would be a truce until midnight on Christmas night. They also agreed to give enough time to bury the dead. In another section, British soldiers heard the Germans singing *Silent Night* and they also began to sing. The guns did remain silent on Christmas Day and German soldiers crossed over to the British lines and talked, and in some cases exchanged gifts of food and personal items. At one location, German and British soldiers began playing football. The spirit of Christmas continued throughout the day, much to the annoyance and irritation of the British high command. As a result a number of British officers were reprimanded. Such an event never took place again throughout either of the world wars.[11]

On 10 March 1915 the British successfully bombarded and attacked the German positions at Neuve Chapelle, some twenty miles south of Ypres. However, they failed to capitalise on this surprise attack and by the end of the offensive were nearly pushed back to their original positions. The bloodshed continued between April and May of 1915 with the second battle at Ypres. Following two days of bombardment by the Germans, the shelling stopped, lulling the British into a false sense of security. However, a more sinister weapon was released and was carried on a slight breeze towards the allied lines. This new weapon of human destruction brought with it excruciating death in the form of poisonous gas. Among its victims was Private John Condon from Waterford, the youngest combatant of the Great War. He was just thirteen years and eleven months when he died huddled in his trench. On 25 September 1915, the British and French forces attempted to regain the mining district around the towns of Loos and Len, and so began the battle of Loos. It was here that the British attempted to use gas as a weapon, but the direction of the wind shifted and the gas attack had to be aborted. During the initial infantry assault, the British lost over 8,000 men, either killed or wounded. The offensive continued into October, by which time they had suffered some 60,000 casualties and again had gained little ground.[12]

While the death toll continued to mount in Europe, the Gallipoli landings in April 1915 also witnessed some savage fighting. As in Europe, both sides suffered horrendous casualties and over the following weeks many more young men suffered in this futile effort to secure the peninsula. The fighting continued in this theatre of war until the autumn of 1915, by which time it had become apparent that the allies would not be successful in forcing the Turks out of their positions. Many of the allied troops were then deployed to Salonika, while others were sent to Mesopotamia and Palestine. Over time these areas of war also saw some bitter fighting and many Irish names are recorded in the cemeteries of Basra, Amara and other such burial grounds.[13]

FIGHT TO A FINISH

During the early months of 1916, battleships of the German High Seas Fleet shelled towns on the English coast. This resulted in the British Grand Fleet, under the command of Admiral Sir John Jelliceo, being put to sea. When both sides met on 31 May, the battle of Jutland, the biggest sea battle of the First World War, began. On board the British battleships the Claddagh village was well represented and a number of its sons are named among the casualties. Although the outcome of the battle favoured the British, they had suffered huge losses with the HMS *Indefatigable*, *Queen Mary*, *Black Prince*, *Defence* and *Invincible* going to the bottom of the sea, taking with them thousands of sailors. The HMS *Tiger*, *Warrior*, *Warspite* and *Princess Royal*, and Admiral David Betty's flagship HMS *Lion*, were also damaged. Despite these losses the British controlled the sea for the remainder of the war.[14]

Just over a month later, on the morning of 1 July 1916, the British officers on the Somme sounded their whistles, and led their men into the most infamous day of the Great War and indeed British military history. Before sunset they had sustained over 60,000 causalities. Although they had bombarded German positions during the week before the battle, firing over a million shells, it had little affect, other than serve as a warning of an impending infantry assault. The German machine guns inflicted horrendous causalities all along the twenty-five mile front. In some areas battalions ceased to exist as wave after wave of troops were sent across the hellish abode of 'no-mans-land'. Sadly, no lessons had been learned from Loos the previous year. The offensive continued throughout the summer and on 3 September the Sixteenth Irish Division was sent into action in a huge assault on the village of Guillemont. Six days later, they were ordered to attack Ginchy. Both assaults were successful, but many more Irishmen fell in these attacks. The battle of the Somme finally concluded in mid-November, when severe weather conditions forced an end to the carnage. One young Irishmen who was killed during the Somme offensive was Private Patrick Larkin of the Irish Guards. Two letters from him were included in *Galway and the Great War*, p. 229, 230. A third letter has since been uncovered; the following is an extract indicating the serious concerns about the loss of life among the troops:

> It's not really known when the war will be over but if it lasts another year or two all the young and good blood in Europe will be cut to ...

The remainder of the letter is missing, but the word 'pieces' comes to mind. As with many of the battles on the western front, little was achieved in terms of military objectives, but enormous loss of life was sustained. The Thiepval Memorial on the Somme records the names of over 72,000 soldiers whose remains were never found.[15]

The following year, the third battle of Ypres, or Passchendaele as it is also known, took place between July and November 1917. It was an allied offensive and was an attempt to capture the Belgian ports held by the Germans. It was fought in the appalling conditions of driving rain and water-logged trenches. As at the Somme a year earlier, the battle continued until November when, again, weather conditions forced an end to the madness, with little ground gained by the allies. Meanwhile, in France, the first battle of Cambrai was fought, with its objective being to break through one section of the formidable Hindenburg Line. Similar to all the Great War battles, the allies opened with a heavy artillery barrage. This was followed by an attack of massed tanks, supported by infantry. Although the attack gained initial success, the Germans again demonstrated their ability to mount a fearsome counter-attack, pushing the British back more to their original starting lines. This fruitless attack cost the lives of some 40,000 men on both sides.

The beginning of the end for the Germans came almost a year later with the second battle of Cambrai, fought between September and October 1918. By 8 October the allies had encircled Cambrai on the southern side and pounded the town with an artillery barrage. Allied tanks then advanced on the town, and were followed by an infantry assault. They also penetrated the Hindenburg Line despite the best efforts of its machine gunners. A short time later the German army was on the way home, many of them disappointed and dejected. All the guns fell silent when hostilities ceased at 11 a.m. on 11 November 1918 following the signing of the armistice earlier that morning.[16]

BROTHERS IN ARMS

The recruiting drives were extremely successful in targeting large families and many sets of brothers joined. In Galway city, four Macken brothers from Eyre Street and four McGowen brothers from Prospect Hill (neighbours) enlisted. In the Claddagh, four Oliver, Flaherty and O'Flaherty brothers joined the colours. In Loughrea, the O'Shaughnessy brothers, Martin, Tommy, William and Jimmy, all joined the Connaught Rangers on the same day, and luckily all of them survived. There are many more examples throughout the city and county, and many remain unknown because they were forgotten over the passage of time. According to a letter received during the research for this book, five Cody brothers from Cloonavadogne, near Turloughmore, were killed in the war. A booklet published in Tuam in 1970 stated that a McCaffrey family, a father and four sons, went off to war and none of them returned.[17]

Some members of the prominent families in the town also left for war, among them the postmaster, W.G. Todd, Captain Mahon of Nile

Lodge and the governor of Galway jail. According to some newspaper reports, there were also records created in Galway. Major Frank Glynn from Tuam became the youngest man in the British army at the time to hold that rank, while the oldest lieutenant was fifty-four-year-old Fred Poyser, a former master of the Galway hounds. However, the military authorities have not confirmed these records. Galway also produced some fine airmen, including Major Robert Gregory of Coole Park, son of Lady Gregory. His details are included in the list of the dead. Flight Lieutenant E.C. Kelly from Ballinasloe transferred from the Connaught Rangers to the Royal Flying Corps. He was wounded and 'mentioned in despatches' in June 1916. Major T. Falcon Hazell shot down twenty-seven enemy aircraft; three of them in one aerial fight alone. He was awarded the military cross, distinguished flying cross with bar and distinguished service order. Squadron Commander, Major William Grattan-Bellew from Mountbellew was also an excellent pilot. He first served with the Connaught Rangers, before transferring over to the Royal Flying Corps. Before leaving for the front on 22 April 1915, he was presented with a sword by the people of Mountbellew in the local town hall. He won the military cross and was 'mentioned in despatches'. He was killed on 24 March 1917.[18]

No account of Galway military families could be complete without discussing the Furey brothers from Loughrea. Although many military records have been explored, they have not yielded definite evidence to substantiate this story. However, there is other evidence available that cannot be ignored which indicates that this family contributed, and suffered, more than most in the horror of the Great War. Under the heading 'A Brave Galway Family, A Loughrea Batch of Heroes', *The Tuam Herald* of 28 August 1915 published a shocking account of ten brothers from Loughrea who enlisted for service at the front. At the time, it was reported that five of them had already been killed. According to the newspaper article, a similar report had been published previously in the *Daily News* and the *Leader* by J. Doughlas. The reporter stated that the story was being recorded so that every man, woman and child in the empire would be able to admire the matchless self-sacrifice and duty done by 'humble souls'. He also stated that it was published to ensure that King George V would be aware of their sacrifice and to have them honoured among the great soldiers of the empire. They were the children of William and Mary Furey. William was from Tynagh and had served in the Connaught Rangers for twenty-one years. He died in 1903. Mary was a member of the Ward family from Ballinasloe. She was seventeen years old when she married William Furey in Ballinasloe on 11 October 1873. According to documents relating to the family there were also three daughters, Bridget, Elizabeth and Catherine. The report described Mary Furey as a mourning widow whose image should be 'chiselled in marble like the mourning widows of the great Serbian sculptor, Mestrovic'. However, she was a quiet, reserved lady who did not wish to have the story of her sons made public. Nevertheless, the reporter felt that it was too tragic and courageous to be ignored, so he published the story and included an apology to her for doing so.[19]

It was while recovering from wounds in Kinsale that her son, John informed J. Doughlas of the fate of his brothers. His commanding officer, Colonel Lewin, DSO, had encouraged him to talk to the reporter. According to John, all of them were mobilised together in August 1914 and five of them had already been killed somewhere in Flanders or France. He also stated that his mother was dreading the first anniversary of the war and that it was his wish to be with her on that day. John's statement that five of his brothers had been killed was confirmed almost two years later in *The Tuam Herald* of 30 June 1917. This report stated: 'From wounds received in action, William Furey (Inniskillings), a native of Loughrea, died in Derry. There were eight brothers in the Army, six of them have now fallen, leaving a widowed mother, but leaving Loughrea an imperishable record of courage and loyalty.' According to the first report, the brothers who lost their lives included *Malachy*, killed in action at Ypres on 7 April 1915, *Martin Francis, Willie, Henry and Willie John*, all Connaught Rangers. The surviving brothers included *Michael* and *Edward*, both Royal Irish Rifles (the latter was wounded at Mons), *Martin, John* and *Thomas* (the latter was captured at Mons). The last three were reported as Connaught Rangers. One immediate problem with the reports is that three brothers had or were called by the same name – Willie, Willie John, William. This is extremely unlikely, but it is also unlikely that their brother would have been inaccurate when naming his own brothers. Or did the reporter simply record the names inaccurately? Nevertheless, if both newspaper accounts are accurate, then this means that six brothers were killed. The state birth records give a number of home addresses for the family in Loughrea, with The Hill being the main location. Bride Street is another address recorded for this family. Another soldier, Private Alick Furey 4240, of the First Connaught Rangers, is recorded by the Commonwealth War Graves Commission as being killed in action on 7 April 1915. He was eighteen years of age and was the son of William and Mary Furey of Bride Street, Loughrea. His death is recorded for the same date that Malachy Furey was reported killed. Given that the names of the parents and the address are the same, is this the same man, with the name recorded inaccurately, or was he a seventh brother to be killed? The following poem was composed in memory of these brothers by Eamonn McNally from Loughrea:

THE FINAL BELL

The hammering sounds of the tinsmith's last, the bantam crows at will.
The piebald pony prances, on the rocky stony hill.
The fiery headed youngsters, who raced around boreen come.
And the women who stood at the doorways, when the final bell was rung.

The flashing light on bayonets, that jerks the youthful mind
The love of an adventure, and the loved ones left behind
Like bluebells on the lakeshore, on that April sunny day
The young enlisted foolish left, to give their lives away.

All the Fureys have enlisted, they have answered to the call
They will fight for king and country, in the nineteen fourteen brawl
Their widowed mother stood beside them, as they line up from the crowd
Somehow through her sadness, she felt, their father would have been proud.

There was John, and Tom, and Mikie, and their brother Willie John
And young Edward who got accepted, when he put his long trousers on.
Their mother was there weeping as they marched down to the glen
The Fureys have enlisted, her little boys are fighting men.

The marching sounds from soldiers' boots, as they set along the way
Down Barrack Street and cross west-bridge, to the outskirts of Loughrea
The sun was shining in their face, the drum was beating loud
They'll fight for king and country, it would make their old man proud.

Tomorrow all the rabbits, can rest on Knock Ash Hill
The half bred one-eyed greyhound, has preformed his final kill
And the half stripped naked fighters, who fought like the great John L
They're all memories now, of life that was then, before that final bell.

One would think that such a tragedy occurring in one family would be well known, and equally well recorded. If it is true, then why was the story ignored for so many years? Perhaps the answer is similar to other soldiers of the Great War; their sacrifice was not recognised because of the change in public opinion following the 1916 Rebellion and the War of Independence, and for the Furey brothers there could also have been an added degree of prejudice as they were members of the travelling community. Many travellers did enlist for service in the Great War, and several of them were killed. It is no surprise that the contribution and sacrifice made by these men was forgotten. One well-known member of this community who survived the war was Martin Ward from Ballinasloe. When he enlisted in Ballinasloe, he boasted that he was the best 'scrapper' in Ireland. In an interview many years later, he said that his proudest moment was when he marched into the Rhineland in 1918, happy in the knowledge that the people of Belgium were free again; the recruiting officers had certainly done their job well. After the war he was honourably discharged from the army, and returned to travelling the roads of Connacht where he plied his trade as a tinsmith. When he passed away in 1951, it was reported that this man was born on the side of the road, had lived all his life on the road, except for the four years he spent in the trenches of the western front, and eventually he died on the side of the road. During an interview carried out some years ago, a former military man mentioned that Irish travellers were a welcome addition to the British army during the First World War. He said that some British officers were delighted to have these people serve under them as they could suffer the hardships of trench life without much complaining.[20]

PEACE AND REMEMBRANCE

News of the armistice was welcomed in Galway, as it was elsewhere. Celebrations followed, and mothers could relax in the knowledge that their sons would not end up as 'cannon fodder' on the western front. From the beginning there had been some opposition to the war by Irish nationalists. But the vast majority of people had supported the war, as can be seen by the sheer numbers of men who enlisted. As the war progressed, there was a shift in attitudes by many Irish people and this became very apparent in the years following the 1916 Rebellion. Failure to implement home rule and the death toll on the western front also contributed to the disappointment and betrayal felt by the soldiers and their families. Sinn Féin defeated the Irish Nationalist Party in 1918 and the wheels were set in motion for an independent Ireland. However, this was only achieved by a bitter war of independence, which was followed by an even more bitter civil war.[21]

The Irish presence on the battlefields of Europe during the Great War was considerable. The cemeteries and memorials bear testament to the courage of these Irishmen. The sheer numbers involved is staggering; the list of the dead which follows is just one county's contribution in lives and makes one wonder how many actually enlisted, considering the death toll. It is estimated that some 49,400 Irishmen never returned, among them at least 1,107 Galwaymen. It has been suggested that one in every ten soldiers in the Great War became a casualty. This would suggest that Ireland's contribution in men was far greater than the numbers generally accepted. Given the numbers involved, it seems incredible that these men were, in a sense, forced to deny, or at least not advertise, the fact that they had fought in the war. When these men marched off to war, they were accompanied by cheering crowds, marching bands and the promise of a glorious heroic welcome when they returned home. However, times had changed dramatically and they were eclipsed by the new political climate which had emerged in Ireland. Because of this, the men of the Great War were ignored and forgotten.[22]

Thankfully there is a new emergence of pride in the people who risked everything and gave their lives on the slaughtering grounds of Europe, in the belief that it was for the greater good of civilisation. During an interview with a woman whose father had fought in the Great War, she said that he was bitterly disappointed in the attitude of many of his own countrymen in the years following the war. He once said to her that, had he died on the 'fields of Flanders or the Somme', he would have been as good an Irishman as those who died in the 1916 Rebellion. His statement reflects the feelings of thousands of Irishmen who believed that the defeat of Germany would secure home rule for Ireland, which would have been acceptable to many people at the time. The ninetieth anniversary of the 1916 Easter Rebellion was commemorated with a huge military parade and fly-over of Irish warplanes. It was celebrated with pride in the Irishmen who, against overwhelming odds, faced the might of the British empire for one bloody week in Dublin. Their sacrifice should never be forgotten, but neither should their brothers who fought in the killing fields of Europe and elsewhere. The change in opinion and attitudes towards these men was demonstrated at government level on 1 July 2006, when the Irishmen who lost their lives at the Somme ninety years earlier were remembered in Dublin. It was with pride and honour that President Mary McAleese and members of the Irish government, led by *An Taoiseach* Bertie Ahern, recognised the sacrifice and contribution made by Irishmen in the First World War. This remembrance continued on 9 September 2006, when the people of the French villages of Guillemont and Ginchy also remembered the Irish who died liberating their villages on 3 and 8 September 1916.

A reception and commemoration ceremony took place over two days, with wreaths being laid by representatives of various organisations and individuals, among them members of the combined Irish regiments association. The London Irish Rifles pipe band and colour parties led the parade of the combined Irish regiments association as they marched through both villages and assembled at the churches for the ceremonies. Two statues of St Patrick were presented, one to each of the village churches. In the 'field of the fallen', located between the two villages, 1,100 poppy crosses were planted in memory of the Irishmen who were killed in the battles. Their names were also read out in Guillemont, close to a German underground bunker which they had attacked and over-run ninety years earlier. After each name was read out, the words 'Died in the Field of Honour' were recited by all those present. It was a haunting experience to visit the bunker and see old bottles, half-burnt candles and rusted rounds of ammunition strewn about in this 'silent tomb'. In many ways, the soldiers of the Great War were victims of their time, cursed by the date of their own birth, and destined to be sacrificed in the most appalling war yet waged on mankind. It was a tragedy that should never be forgotten. I composed the following poem in memory of the Galwaymen who fell in the Great War:[23]

REMEMBER

In days long past; a whistle blast sent men out to their doom,
The thunderous roar of heavy guns was the last sound that they knew,
Now the battlefields lie silent; and there are no soldiers there;
The stench of death and gas no longer fills the air.
The slaughter of the innocents across this muddy 'no-mans-land'
Replaced by fields of wheat and maze; with bird songs close at hand.

An eerie silence steals across those once such bloody plains;
Where broken-hearted mothers paid tribute to their slain.
The hopes of these young Irishmen whose hearts were turned to clay;
Twas theirs to know the price of war, and there they had to pay.

They lay upon the place they fell, those blessed to have a grave,
For thousands more there is just the memory of a soldier's name;
Recorded on the monuments across the battle plains;
Are those who fell without the honour of a shallow grave.

Today the pleasant sunshine brings brightness to a place;
Where thousands died 'mid darkness of smoking guns insane.
The cemeteries and monuments now dot the western front;
With many more in Gallipoli; and Palestine and Kut.

Remember them forever; it's the least that we might do;
For this lost generation bore horrors known to few.
The time has come to honour them in a most appropriate way;
To carve their memory on Irish stone; so far from where they lay.

ARMY AND NAVY PROFILES

ABLE SEAMAN DOMINIC BURKE

Born on 5 August 1894, the son of Joe & Bridget Burke, he joined the navy and one of the first ships on which he served was the RMS *Alaunia*. He also served on the RMS *Carpathia*, the ship that went to the rescue of the *Titanic* victims in April 1912. In September 1915, he enlisted for service on the passenger ship SS *Transylvania*; it was later converted into a troopship, capable of carrying 3,000 men. On 4 May 1917, the German submarine, *U-63*, fired a torpedo which struck the *Transylvania* in the port engine room. The badly damaged ship made a futile attempt to reach the nearby Italian town of Savona. Although two allied Japanese destroyers, the *Matsu* and *Sakaki*, came to its rescue, the *Transylvania* was hit by a second torpedo, sending her to the bottom of the sea, taking with her 414 lives. The Japanese destroyers picked up the survivors, among them Dominic Burke.

On 26 June 1917, he enrolled in the Royal Naval Reserve and was assigned to the shore establishments HMS *Colleen*, Queenstown and HMS *Vivid*, Davenport. Other royal naval ships on which he served during the war included HMS *Queen, Caesar* and *Europa*. He married Nelly Lynskey from Barna, and they had five children. They first lived at the Halls in Quay Street and later moved to 9 Beattystown, Claddagh. He died in the 1940s and was buried in St Mary's (new cemetery), Bohermore. *(Courtesy of Anne O'Flaherty.)*

SERGEANT EDWARD JOHN CARR 25998
(Royal Inniskilling Fusiliers)

Although born in Donegal on 14 October 1894, he lived all his life in Galway. Son of Patrick & Mary Ann Carr (*nee* Molloy), he enlisted when the war began and was wounded in both legs and taken prisoner by the Germans. Because he was a tailor, he was assigned to this work in a POW Camp. After the war he was repatriated to Galway where he joined the IRA during the War of Independence. He later enlisted in the Irish Free State army, in which he served until his retirement. He married Bridget King, and the family home was at Spanish Parade. The family also lived in the married quarters in Renmore barracks for a time. In later life his daughter Barbara remembered his expression of sadness upon seeing a documentary on the Great War. He held no bitterness against the German soldiers, as he believed that, similar to himself and his comrades, they were also fighting to survive. He died on 21 February 1965 and was buried in St Mary's (new cemetery), Bohermore. *(Courtesy of the Carr Family.)*

PRIVATE PATRICK CARRICK 24159
(First Royal Inniskilling Fusiliers)

Killed in action on 1 July 1916, Somme, France, he was the son of Michael & Mary Carrick (*nee* O'Farrell) of Fair Hill, Claddagh, Galway. *(Courtesy of Mary Smith.)*

PRIVATE CHARLIE CARRY
(South Irish Horse)

Born in Ballinasloe in 1886. He served throughout the war and survived. He died on 7 March 1966. *(Courtesy of Douglas Rafter & Pádraig Maloney.)*

PRIVATE THOMAS CASSERLY 668584
(Battery A Field Artillery US army)

He was born in 1887, the son of Martin & Catherine Casserly (*nee* Small) of Kiloughter, Castlegar. He had three brothers and one sister. He survived the war and was honourably discharged from the army in Camp Devens, Massachusetts on 18 January 1919. Returning to Galway he married Bridget Leonard from Angliham. They had eight children and the family home was 73 Bohermore, where two of his sons, James and P.J., still live. Another son, Frank, served in the US army during the Cuban missile crisis of 1962. Thomas died in 1968 and was buried in St Mary's (new cemetery), Bohermore. *(Courtesy of James Casserly.)*

PRIVATE JOHN CAULFIELD 364396
(Royal Irish Fusiliers)

His wife and one of his children also feature in the photograph. He survived the war and returned to his home town, Ballinasloe. The area in which he lived was St Grennan's Terrace, and was known locally as Hill 60, so-called after the infamous hill in Gallipoli which saw much action during that campaign. He died in 1956 and was buried in Ballinasloe. *(Courtesy of Ned Caulfield.)*

MAJOR WILLIAM UTTING COLE

Major Cole lived in St Clerans, Craughwell and served in the military all his life. He married Mary de Vere, niece of Robert O'Hara Burke, the famous Australian explorer. He had two sons and one daughter. One of his sons, Lieutenant Colonel John James Cole, served in both world wars. He was wounded three times during the Great War and was awarded the French Croix de Guerre. His daughter, Anne, married Neville Chamberlain, who later became prime minster of Great Britain. *(Courtesy of Francis Chamberlain.)*

DRIVER JAMES (JIM) COMBER
(Royal Field Artillery)

He was born on 22 January 1896, the son of James Comber of Blake's Lane, Bohermore, Galway. Jim had an older brother, John, and both men worked at Galway docks. On 27 December 1914, along with a number of neighbours and friends, he walked the old military path along the railway line to Renmore barracks and enlisted. He was wounded at Ypres when enemy fire obliterated his field gun and crew. According to the family, his wounds were at times painful throughout his life. He also suffered respiratory problems, caused by a gas attack. He was honourably discharged on 30 April 1919, and resumed his old job at Galway docks.

He married Delia Folan from Long Walk and they had one son, Jimmy. Jim died in the early 1960s and was buried in St Mary's (new cemetery), Bohermore. *(Courtesy of Gerald Comber.)*

ABLE SEAMAN PATRICK CONNEELY 1791

Born in Spanish Parade, Galway, about 1876, he married Bridget 'Delia' Griffin from the Claddagh and they had seven children. As a young man he joined the Royal Navy. During the First World War, he served at the shore establishment HMS *Victory I*, Portsmouth. On 21 July 1916, he was injured while serving on another ship, the HMS *Baunbuam*. He died in 1944 and was buried in Fort Hill Cemetery. *(Courtesy of Anne Campbell.)*

PRIVATE JAMES CONNOLLY 1567
(Second Irish Guards)

From Ballinaboy, Clifden, Connemara, he enlisted on 7 August 1914. He was wounded twice; the first time on 13 January 1915 when he was shot in the shoulder near La Bassee. On 9 October 1917, he received a gunshot wound to the foot at Cambrai, which put him out of action. He was honourably discharged because of the wound on 30 April 1918. *(Courtesy of Noel & Madeleine King.)*

PRIVATE JAMES CONNOLLY 61965
(Company K 101st infantry division, 26th brigade US army)

He was from Rossaveal, Connemara and had three sisters and five brothers. He wrote his last letter to his mother on 12 October 1918, as he was killed in action on 23 October. On 24 March 1919, his brother, William, wrote to the military authorities requesting to know the whereabouts of his brother, as the family were not receiving any communication from him. It was only then that they were informed of his death. Another brother, Thomas, also served in the war, and had a poem composed in memory of his brother. *(Courtesy of Seán Malone.)*

LANCE CORPORAL THOMAS CORCORAN 10189
(Second Irish Guards)

Son of James & Bridget Corcoran of Eyrecourt, he was killed in action at Bourlon Wood, France on 28 November 1917. *(Courtesy of Mary Corcoran Deely.)*

PRIVATE JOHN CRAUGHWELL
(Thirteenth Northumberland Fusiliers)

Born on 26 August 1889, he was the son of John & Mary Craughwell (*nee* Gaffney) of Mayo, and later of Munster Avenue, Galway. The family are recorded at the latter address in the 1901 census. He was wounded during the Somme offensive of 1916. He survived the war and went to live in the Isle of Wight. Brother of Patrick Craughwell. He is in his musician's uniform. here. Another brother, Private Danny Craughwell, also fought in the war and survived. *(Courtesy of Christy Craughwell.)*

SERGEANT PATRICK CRAUGHWELL 15524
(Thirteenth Northumberland Fusiliers)

Brother of John and Danny Craughwell, he was born on 13 June 1893. He was killed in action on 4 July 1916, during the Somme offensive. *(Courtesy of Christy Craughwell.)*

PRIVATE JOSEPH CUNNINGHAM
(Third London Post Office Rifles)

He lived at 47 Prospect Hill, Galway. His father was a member of the Royal Irish Constabulary. In 1902, he married Mary Fleming of the Lock House, Dominick Street and they had one daughter, Josephine. After the war he returned to his job in Galway post office. He died in the early 1950s and was buried in Forthill cemetery. *(Courtesy of Mary Raftery.)*

PETTY OFFICER STEPHEN CURRAN & MARTIN O'DONNELL

Both men were from the Claddagh and served on the *Alcantara* and survived its encounter with a German warship. The story of the sinking of the *Alcantara* was recorded in *Galway and the Great War*, p. 93. *(Courtesy of Tom O'Donnell and Paddy Curran)*

PRIVATE MICHAEL DEELEY

From Aughrim, he is on the left of the photograph which was taken in Egypt, just before the campaign in Palestine. The soldier on the right is unknown. *(Courtesy of Mary McLoughlin.)*

SECOND LIEUTENANT ROBERT DE STACPOOLE

(Connaught Rangers)

Son of the Duke & Duchess de Stacpoole of Mount Hazel, Woodlawn. He was killed in action at either the battle of Marne or the Aisne on 20 September 1914. Brother of Roderick de Stacpoole, killed in March 1915. *(Courtesy of Richard de Stacpoole.)*

SECOND LIEUTENANT RODERICK DE STACPOOLE

(Royal Field Artillery)

Brother of Robert de Stacpoole, he was 'Mentioned in Despatches'. He was killed in action at the battle of Neuve Chapelle on 11 March 1915. *(Courtesy of Richard de Stacpoole.)*

PRIVATE CHARLES DEVLIN
(Australian Commonwealth Regiment)

In his naval uniform. Son of Charles & Catherine Devlin; husband of Margaret Devlin of St John's Terrace, Galway. He was wounded twice, in Belgium and France, but survived the Great War. However, he was killed on 5 July 1940 when his merchant navy ship, SS *Elmcrest*, was attacked and sunk by a German U-boat during the Second World War. *(Courtesy of Cathal Devlin and the late Bunny Devlin.)*

ABLE SEAMAN PATRICK DIRRANE

Son of Michael Dirrane of Inishmore. His wife was Mary Geary, also in the photograph, and they had five children. He survived the war and lived in the Claddagh. *(Courtesy of Paddy Moore Flaherty.)*

PRIVATE MICHAEL DONOHUE
(US army)

From Spiddal, Connemara., he emigrated to the United States, where he enlisted in the army. He survived the war, but there is no other information available regarding any personal details. *(Courtesy of Thomas Feeney.)*

RIFLEMAN THOMAS DONOHUE 373540
(Eighth London Post Office Rifles)

He was from Esker, Athenry and died from his wounds in London on 12 June 1917. Before going into action, he wrote a letter to his wife Bridget, which was included in *Galway and the Great War*, p. 164–165. *(Courtesy of Marcella Jordan.)*

ABLE SEAMAN JAMES FAHERTY

From the Claddagh, he fought at the battle of Jutland in May 1916. He survived the war and married Mary Moore who was also from the Claddagh, and they had seven children. He died in the early 1930s. *(Courtesy of Mary Smith.)*

LANCE CORPORAL BERNIE FAHY 4/1423
(New Zealand Engineering Tunnel Company)

He was from Cregmore, Claregalway and was killed in action in France on 20 April 1917. He had emigrated to New Zealand before the outbreak of the war. During the war, he wrote many letters to his family, some of which were included in *Galway and the Great War*, p. 161, 162. *(Courtesy of Brian Fahy.)*

PRIVATE COLMAN FARMER 410392
(Second Canadian Expeditionary Force)

Born on 16 January 1885, he was the son of Lawrence Farmer of Trabane, Lettermore, Connemara. He emigrated to Canada as a young man and enlisted in the Thirty-eight battalion Canadian army at Ottawa, Ontario on 1 March 1915. He was subsequently transferred to the Second Canadian Expeditionary Force. During action in Wulverghem-Lindenhoek (Ypres), Belgium on 8 December 1915, he received severe gunshot wounds to both legs, and was also wounded several times in the body and head by grenade shrapnel.

He was admitted to the Canadian military hospital at Etaples, France (admission No. 23). Having been transferred to a number of hospitals in the UK, he was eventually sent to Elmhurst hospital in Ontario, Canada. He was awarded the 1914–1915 Star and British War and Victory medals. He was honourably discharged on a disability pension from the Canadian army on 8 February 1917. His wounds caused him much suffering for the remainder of his life. He died in the 1960s and was buried in a military cemetery in Toronto, Canada. Brother of Larry Farmer. *(Courtesy of Colm Walsh and the late Julia Walsh.)*

PRIVATE LARRY FARMER 2245988
(Seventeenth Regiment of Infantry Canadian Expeditionary Force)

He was born on 1 March 1891 and emigrated to Canada on 28 March 1910 from Queenstown on board the SS *Saint Louis*. He initially worked as a lumberjack in Portland, Maine before going to Canada to enlist. He enlisted in the Canadian army at Levis, Quebec on 12 December 1917 and saw active service at Amiens, Canal Du Nord, Cambrai and Moreuil Wood. He survived the war without being wounded or injured. He was honourably discharged from the Canadian army on 18 June 1919. He went to live in the United States, where he remained for the rest of his life. He was awarded the British War and Victory medals and the War Service Badge Class 'A'. He was a brother of Colman Farmer. (*Courtesy of Colm Walsh and the late Julia Walsh.*)

PRIVATE JOHN FINNERTY 7996
(Second Connaught Rangers)

From Ballinasloe, he enlisted at Renmore barracks in 1901. He served in India on several occasions. He was one of the survivors of the second battalion, which was amalgamated with the first battalion Connaught Rangers, following the first battle of Ypres in November 1914. He was wounded in action at St Julian. He also served in Mesopotamia. He was honourably discharged in March 1919 and returned home. He died in 1953, and was buried in Ballinasloe. (*Courtesy of Tony Finnerty.*)

ABLE SEAMAN OWEN FITZGERALD
He is on the left in the photograph and his son Christopher is on the right. Owen

was born in the Claddagh in 1895, the son of Seán Fitzgerald. He married Mary Hehir and they had four children, Christopher, Mickey, Nora and Maureen. He died on 2 August 1946 and was buried in St Mary's (new cemetery), Bohermore. Christopher served in the royal navy during the Second World War. (*Courtesy of Mickey Fitzgerald.*)

PRIVATE THOMAS FLAHERTY
(Third Irish Guards)

Son of Patrick & Kathleen Flaherty (*nee* Egan) of Oughterard, he enlisted in Dublin on 25 April 1915 and saw action at the Somme and Ypres. He was wounded on 11 April 1916, and on two other occasions. He was also gassed. He was present when his friend, Arthur O'Flaherty from St Bridget's Terrace, was killed. Thomas survived the war and married Mary Glynn from Waterlane, Bohermore. They had nine children. The family eventually moved to Hidden Valley, where his son Johnny still lives. Thomas died in 1960 and was buried in St Mary's (new cemetery), Bohermore. *(Courtesy of Johnny Flaherty.)*

ABLE SEAMAN McDARA FLAHERTY

He was from Ardmore, Carna, Connemara. No other information was available about this man, except that he served for at least the duration of the war and survived. *(Courtesy of Anne O'Flaherty.)*

PRIVATE STEPHEN FLYNN 612655
(Hussars & Royal Engineers)

A rope-maker from the Claddagh, Galway, he enlisted at Renmore barracks in 1899, when he was sixteen years old, telling the authorities that he was eighteen. He served in India until 1907 when he resigned. He re-enlisted on 4 August 1914. According to family documents, he saved the life of a wounded officer by carrying him back to safety from 'no-mans-land'. It seems that the officer's peerage family were forever grateful and awarded him a private pension. During the war he was wounded several times, the first time on 9 July 1915, when he received a head wound.

On 1 January 1916 he was wounded again, this time in the buttocks. However, his most severe wounds were received seven days later at Loos, France, when he was recorded as having received gunshot wounds to the back and buttocks, and also suffered multiple shrapnel wounds. He was transferred to a hospital in England. He was discharged on 18 June 1919. He married Sarah

Geary and they had three children, William, Michael and Patrick. The family address was 23 St Finbarr's Terrace, Bohermore. As he got older, his wounds caused him much discomfort and he had to walk with the aid of sticks. He died on 16 January 1970 and was buried in St Mary's (new cemetery), Bohermore. *(Courtesy of Mike Flynn.)*

PRIVATE THOMAS FOLAN & SERGEANT THOMAS O'TOOLE
(Fifth Connaught Rangers)

Thomas Folan of Derrygimla, Clifden is on the left, standing. He enlisted in Galway on 31 January 1916. He was badly wounded on 21 March 1918 and was discharged on 4 April 1919. However, he enlisted in the Highland Infantry on 3 July 1919 and was discharged on 17 February 1920 and returned home. He subsequently joined the Irish Free State army and rose to the rank of captain. Two of his brothers, John and Patrick, were also Connaught Rangers, and both were killed in the war, see p. 123. Sergeant Thomas O'Toole, who is standing on the right of the photograph, was the son of Thomas and Margaret O'Toole from Cloghaunard, Clifden. He enlisted on 6 October 1915, and also served in the Third Connaught Rangers. He was discharged on 24 June 1919. He joined the Royal Irish Constabulary and served in Tipperary south riding. Following the disbandment of the RIC, he joined the Palestine police. He later returned to Connemara, where he married and had two children. When the Second World War broke out, he rejoined the British army, and served for the duration of the war. He returned to Clifden, where he remained until his death in 1954. The soldier seated is O'Hara, but there was no additional information available about this man. *(Courtesy of Kathleen Villiers-Tuthill.)*

FIELD-MARSHAL SIR JOHN FRENCH

Commander of British Expeditionary Force in 1914. He was born in Ripple Vale, Kent in 1852. In 1866, he joined the royal navy, and eight years later transferred to the army. He served in the second South African war 1899–1902, where he saw action at Elandslaagte, Reitfontein and Lombard's Kop. Sir John French was descended from the French family of French Park, Co. Roscommon. This family was a branch of the well-known Tribes of Galway. *(Courtesy of Eamonn McNally.)*

MAJOR GENERAL SIR NOEL GALWAY-HOLMES
(British Expeditionary Force)

One of the founding members of the Galway Lawn Tennis Club, he survived the war and returned to Ireland. He played in the Davis cup for Ireland in 1929. Possibly related to Captain Reginald Holmes of the royal army medical corps, who died in the military hospital in Malta in April 1916, see p. 141. *(Courtesy of Peadar O'Dowd & Galway Lawn Tennis Club.)*

PRIVATE TOMMY GARDINER

Originally from Annaghdown, his family had a grain store in Forster Street, Galway. According to the family, he arrived in France the day the war ended. He later joined the Red Cross. He worked for Young's Distillery, Galway. *(Courtesy of Heather Gardiner.)*

PRIVATE JAMES GARVEY 40124
(Second Connaught Rangers)

From Parkavera, Galway., he is seated in the centre and the photograph was taken in India. He received the 1914–15 Star and managed to survive the slaughter of his battalion during the first battle of Ypres in November 1914. He also served with the Sixth Connaught Rangers 4271, and the Seventh & Eighth Royal Inniskilling Fusiliers 48415. He died on 5 March 1964 and was buried in St Mary's (new cemetery) Bohermore. *(Courtesy of Jimmy Gillespie.)*

PRIVATE JOHN GILMORE
(British Expeditionary Force)

Born in Galway in 1897, he survived the war. He died in 1941, and was buried in Rahoon cemetery. *(Courtesy of Christy Craughwell.)* `

GUNNER MALACHY GOODE 1016394
(Royal Field Artillery)

He is on the left of the photograph. He was born on 13 August 1895, the son of Malachy & Sarah Goode (*nee* Leonard) of Aughrim. He enlisted on 6 November 1916 at Ballinasloe. He received either gun-shot or shrapnel wounds to the face on 28 September 1918 and he was discharged on 9 July 1919. On 26 November 1919, he married Ellen Corr from Rush, Co. Dublin. They had four children, Malachy, Mary, James and William. He worked as a tram driver in Dublin. He died on 19 October 1990, and was buried in Whitestown cemetery, Rush, Co. Dublin. *(Courtesy of Mary McLoughlin.)*

PRIVATE MARTIN GEARY 3812A
(Forty-ninth Australian Infantry)

Born on 3 September 1894, the son of Patrick & Honor Geary of Carna, Connemara. While he was still young, the family moved to 21 Long Walk, Galway. He was killed in action on 3 September 1916 (twenty-second birthday) during the Somme offensive. *(Courtesy of Paddy Moore Flaherty.)*

CHIEF PETTY OFFICER MICHAEL GRIFFIN

From the Claddagh, his wife Catherine 'Kate' O'Brien from Rope Walk, Claddagh also features in the photograph. They were married on St Stephen's day 1905, and they had nine children. His best man was Stephen King, who later became a casualty of the Great War. After the war Michael returned to the Claddagh and began working for himself on a newly purchased Galway hooker. He also opened a shop and later worked in the IMI at Earl's Island. He died in 1950 and was buried in Rahoon cemetery. *(Courtesy of Anne Eversis.)*

CORPORAL JIM 'RUCÁN' HEANEY
(Royal Field Artillery)

He was from Woodquay, Galway and enlisted at Renmore barracks at sixteen years of age, but because of his youth, his father was able to secure his release. However, a short time later, his second attempt was successful. He was an excellent horseman, and it was his love of horses that prompted him to join the forces. His brother, Paddy, also served in the Great War and survived. After the war, Rucán followed the family trade and set up a butcher shop in Woodquay, which was later converted to a grocery shop. He was married twice; his second wife was Julia Corcoran and they had three children, Frank, Collette and the late Patrick Heaney. He was a noted sportsman throughout Ireland, and had a life-long association with the Galway Rowing Club. He died on 15 December 1976 and was buried in St Mary's (new cemetery), Bohermore. *(Courtesy of the late Patrick Heaney.)*

PRIVATE BARTHOLOMEW HEHIR
(South Irish Horse)

Born in 1898, the son of Bartholomew & Honor Hehir (*nee* Comber) of Bohermore, he survived the war. He married May Barrett and they had eleven children. He died in 1981 and is buried in London. *(Courtesy of Teresa King & Mickey Fitzgerald.)*

SERGEANT MAJOR STEPHEN HIGGINS

(Second Connaught Rangers)
In his Second World War uniform. Born in November 1889, the son of Thomas & Mary Higgins, he enlisted at Renmore barracks on 28 August 1906. He was also attached to the York & Lancaster regiment. He survived the war and married Maria Keegan, and they had ten children. He was awarded the 1914 Star, British War and Victory medals, the Long Service and Good Conduct medals. He was a military man for most of his life and also served in the Second World War. He died in January 1980 and was buried in Rahoon cemetery. *(Courtesy of Simon McKiernan.)*

SERGEANT HARRY HOWETT
(Army Pay Corps)

Originally from the Claddagh, his wife was Kate Burke from Palmyra Avenue, Galway, and also features in the photograph. He also saw service in China and Gibraltar. Note the red cross badge on his uniform indicating that he also served with a medical corp. *(Courtesy of Michael Conneely.)*

PRIVATE MICHAEL HUGHES
(Royal Field Artillery)

He was born in 1876, the son of Thomas & Bridget Hughes (*nee* Connell) of Bohermore, Galway. He married Bridget Lenihan from Claregalway, and they had seven children, Mary, Bridie, Eileen, Tommy, Charlie, Patsy and Michael. The three girls were born before the war. His daughter, Mary, also features in the photograph, and was five years old at the time. Mr Hill of Dominick Street took the photograph in 1916. Michael Hughes was home on compassionate leave at the time because one of his daughters was extremely ill. Before returning to war he had a number of family photographs taken, the photographer gave this one to Mary, and she has treasured it all of her life. Because of his expertise with horses, he served with the Royal Field Artillery. He saw action in various theatres of war and while serving in Egypt, he sent Mary her Holy Communion medal. After the war, he worked in Renmore barracks for a short time before taking up a position with McDonogh's, driving a horse and cart. He died on 18 November 1931 and was buried in St Mary's (new cemetery), Bohermore. *(Courtesy of Mary McGrath.)*

LIEUTENANT COLONEL HENRY FRANCIS JOURDAIN
(Connaught Rangers)

Commander of the Connaught Rangers at Renmore barracks, he was a veteran of the Boer War, during which the local media reported him as having been killed in action. He received the mobilisation orders for Galway in 1914. He took an active part in the Great War and was well respected by all who served under him. He was also the man who introduced golf to Galway, when, along with a fellow officer, he constructed a nine-hole golf course at the rear of Renmore barracks in 1894. According to one source, Lieutenant Jourdain was approached by Michael Collins to become Commander-in-Chief of the newly formed Irish Free State army in 1922. *(Courtesy of Ray Duke.)*

PRIVATE JOSEPH KEANEY
(US army)

Born on 14 April 1889, the seventh child of Thomas 'An Greasai Mor' and Margaret Keaney (*nee* Joyce) of Glynsk, Cashel, Connemara. In 1911 or 1912, he emigrated to the United States and settled in Pittsburgh, Pennsylvania. He saw action in France after the US entered the war in 1917. He married Rose Donovan on 14 November 1919 and they had three children. One of his sons, Sergeant William Keaney, later served with the US Marine Corps, and saw action in Korea and Vietnam. He was awarded a Purple Heart. *(Courtesy of Francis Keaney.)*

LANCE CORPORAL THOMAS KEANEY 5978
(First & Second Irish Guards)

Thomas Keaney is seated in the photograph; (the other soldier has not been identified). He was born on 17 December 1894, the twelfth child of Thomas 'An Greasai Mor' & Margaret Keaney (*nee* Joyce) of Glynsk, Cashel, Connemara. It was while working as a shipyard labourer in Dumbarton, Scotland that he decided to enlist on 15 November 1914. He did two tours of duty, from 1 June 1915 until 9 October 1917, with the first battalion and from 31 March 1918 until 26 December 1918 with the second battalion. His was a Lewis gunner. The war diaries recorded on 21 April 1918 near Hondeghem give a flavour of what life was like for him at the front line:

At 10.15 pm the Germans threw over many gas shells – so bad was the gassing that the battalion HQ were obliged to move into the wood to the south. This shelling continued until 2am and caused rather a number of casualties. The gas fumes hanging in the thick undergrowth for a considerable time. No. 1 and 3 company replaced No. 2 and 4 company in the front line during the night. On 23 April 1918, German

*prisoners (25) were taken, those who could speak English expressed their distaste for
the war, and said that they were delighted to be taken prisoner.*

Quoted from military record held by the family

On 25 November 1918, he was diagnosed with influenza and was transferred to Brook
war hospital in Woolwich, and later to the dispersal hospital in Portobello, Dublin. He
was awarded a pension because he suffered from chronic bronchitis for the remainder
of his life. He married Anne Keane from Inishnee, Roundstone, Connemara on 7
March 1923, and they had ten children. Two of his sons, Thomas and John, joined the
Irish army. He died on 9 August 1961. *(Courtesy of Francis Keaney.)*

LANCE CORPORAL MARTIN KEARNEY 8/238
(Otago Regiment NZEF)
Son of Peter & Anne Kearney of Ballinacourty, Oranmore,
he was killed in action in Gallipoli on 29 April 1915. *(Courtesy of Martin Kearney.)*

PRIVATES MARK & WILLIE KELLY
(Supply & Transport US army)

The sons of Michael & Mary Kelly (*nee*
Madden), who had six children. Mark (right)
was born on 18 May 1892. On 12 December
1917, both brothers enlisted together, and
both of them survived the war. They were
also discharged together on 12 March 1919.
Mark returned to Ireland and lived in Ballykeaghra, Tuam. He died on 10 February
1966 and was buried in Tuam. Willie was
born on 25 April 1887. He married Margaret
Mullin on 16 October 1927 in the United
States and they later returned to Ireland and
lived in Cussane, Athenry. He died on 16
September 1979 and was buried in Athenry
cemetery. *(Courtesy of Maureen Kelly.)*

RIFLEMAN PATRICK KENNEDY-LYDON, 77133
(Third New Zealand Rifle Brigade)

He was born in 1890, the son of John & Honora Kennedy-Lydon (*nee* Cunniffe) of Cahercrin, Athenry. He was one of eight children. and emigrated to New Zealand as a young man, where he enlisted in the army when the war broke out. He was mortally wounded in France, and died on 6 November 1918. He was buried in Cannock Chase war cemetery – Staffordshire – United Kingdom (4. A. 8). His brother, John, took part in the 1916 Easter Rebellion. *(Courtesy of the Kennedy-Lydon family.)*

LIEUTENANT JACK KING
(Royal Field Artillery)

Son of John & Lena King (*nee* Casey). His father was clerk of the petty sessions. Jack was educated by the monks at Ardbear and later in St Jarlath's college, Tuam. Following the armistice, he returned to complete his education and graduated in law. He joined the civil service. He later contracted TB and having sought medical advice, he moved to the warmer climate of South Africa, where he spent the remainder of his life. *(Courtesy of Kathleen Villiers-Tuthill.)*

CAPTAIN LEO KING
(Connaught Rangers)

A brother of John King, he followed the same educational path as his brother, and also graduated in law. After the war he worked for the Electricity Supply Board in Dublin. On 28 July 1935, he was killed in a motorcycle accident. *(Courtesy of Kathleen Villiers-Tuthill.)*

ABLE SEAMAN JOHN 'TOGO' LALLY

From O'Donohoue's Terrace, Galway, he had served in the royal navy before the war. He survived the war. This image of Togo was drawn by an unknown street artist in Cairo before the war. *(Courtesy of Billy Lally.)*

ABLE SEAMAN MARTIN LARNER
(US navy)

Son of Thomas & Kate Larner from Doogara near Tuam, he emigrated to the United States sometime during the Great War, where he enlisted in the navy. Following the war he returned home and married Winfired Giblin of Lavally. They moved to Cloondahamper where they had three children, Mary, Margaret and Tom. He died in 1984. *(Courtesy of Mary Potter.)*

LIEUTENANT MICHAEL LAVELLE
(Fourth Connaught Rangers)

Master of the Clifden workhouse before enlisting for service in the Great War, he received his commission on 7 July 1915. Lieutenant Lavelle was sent to France in July 1916 and was immediately attached to the Ninth (Service) Royal Innishkilling Fusiliers. Within three months of his arrival, he was awarded the Military Cross for bravery at the Spanbroek sector. On the night of 11–12 October, Lieutenant Lavelle and three other officers led some eighty men in a raid on German trenches. The attack was a success, but his three fellow officers and a large number of men were lost. Among the dead was his friend, Lieutenant K. Kempston.

After the mission was accomplished, at considerable risk to his own life, Lieutenant Lavelle returned to 'no-man's-land' to recover the body of his friend. It was a promise the men had made to each other the night before the attack, that neither man would be left in 'no-man's-land' should the other survive. Lieutenant Lavelle was 'brave to a fault' and proved himself a great leader of men. In 1917, he saw action in Palestine with the Fifth Connaught Rangers and returned to France in 1918. On 11 December 1919, he received the Military Cross from King George V at Buckingham Palace. Lieutenant Lavelle resigned from the army on 16 March 1920. He returned to his former position in Clifden workhouse and was later the rate inspector for the Connemara district.

He married twice and had three children, Michael, Barbara and Kathleen Villiers-Tuthill (author and historian). The children were born to his second wife, Teresa Joyce; his first wife, Mary Cloherty, died childless. Two of his brothers, William and Joseph, also served in the Great War, and survived. William served with the Fifth Connaught Rangers and was wounded several times. It is not known which regiment Joseph served with, but he was demobbed in 1919. *(Courtesy of Kathleen Villiers-Tuthill.)*

PRIVATE JOHN JOE LEONARD
(Black Watch)

Born in 1894, the youngest of eleven children of James & Belinda Leonard of Prospect Hill, Galway, and educated in St Ignatius college. He enlisted for service with the Black Watch when the war began, and was severely wounded at the battle of the Somme on 1 July 1916. He was sent to hospital in England and was later transferred to Galway, where he was discharged from the army because of his wounds.

In 1917, he joined Sinn Féin, and shortly afterwards became a senior member of the IRA. According to his family, he ranked amongst the ten most wanted men in Ireland during the war of independence. In 1928, he married Rita Brennan from Mayo and they settled in Lenaboy Park, where they had four daughters. He was a great admirer of Eamon de Valera, and named his second daughter Valera, as a tribute to his friend and colleague. In 1932, he became a member of Galway County Council. He died suddenly in 1935 and was buried in St Mary's (new cemetery), Bohermore. *(Courtesy of Valera Raftery.)*

PRIVATE JOHN LYNCH R4/062612
(Royal Field Artillery)

He was born in Loughrea in 1877 and enlisted on 5 March 1915. He survived the war and remained in the army until the late 1930s. He died in 1967 and was buried in the new cemetery, Loughrea. *(Courtesy of Gerry Carthy.)*

CORPORAL PATRICK LYNSKEY 9607
(First Connaught Rangers)

From Waterlane, Bohermore, Galway, he was born on 2 February 1892. He joined the Connaught Rangers at Renmore barracks on 2 February 1909. The following year he met Bridget Burke from the Claddagh, who later became his wife. In 1910, he was sent to India, and Bridget left for the US. However, they continued to write to each other, even throughout the war years.

During the war he saw service in Egypt, Palestine, Mesopotamia and France. He was wounded twice, the first time in France in 1916 when a bullet penetrated his helmet and clipped his skull. While serving in Palestine he was wounded in the buttocks. When the war ended, he returned home and worked as a cobbler. In 1920, he married Bridget. They had nine children and the family home was in the Claddagh. He died in 1966 and was buried in St Mary's (new cemetery), Bohermore. In 1998, his son Michael Lynskey became King of the Claddagh. *(Courtesy of Michael Lynskey.)*

PRIVATE WALTER MACKEN G/18392
(Fourth Royal Fusiliers)

He was from St John's Terrace, Galway, and was born in 1889, the son of Walter & Mary Macken of Eyre Street. He married Agnes Brady of 18 St Joseph's Avenue, Galway. He was killed in action on 27 March 1916. He had three other brothers, John, Michael and Tom, who also served at the front. His letters to Agnes have formed a valuable collection of Great War letters. Two of his letters were included in *Galway and the Great War*, pp. 245, 246, 247, 248. He was the father of the renowned author, Walter Macken. *(Courtesy of Ultan Maken.)*

JOHN MADDEN 33974
(Royal Engineers)

John Madden is seated in the photograph. He was born in 1871 at Garrybreeda, Loughrea and worked in Woodlawn House, where he met his wife, Catherine Kavanagh. They had seven children, five of whom were born before the war. He enlisted in February 1915, and was first stationed at Dunstable, England. Later that year he was sent to France and saw action in the Somme offensive of 1916.

He survived the war and after his return to Ireland became embroiled in the national conflict. During this period, his house was raided by Black and Tans, but his years of military service enabled him to handle the situation without them causing too much damage to his home. He was a gifted raconteur, and great advocate of education. He died in 1965 and was buried in Garrybreeda cemetery, a few metres from where he was born. The other soldier in the photograph remains unknown. *(Courtesy of Anna Cronin & Finbarr O'Shea.)*

PRIVATE PATRICK McDERMOTT
(Thirteenth Northumberland Fusiliers & Royal Field Artillery)

He was born in 1897, the son of Patrick & Kate McDermott (*nee* Martyn) of Munster Avenue, Galway. His mother was possibly from the Claddagh. He was killed in action on 1 July 1916 during the Somme offensive. He was related to the Craughwell brothers, see p. 40. *(Courtesy of Christy Craughwell.)*

ABLE SEAMAN BARTLEY McDONAGH

He was from the Claddagh and served in the royal navy before the war, and was a naval champion boxer. He married Margaret Burke and they had five children. After the war he worked as a caretaker in the University College Galway rowing club and lived on the premises for a time. He died in 1940. *(Courtesy of Michael Lynskey.)*

LANCE SERGEANT JOHN McELROY 6643

(Third Irish Guards)

Born in 1886, the son of William McElroy of Co. Roscommon, he enlisted in Dublin on 24 January 1915. He was 'Mentioned in Despatches' following the battle of Loos in September 1915. During the action he showed tremendous courage, carrying back to safety a number of wounded comrades, including a mortally wounded officer, Captain Wynter, while under heavy fire at Chalk Pit Wood. He was awarded the Military Medal in 1916 and was wounded in April of that same year. He was discharged on 23 January 1919 and took up his former position as an RIC constable, and was stationed in Tuam. He remained in Tuam for the rest of his life, dying in 1968. He is buried in Tuam cemetery. *(Courtesy of Jimmy McElroy.)*

DECK HAND THOMAS McHUGH SD1562

(Royal Naval Reserves)

He was born in 1874, the son of Patrick & Ann Mc-Hugh of Bohermore, Galway. He lived with his wife Delia at 33 Upper Bohermore. He enlisted in the navy on 10 June 1915. Following two months training he was assigned to HMS *Thetis*. Four months later he was transferred to the lightly armed trawler, HT *Daisy II*, which had been commandeered for service. His next ship was the *Manzanita*, on which he served for seven months. He then transferred to the *Admirable*, which was sunk by the enemy cruiser *Helgoland* in May 1917 during action in the Otranto Straits. Six months later he was admitted to Comino military hospital, Taranto, Italy with peritonitis. The log of HMS *Queen* records that he died at 5.30 p.m. on 27 November 1917. He was buried in Taranto Town Cemetery Extension (S. IV, R. F, P. 9). *(Courtesy of Anne O'Flaherty.)*

PRIVATE JACK MONAGHAN 7782
(Third Irish Guards)

Born in 1894, the son of Patrick & Elizabeth Monaghan (*nee* Darcy). They had nine children, and the family home was in Middle Street and later St Patrick's Avenue, Galway. He enlisted at the Royal Hotel, Eyre Square during an Irish Guards recruiting meeting. He was a member of a local choir and, similar to other organisations, they decided to enlist together. It seems that the decision was made in their local pub, 'Ma Hoey's' (where the 'Living Room' pub is presently), when it was decided that they would go to France and 'sort out the Kaiser'.

He was wounded in the arm in 1917 during action in the Somme area. After the war, he worked as a carpenter. He married Bridie Griffin and they had four children, Paddy, Joan, Collette and Jack. He died in 1952 and was buried in St Mary's (new cemetery), Bohermore. *(Courtesy of Johnny Flaherty.)*

MARTIN WILLIAM MOLLOY 6649
(Second Irish Guards)

He was born in 1887, at Carrowmoreknock, Rosscahill. This photograph, in his Royal Irish Constabulary uniform, was taken shortly before he joined the colours. He was stationed in Limerick when the Great War began. He immediately joined the British army and was sent to France. He was killed in action on the Somme on 13 September 1916. *(Courtesy of Mary Jane Carter.)*

PRIVATE THOMAS MOYLAN
(New Zealand Expeditionary Force)

Born in Clonboo in the late 1800s, Thomas Moylan was raised by Thomas & Mary Leonard of Addergoole. He emigrated to New Zealand as a young man. When the war began he enlisted in the army and saw action at Gallipoli and France. He survived the war and returned to New Zealand, but there is no additional information available about Thomas. *(Courtesy of Johnny Murphy.)*

PRIVATE JAMES MURPHY
(Connaught Rangers)

Son of James & Nora Murphy (*nee* Fahy) of Clooncun West, Glenamaddy. He was discharged because of wounds received during action in France. He later married Ellen Keaveney from Bushtown and they had one daughter. He died on 2 July 1949 and was buried in the old graveyard, Glenamaddy. *(Courtesy of Paddy Cunningham.)*

BOATSWAIN COLMAN NEE

Third from the right in the photograph, he was born in 1876, the son of Martin & Mary Nee of the Claddagh. He married a lady named Delia and they had one daughter, Della. They lived at Lower Fairhill Road, Claddagh. As a young man he served on the SS *Granuaile*, a Congested Districts Board vessel, which carried supplies to offshore islands. He also served with the *Gunnamor* in the Claddagh. When the Great War began he was transferred to the Mercantile Marine Reserves and served on the HM water tanker

Progress. He was killed on 21 December 1916, when his ship was torpedoed off Hull. The photograph was taken just before the ship set off on its last journey. According to military records he is buried in Cruden parish churchyard & extension, Aberdeenshire, Scotland. *(Courtesy of Michael Conneely.)*

ABLE SEAMAN JOHN O'BRIEN

From the Claddagh, he served as a signalsman in the royal navy. He survived the war and later joined the Irish Free State army. *(Courtesy of Francie O'Brien.)*

ABLE SEAMAN MICHAEL O'BRIEN 1140

Born on Inishmore, Aran islands, he married Barbara Conneely from Inisheer, and they had three children, Edmond, Mary and Michael. He was killed in an accident on board his ship on 1 February 1917. His youngest son Michael was later killed at Monte Cassino during the Second World War. *(Courtesy of Rita O'Connor.)*

LIEUTENANT MICHAEL O'CONNOR & CAPTAIN THOMAS O'CONNOR
(Connaught Rangers)

From Loughrea, the photograph was taken in Dover in 1915 or 1916. The cap and collar badges indicate that Captain O'Connor [on right] was a chaplain. *(Courtesy of Ray Duke.)*

PRIVATE MICHAEL O'DONNELL 4628
(Sixth Connaught Rangers)

Enlisted Galway. Son of Michael & Mary O'Donnell (*nee* Conneely) of Tiernee, Lettermore, Connemara. He was killed in action in France on 20 November 1917, and was buried in Croisilles Railway Cemetery – Pas de Calais – France (I. D. 21). *(Courtesy of the O'Donnell Family & Val Folan.)*

CHIEF PETTY OFFICER PATRICK O'DONNELL M12224

Born on 8 June 1893, he had a long naval career serving on the shore establishments HMS *Victory, Fisgard*, and *Ebro, Pembroke*, and the light cruiser HMS *Cleopatra*. He died on 18 January 1976 and was buried in St Mary's (new cemetery), Bohermore. *(Courtesy of Alice Scanlan.)*

O'FLAHERTY BROTHERS

From the Claddagh, from left: Laurence (HMS *Victory*); John and Dominick (HMS *Excellent*). Laurence was reported as missing following action at sea, but later turned up wounded and survived. His story is recorded in *Galway and the Great War*, p. 33, 34, and *The Claddagh Boy*, published in 1963. *(Courtesy of Tony Flannery.)*

LANCE CORPORAL JAMES OLLINGTON
(First Connaught Rangers)

He lived in Beattystown, the Claddagh and was in the rangers for some twenty years. He served in the Boer War, saw service in Malta and India, and later in France and Belgium during the First World War. He was wounded in France, but survived the war. There are many images of the Great War captured on film, but one in particular is of a soldier carrying a badly wounded comrade through a trench. As he moves quickly through the trench, he is looking directly at the camera, with a haunting expression of shock on his face. It is sometimes described as the iconic image of the Great War. This man has never been positively identified, but some believe that he was James Ollington. A number of years ago, his daughters Peggy and Lila, were watching a television documentary on the Great War and when this image appeared, they were immediately convinced that this man was their father. The BBC and the Imperial War Museum authorities were informed. However, there have been many claims to this man's identity. He died on 17 January 1954 and was buried in St Mary's (new cemetery), Bohermore. *(Courtesy of the Ollington family.)*

LANCE CORPORAL THOMAS PARSLOW
(Connaught Rangers)

The family say that Lance Corporal Parslow was definitely a Connaught Ranger. However, the cap badge seems to be from some other regiment, or maybe it's simply the condition of the photograph that is distorting the shape of the badge. He was from St Bridget's Place, Galway. Awarded the Distinguished Conduct Medal during the Boer War. He was married to Monica Derrick from College Road, possibly a sister of John Derrick of the Royal Field Artillery, who died of wounds on 21 August 1917. His eldest son, Tommy, also features in the photograph. Thomas Parslow survived the war and had eleven children. One of his sons, John, joined the British army as a bugler at sixteen years of age, and rose to the rank of captain during the Second World War. Thomas died in 1947 and was buried in St Mary's (new cemetery), Bohermore. *(Courtesy of Maureen Parslow.)*

PRIVATE PAT PURCELL
(Connaught Rangers)

He is seated in the photograph and wearing his Irish Free State army uniform. Born in 1889 at Isserkelly, Ardrahan, he had three brothers, Tommy, Jim and Mike, who also served in the Connaught Rangers. Pat served in the rangers for the duration of the Great War. Having returned home, he became involved in the national struggle for independence, and served on the side of the Free State in the civil war. However the photograph is interesting, in that the other two unknown men are wearing paramilitary uniforms. The photograph was possibly taken about 1922. He married Miara Fahy from Ardrahan and they had five children. Miara was president of the local Cumann na mBan. Pat died in 1957 and is buried in Labane cemetery. *(Courtesy of Seán Purcell.)*

PRIVATE TOM RUFFLEY
(Connaught Rangers)

One of five brothers from Bohermore who served in the Great War, he was killed in India in 1922. James served with the Royal Dublin Fusiliers and John was killed in action on 15 September 1916, see p. 209. There is no information available on the other brothers. *(Courtesy of the Ruffley family.)*

ABLE SEAMAN REDMOND SULLIVAN
(Royal Navy)

From Middle Street, Galway, his brother Stephen, served with the Irish Guards, both of them survived the war. *(Courtesy of Nuala Nolan).*

PRIVATE MICHAEL JOHN SUMMERLY 40624
(Royal Inniskilling Fusiliers)

From Bohermore, Galway, he enlisted when he was fifteen years of age. In one of the actions of the war he saved the life of an officer and was awarded the Military Medal. After the war he went to live in Ennis, Co. Clare where he married in the 1920s. His wife Catherine also features in the photograph.

He remained in Ennis until his death in 1975. His brother, William, also served in the Great War. They met once during the war, close to the front, but only managed to wave to each other. Following the war, William went to the US were he remained until his death in 1960. *(Courtesy of P.J. Summerly.)*

SECOND LIEUTENANT CHARLES JAMES WAITES
(Sixth Connaught Rangers)

Born in 1887, the son of William & Mary J. Waites of Kilcolgan, he was killed in action in France on 10 October 1918. *(Courtesy of Agatha Mahon.)*

CORPORAL JOHN WALSH 4506
(Second Leinster Regiment)

He was born in 1896, the son of Philip Walsh of the Tram Yard, Forster Street, Galway. Formerly of the Royal Field Artillery 100275. Before enlisting, John played with St Patrick's band. He was killed in action on 31 July 1917 at the third Battle of Ypres (Passchendaele). He wrote a letter to his mother, just six days before he was killed. The letter was included in *Galway and the Great War*, p. 184, 185. *(Courtesy of Valerie Noonan.)*

ABLE SEAMAN MARTIN WALSH & PETTY OFFICER STEPHEN CURRAN

Martin Walsh was from Long Walk, Galway. Stephen Curran also appears in another photograph with Martin O'Donnell, p. 41. *(Courtesy of Paddy & Stephen Curran.)*

SERGEANT PATRICK WALSH
(Connaught Rangers)

From Oughterard, two of his brothers, Michael and Peter, also served in the Connaught Rangers, and according to the family both were killed during the war. However, they were not mentioned in any of the records explored in compiling the list of dead for this book. One was allegedly killed at Mons in 1914, while the other brother was killed in 1918. Patrick survived the war and having returned home, he began working as a tailor in Moons of Galway (Brown Thomas). He married Sabina Coyne from Moycullen and they first lived in a thatched house at 76 Lower Salthill, but later the family moved to Raleigh Row. They had seven children, one of whom, Sheila Jordan, became mayor of Galway in 1977. *(Courtesy of the late Shelia Jordan.)*

CORPORAL PETER JOHN WALSH
(Connaught Rangers)

Born 18 June 1896, Corporal Walsh was from St John's Terrace, and later lived in Fursey Road, Shantalla, Galway. He was an exceptionally brave man and his courage was put to the test during action at the Somme. Under heavy fire he managed to pull one of his comrades to safety with little regard for his own life. He returned to the fighting line and managed to help a badly wounded officer, Captain Joe White, who lay tangled in barbed wire. He was awarded the Distinguished Conduct Medal. Two of his brothers also served – James with the Royal Engineers and Frank with the Irish Guards. He was stationed in India after the war and was arrested following the Connaught Rangers mutiny. Peter also fought in the Second World War, and was almost killed near Dunkirk. He married Kate Power from Waterford and they had eight children. In later years he was affectionately know as 'Daddo'. He never forgot the years he served in the Connaught Rangers. During an interview many years ago, he said: 'I had some great times in the army and would do it all over again if I could join the Connaught Rangers. I often reflect on those marvellous times and they are a great source of pleasure in my old age.' He died on 7 September 1982 and was buried in St Mary's (new cemetery), Bohermore. *(Courtesy of Mary Lambe.)*

LANCE CORPORAL MICHAEL WHITE
(First Connaught Rangers)

He was born in 1877 in Portumna, was a military chiropodist and served in the Boer War. His medals included the South African Campaign Medal & Bars and the Good Conduct Medal. He also served in India. He married Margaret Burke, sister of Katy Burke who was married to Private Harry Howett, and they had six children. After the war he served as chiropodist with the Irish Free State army for a number of years. His brother, John, was invalided out of the Royal Field Artillery. Some time later he re-enlisted in an infantry regiment under an assumed name and was killed on the western front. Michael died in 1956 and was buried in St Mary's (new cemetery), Bohermore. Brother of Pat White. *(Courtesy of Michael Conneely.)*

PRIVATE PAT WHITE
(First Connaught Rangers)

Brother of Michael White, Pat survived the war and lived in Portumna for the remainder of his life. *(Courtesy of Michael Conneely.)*

GALWAY
ROLL OF HONOUR

[See Introduction for explanations on age differences, Death 1614–1918, France or Flanders, Address, Killed in Action or Died of Wounds. Numbers/figures in brackets indicate the grave number or memorial panel.]

AGNEW, Michael (Myles)   Private 4863   Connaught Rangers
Death: (Galway) 4 April 1915.
Supplementary Notes: Wounded on the western front in 1915. Sent to a Liverpool hospital. From there he was sent to Galway to rejoin his regiment at Renmore barracks. On the morning of 4 April 1915 he was found dead in his bunk; his throat had been cut. A small safety razor was found close to his bed. The verdict of the medical examiner was death by suicide. It was believed that he had suffered deeply because of experiences at the front, and was a victim of the Great War. Born: Galway.
Buried: St Mary's – (new cemetery) – Bohermore – Galway – Ireland (R.C.A. 13. 49).

ACTON, Armar Edward   Chaplain Fourth Class   Second Border Regiment
Death: (France) 4 November 1917. Age 28.
Supplementary Notes: 'Mentioned in Despatches'. Son of Lieutenant Colonel J.L.C. (First Connaught Rangers) & Maud J. Acton. Born: Galway.
Buried: Wimereux Communal Cemetery – Pas de Calais – France (IV. L. 2).

ALLCOCK, S.   Gunner 58673   Nineteenth Royal Garrison Artillery
Death: (Belgium) 19 October 1917. Age 29.
Supplementary Notes: Son of Richard & Jessie Allcock of Church View, Tuam.
Buried: Canada Farm Cemetery – Ieper – West-Vlaanderen – Belgium (III. E. 3).

ANDERSON, James   Seaman 3912/A   HMS *Pembroke*   Royal Navy Reserves
Death: 3 September 1917. Age 25.
Supplementary Notes: Son of Thomas & Mary Anderson of Fairhill, Claddagh, Galway.
Buried: Gillingham (Woodlands) Cemetery – Kent – United Kingdom (R.C. 5. 230).

ANDERSON, James   Private 47112   Connaught Rangers
Killed in Action: (France) 18 August 1917. Age 30.
Supplementary Notes: Born: Galway.
Buried: Boulogne Eastern Cemetery – Pas de Calais – France (VIII. B. 73).

ARMSTRONG-LUSHINGTON-TULLOCH, Graham   Lieutenant   First
Connaught Rangers
    Killed in Action: (Ypres, Belgium) 4 or 5 November 1914. Age 28 or 29.
    Supplementary Notes: Son of William Cairns & Kate Lushington-Tulloch- Armstrong
of Shanbolard, Moyard (Clifden).
    Buried: Rue-du-Bacquerot No. 1 Military Cemetery – Laventie – Pas de Calais –
France (I. A. 17).

BANKS, Thomas   Seaman 8197A   HMS *Samia*   Royal Navy Reserves
    Killed in Action: (Mediterranean) 12 September 1918. Age 20.
    Supplementary Notes: Killed during action with an enemy submarine. Son of Michael
& Bridget Banks of Rope Walk, Claddagh, Galway.
    Remembered: Portsmouth Naval Memorial – Hampshire – United Kingdom.

BANKS, Thomas   Private 13711   Connaught Rangers
    Killen in Action: (France) 11 July 1915. Age 29.
    Supplementary Notes: Born: Galway.

BARNETT, Joseph Thomas   Lance Corporal 23357   Eighth Royal Irish Fusiliers
    Killed in Action: (France) 26 or 27 April 1916. Age 18 or 31.
    Supplementary Notes: Son of Joseph T. & Fanny Barnett of 2 Frenchville, Galway.
    Buried: Bois-Carre Military Cemetery – Haisnes – Pas de Calais – France (D. 2).
    Remembered: Great War monument – St Nicholas' Collegiate Church – Galway
– Ireland.

BARRETT, James   Private 24960   Second Royal Irish Fusiliers
    Died of Wounds: (Egypt) 27 November 1917.
    Supplementary Notes: Born: Mountbellew.

BARRETT, John   Private 3986   Royal Munster Fusiliers
    Killed in Action: (Dardanelles) 9 May 1917. Age 26 or 36.
    Supplementary Notes: Because of the date and location of Private John Barrett's death,
it is necessary to say that this is the official recorded information. Born: Galway.

BARRETT, John Patrick   Private G/515   First Royal Irish Fusiliers
    Death: 24 September 1918. Age 32.
    Supplementary Notes: Enlisted: Oranmore. Formerly of the Connaught Rangers
2933. Son of James & Mary Barrett of Rope Walk, Claddagh, Galway.

Buried: Taukkyan War Cemetery – Myanmar (26. J. 15).

BARRETT, Matthew   Sergeant 420826   Sixteenth Canadian Infantry
    Death: (France or Flanders) 8 August 1918. Age 29.
    Supplementary Notes: Enlisted Canadian Infantry (Manitoba Regiment). Born Galway.
    Buried: Demuin British Cemetery (A. 18).

BARRETT, Mattie   Private   British Expeditionary Force
    Killed in Action: (France) 1914–1918.
    Supplementary Notes: Born Cullen, Carna, Connemara.

BARRETT, Patrick   Private 9995   Royal Inniskilling Fusiliers
    Died of Wounds: (Loughrea, Co. Galway) 13 August 1917. Age 24.
    Supplementary Notes: Born: Loughrea.
    Buried: Loughrea (Garrybreda) Cemetery – Loughrea – Ireland (north-east part).

BARRETT, Patrick   Acting Sergeant 48190   Thirteenth Royal Inniskilling Fusiliers
    Killed in Action: (France) 13 November 1917. Age 32.
    Supplementary Notes: Born: Galway.
    Buried: Pont-de-Nieppe Communal Cemetery (II. H. 13).

BARRETT, Patrick   Sergeant 48910   Thirteenth Royal Inniskilling Fusiliers
    Died of Wounds: (France) 29 October 1918.
    Supplementary Notes: Enlisted: Galway. Formerly of the Royal Irish Rifles 6887. Born: Galway.

BARRETT, Patrick   Private 8792   Connaught Rangers
    Killed in Action: (France) 17 July 1918. Age 24.
    Supplementary Notes: Born: Galway.

BARRETT, Michael   Lance Sergeant 29345   (4 Depot) Royal Garrison Artillery
    Death: (England) 1 June 1920. Age 32.
    Supplementary Notes: Husband of M.A. Barrett of Lower Abbey Gate Street, Galway.
    Buried: Ripon Cemetery – Yorkshire – United Kingdom (G. 244).

BEIRNE, Eugene Private 3959 Sixth Connaught Rangers
Killed in Action: (France) 21 March 1918.
Supplementary Notes: Born: Galway.
Remembered: Pozieres Memorial – Somme – France (77).

BEIRNE, Michael Private 4202 Second Connaught Rangers
Death: 29 October 1914.
Supplementary Notes: From Ballinasloe.
Remembered: Ypres (Menin Gate) Memorial – Ieper – West–Vlaanderen – Belgium (42) & Roll of Honour – Killed in Action – 1914–1918 – Ballinasloe – Ireland.

BEIRNE, Thomas Private British Expeditionary Force
Death: 1914–1918.
Supplementary Notes: From Ballinasloe.
Remembered: Roll of Honour – Killed in Action – 1914–1918 – Ballinasloe – Ireland.

BELL, Alfred Roy Second Lieutenant Second Royal Dublin Fusiliers
Killed in Action: (Ypres, Belgium) 17 March 1915. Age 19.
Supplementary Notes: Born: Ballinasloe.

BELL, William John Sergeant 12087 Sixth Royal Irish Fusiliers
Death: (Salonika) 22 November 1915.
Supplementary Notes: Enlisted: Sheffield. Born: Galway.
Buried: Mikra British Cemetery – Kalamaria – Greece (1372).

BELTON, John Seaman 5003A *Lady Cory Wright* Royal Navy Reserves
Killed in Action: (English Channel) 26 March 1918. Age 23.
Supplementary Notes: Killed during action with an enemy submarine. Son of John & Honor Belton of 5 Lower Merchants Road, Galway.
Remembered: Portsmouth Naval Memorial – Hampshire – United Kingdom (31).

BELTON, John Private 31191 Connaught Rangers
Killed in Action: (France) 2 September 1916. Age 33.
Supplementary Notes: Born: Galway.

BERNE, Patrick William   Sergeant 77478   First Canadian Division
Death: (France) 9 April 1917. Age 29.
Supplementary Notes: Enlisted: Canada 1914 (Central Ontario Regiment). Son of Connor Berne of St Mary's Terrace, Galway.
Buried: Nine Elms Military Cemetery – Thelus (Arras Road Cem. Men. 6).

BERRY, Colman   Private 4939   Sixth Royal Irish Regiment
Killed in Action: (Guillemont, France) 3 September 1916.
Supplementary Notes: Born: Caislean, Lettermullen, Connemara.
Remembered: Thiepval Memorial – Somme – France (3 A).

BERRY, Edward Fleetwood   Captain & Adjutant   Ninth Gurkha Rifles
Killed in Action: (Aiesa, Mesopotamia) 17 April 1916. Age 27.
Supplementary Notes: Only son of Canon Fleetwood Berry, Rector of St Nicholas' Collegiate Church, Galway.
Remembered: Basra Memorial – Iraq (51) & Great War monument – St Nicholas' Collegiate Church – Galway – Ireland.

BERRY, Martin   Leading Stoker K6653   HMS *Defence*   Royal Navy
Killed in Action: (Jutland) 31 May 1916. Age 24.
Supplementary Notes: Son of Festus & Ellen Berry of Ballycource, Clifden.
Remembered: Plymouth Naval Memorial – Devon – United Kindom (14).

BETTS, Conrad Coryton   Lieutenant   G (Mudros) Royal Air Force
Death: 17 April 1918. Age 19.
Supplementary Notes: Son of Cecil Coulter Betts & Louisa Alice Betts of Knockboy House, Recess, Connemara.
Buried: East Mudros Military Cemetery – Lemnos – Greece (III. H. 240).

BINGHAM, George   Sergeant 200016   Duke of Cornwall Light Infantry
Death: (Persian Gulf) 18 August 1916. Age 30.
Supplementary Notes: Born: Roundstone, Connemara.
Buried: Baghdad (North Gate) War Cemetery – Iraq (XXI. A. 42).

BIRMINGHAM, William Arthur   Second Lieutenant   Sixth Royal Irish Fusiliers
Death: 9 August 1915. Age 35.
Supplementary Notes: Son of John Birmingham of Galway; husband of Margery R. Bermingham (*nee* Cooke) of 50 Upper Leeson Street, Dublin.

Remembered: Helles Memorial – Turkey (178 to 180).

BIRKETT, P.   Private   Royal Irish Fusiliers
    Killed in Action: (France) 20 November 1917.
    Supplementary Notes: Awarded Military Medal. Born: Magdalen Terrace, Galway.

BLYTHE, Patrick   Lance Corporal 19657 Tenth Yorkshire & Lancaster Light Infantry
    Died of Wounds: (France) 28 September 1917.
    Supplementary Notes: Born: Galway.
    Remembered: Tyne Cot Memorial Zonnebeke – West-Vlaanderen – Belgium (126 to 128).

BOHAN, Stephen   Able Seaman 152004   HMS *Doris* Royal Navy
    Death: 23 June 1918. Age 44.
    Supplementary Notes: Husband of Mary Bohan (*nee* Ruane) of Shantalla, Galway. Born: Galway.
    Remembered: Kirkee 1914–1918 Memorial – India (A).

BOHEN, Stephen   Able Seaman 43491   Royal Navy
    Died of Wounds: (Bombay) 25 June 1918. Age 45.
    Supplementary Notes: Born: Galway.

BONE, John   Private 3/21693   Eighth Royal Dublin Fusiliers
    Killed in Action: (France) 1 April 1916. Age 36.
    Supplementary Notes: Born: Tuam.
    Buried: Bois-Carre Military Cemetery – Haisnes – France (Sp. Men. 2).

BOOTH, Lawrence Howard   Second Lieutenant   Royal Flying Corps
    Killed in Air Crash: (Dromore, Co. Tyrone) 13 November 1918. Age 20.
    Supplementary Notes: (Royal Air Force) Killed in mid-air collision. Newspaper report states that he was a Galwayman.
    Buried: Omagh new cemetery – Ulster – Ireland (Special Section 128).

BOYLE, James   Private 6420   First Connaught Rangers
    Killed in Action: (France) 17 April 1916. Age 26.
    Supplementary Notes: Born: Belclare.
    Remembered: Basra Memorial – Iraq (40 & 64).

BRACKEN, Hugh Alexander   Corporal 521   Tenth Royal Warwickshire Regiment
Killed in Action: (France) 22 March 1918.
Supplementary Notes: Born: Ballinasloe.
Remembered: Arras Memorial – Pas de Calais – France (3).

BRADLEY, John   Private   Connaught Rangers
Killed in Action: (Belgium) 15 November 1917. Age 22.
Supplementary Notes: Born: Galway.

BRADLEY, John   Private 4625   Sixth Connaught Rangers
Killed in Action: (France) 3 July 1916. Age 21.
Supplementary Notes: Enlisted: Galway. Son of John Bradley of Pouleywerrin,
Lettermullen, Connemara.
Buried: Dud Corner Cemetery – Loos – Pas de Calais – France (II. G. 14).

BRADSHAW, Thomas George   Corporal 54100   Royal Flying Corps
Killed in Air Crash: (Dromore, Co. Tyrone) 13 November 1918. Age 20.
Supplementary Notes: (Royal Air Force) Killed in mid-air collision. Newspaper report
states that he was a Galwayman.
Buried: Northampton (Kingsthorpe) Cemetery – United Kingdom.

BRENNAN, John   Private 34500   Machine Gun Corps
Killed in Action: (France) 9 April 1917. Age 19.
Supplementary Notes: Enlisted: Dublin. Formerly of the Royal Dublin Fusiliers
4/23843. Born: Galway.
Remembered: Arras Memorial – Pas de Calais – France (10).

BRENNAN, Michael   Private, 4048   First Irish Guards
Death: 6 November 1914. Age 24.
Supplementary Notes: Son of James Brennan of Kilkerrin, Ballinasloe.
Remembered: Ypres (Menin Gate) Memorial – Ieper – West-Vlaanderen – Belgium (11).

BRIEN, William   Lance Corporal 24876   First Royal Irish Fusiliers
Killed in Action: (France) 6 or 11 April 1917. Age 28.
Supplementary Notes: Enlisted: Ballinasloe. Formerly of the Royal Irish Fusiliers.
Born: Kilclooney, Ballinasloe.
Buried: Brown's Copse Cemetery – Roeux – France (I. C. 29).

BROSNAN, Patrick   Sergeant Major 15231   Royal Irish Fusiliers
Death: (Dublin) 25 April 1916. Age 50.
Supplementary Notes: Born: Galway.
Buried: Grangegorman Military Cemetery – Dublin – Ireland (RC. 477).

BROWN, Hugh   Private 198943   Fifth Canadian Infantry
Death: (France) 27 September 1916.
Supplementary Notes: (Saskatchewan Regiment). Husband of Elizabeth Brown of Upper Dunlo Hill, Ballinasloe.
Remembered: Vimy Memorial – Pas de Calais – France & St John's Church Roll of Honour – Ballinasloe – Ireland.

BROWN, Stephen   Private   British Expeditionary Force
Death: 1914–1918.
Supplementary Notes: From Ballinasloe.
Remembered: Roll of Honour – Killed in Action – 1914–1918 – Ballinasloe – Ireland.

BROWNE, Joseph   Private 7145   Sixth Connaught Rangers
Killed in Action: (France) 20 November 1917.
Supplementary Notes: Enlisted: Athlone. Born: Ballinasloe.
Buried: Croisilles Railway Cemetery – Pas de Calais – France (I. C. 8).

BURKE, Edmond   Private   British Expeditionary Force
Killed in Action: (France) 1914–1918.
Supplementary Notes: Born Dooyher, Carna, Connemara.

BURKE, Edward   Private 10746   Tenth Cheshire Regiment
Killed in Action: (France) 17 February 1917. Age 25.
Supplementary Notes: Born: Carna, Connemara.
Remembered: Ploegsteert Memorial – Comines – Warneton – Hainaut – Belgium (4 & 5).

BURKE, George   Sapper WR/175524   Royal Engineers
Death: (France) 27 October 1918. Age 21.
Supplementary Notes: Son of Mrs A. Burke of Galway.
Buried: Terlincthun British Cemetery – Wimille – Pas de Calais – France (VI. D. 30).

BURKE, James   Private 1228   First Irish Guards
Killed in Action: (France) 18 May 1915. Age 34.
Supplementary Notes: Awarded Mons Star. Son of John & Bridget Burke of Bishop Street, Tuam. Just before the attack in which he was killed, it was reported that he jokingly said that the Kaiser never got the range of him or never would.
Remembered: Le Touret Memorial – Pas de Calais – France (4).

BURKE, John   Private 11052.   First Irish Guards
Death: (France) 16 December 1917. Age 19 or 21.
Supplementary Notes: Son of John & Catherine Burke of Doon, Kilrickle, Loughrea.
Buried: St Sever Cemetery Extension – Rouen – Seine-Maritime – France (P. V. F. 3A).

BURKE, John   Private   Sixth Connaught Rangers
Killed in Action: (France) December 1916. Age 34.
Supplementary Notes: Born: Galway.

BURKE, John   Private 5812   Fifth Connaught Rangers
Killed in Action: (Gallipoli) 2 November 1915.
Supplementary Notes: Enlisted: Hull. Born: Inishmore, Aran Islands.
Buried: East Mudros Military Cemetery – Lemnos – Greece (III. C. 78).

BURKE, Joseph   Private 10811.   Second Connaught Rangers
Killed in Action: (France) 14 or 23 November 1914. Age 23.
Supplementary Notes: Son of William & Delia Burke of Kilconnell, Ballinasloe.
Remembered: Ypres (Menin Gate) Memorial – Ieper – West-Vlaanderen – Belgium (42).

BURKE, Joseph   Private 25897   Eighth Royal Dublin Fusiliers
Killed in Action: (France) 9 September 1916. Age 28.
Supplementary Notes: Son of Joseph & Mary Burke; husband of Eva E. Burke of Hill House, Clifden. Born: Galway.
Remembered: Thiepval Memorial – Somme – France (16 C).

BURKE, Michael   Private 5244   First Irish Guards
Died of Wounds: (France) 1 September 1915.

Supplementary Notes: Born: Galway.
Buried: Chocques Military Cemetery – France (I. D. 46).

BURKE, Michael   Private 7112   First Shropshire Light Infantry
  Died of Wounds: (France) 23 August 1915.
  Supplementary Notes: Born: Portumna.

BURKE, Michael   Private 13320   Sixth Royal Dublin Fusiliers
  Killed in Action: (Gallipoli) 15 August 1915.
  Supplementary Notes: Born: Kilkernan.
  Remembered: Helles Memorial – Turkey (180 to 186).

BURKE, Patrick   Private 2174   First Gloucestershire Regiment
  Died of Wounds: (France) 16 September 1918.
  Supplementary Notes: Enlisted: Cardiff. Born: Galway.
  Buried: Heath Cemetery – Harbonnieres – France (X. B. 20).

BURKE, Patrick   Private or Lance Corporal 7317   Sixth Connaught Rangers
  Killed in Action: 2 August 1917. Age 25 or 26.
  Supplementary Notes: Enlisted: Sligo. Awarded Mons Star. Son of John & Catherine Burke of Doon, Kilrickle, Loughrea.
  Remembered: Ypres (Menin Gate) Memorial – Ieper – West-Vlaanderen – Belgium (42).

BURKE, Patrick   Private 6933   Sixth or Seventh Royal Irish Regiment
  Killed in Action: (France) 2 September or 2 November 1918. Age 18.
  Supplementary Notes: Enlisted: Ballinasloe. Son of Ellen Burke of Haymarket Street, Ballinasloe.
  Buried: Wulverghem-Lindenhoek Road Military Cemetery – Heuvelland – West-Vlaanderen – Belgium (V. E. 21).

BURKE, Patrick   Private 45280   First Machine Gun Corps
  Killed in Action: (France) 23 April 1917.
  Supplementary Notes: Born: Woodford.
  Remembered: Arras Memorial – Pas de Calais – France (10).

BURKE, Patrick Thomas   Private 29078   Canadian army
Death: (France or Flanders) 1914–1918.
Supplementary Notes: Enlisted: Canada. Born: Galway.

BURKE, Richard   Private 9002   First Irish Guards
Died of Wounds: (France) 23 April 1917 or 29 March 1918.
Supplementary Notes: Born: Annaghdown.
Buried: Doullens Communal Cemetery Extension No. 1 – Somme – France (V C. 2).

BURKE, Thomas   Bombardier 50699   Royal Garrison Artillery
Died of Wounds: (Home) 8 May 1917.
Supplementary Notes: Born: Loughrea.
Buried: Edinburgh (Comely Bank) Cemetery – Scotland (D22).

BURKE, William   Private 9908   Fifth Connaught Rangers
Death: (Salonika) 18 September 1916. Age 24.
Supplementary Notes: Enlisted: Galway. Born: Headford.
Buried: Salonika (Lembet Road) Military Cemetery – Greece (422).

BURNS, Thomas   Private (Sergeant) 705   Second Connaught Rangers
Killed in Action: (Gallipoli) 22 August 1915. Age 44.
Supplementary Notes: Enlisted: Ballinasloe. Born: Kilclooney, Ballinasloe.
Remembered: Helles Memorial – Gallipoli – Turkey (181 to 183).

BUTLER, John   Private 5364   Fifth Connaught Rangers
Killed in Action: (Salonika) 7 December 1915. Age 19.
Supplementary Notes: Enlisted: Galway. Son of James & Bridget Butler of Curraun,
Oughterard.
Remembered: Doiran Memorial – Greece.

BYRNE, Michael   Private 25070   Seventh Royal Irish Regiment
Killed in Action: (France) 21 March 1918.
Supplementary Notes: Enlisted: Athlone. Formerly of the South Irish Horse 1213.
Son of the late William & Bridget Byrne of Front Gate Lodge, Mental Hospital,
Ballinasloe. Brother of Thomas Byrne, p. 81.
Buried: Templeux-le-Guerard British Cemetery – Somme – France (I. C. 7).

BYRNE, Thomas   Private 983   South Irish Horse
Killed in Action: (France) 12 October 1916. Age 20 or 22.
Supplementary Notes: Enlisted: Athlone. Intelligence Dept, XV Corps. Son of the late William & Bridget Byrne of Front Gate Lodge, Mental Hospital, Ballinasloe. Brother of Michael Byrne, p. 80.
Remembered: Thiepval Memorial – Somme – France (1A).

CAFFERY, Joseph   Private 3988   Third Connaught Rangers
Death: (Cork or Galway) 12 August 1914.
Supplementary Notes: Enlisted: Tuam. Son of the late P. Caffery of Tulindaly Road, Tuam.
Buried: Alternative Commemoration – Cork Military Cemetery (Special Memorial).

CAFFREY, Michael   Private 3872   Second Connaught Rangers
Killed in Action: (France) 8 November 1914. Age 20.
Supplementary Notes: Enlisted: Galway. Born: Gort.

CAFFREY, Phillip   Private 9729   Thirty-second East Lancashire Regiment
Killed in Action: (France) 9 May 1915.
Supplementary Notes: Born: Tuam.

CAHALIN, Francis   Private 25097   Seventh Royal Irish Regiment
Killed in Action: (France) 21 March 1918. Age 22.
Supplementary Notes: Enlisted: Ballinasloe. Formerly of the South Irish Horse 1587. Born: Lismanney.
Remembered: Pozieres Memorial – Somme – France (30 & 31).

CAMPBELL, Donald   Lieutenant   Coldstream Guards
Killed in Action: (Ypres, Belgium) 19 July 1916. Age 20.
Supplementary Notes: Eldest son of Captain The Hon. John B. Campbell, D.O.S., D.L., of Moycullen House. His father was also killed, p. 82.
Buried: Essex Farm Cemetery – United Kingdom (II. V. 8).
Remembered: Great War monument – St Nicholas' Collegiate Church – Galway – Ireland.

CAMPBELL, James   Private 10955   First Royal Irish Fusiliers
Killed in Action: (France) 10 December 1916. Age 19 or 21.

Supplementary Notes: Son of Patrick & Anne Campbell of Haymarket Street, Ballinasloe.

Buried: Sailly-Saillisel British Cemetery – Somme – France (V. E. 6).

CAMPBELL, James   Private 10958   First Royal Irish Fusiliers
Killed in Action: 10 October 1916. Age 19.
Supplementary Notes: Born: Kilclooney, Ballinasloe.

CAMPBELL, John Beresford   Captain D.O.S., D.L.   Second Coldstream Guards
Killed in Action: (Guinchy, France) 25 January 1915. Age 49.
Supplementary Notes: Son of Lord Stradtheden & Campbell. On the day that war was declared he left his home in Moycullen and re-joined his regiment. Father of Donald Campbell, listed above.
Remembered: Le Touret Memorial – Pas de Calais – France (2 & 3); and Great War monument – St Nicholas' Collegiate Church – Galway – Ireland.

CAMPBELL, Thomas   Private / Drummer 5682.   Sixth Connaught Rangers
Killed in Action: (France) 8 March 1917. Age 17 or 18.
Supplementary Notes: Enlisted: Ballinasloe. Son of Patrick & Anne Campbell of Haymarket Street, Ballinasloe (Kilclooney).
Buried: Kemmel Chateau Military Cemetery – Heuvelland – West-Vlaanderen – Belgium (M 74).

CANAVAN, John   Private 4663   Connaught Rangers
Death: 5 November 1918. Age 20.
Supplementary Notes: Also served under the alias, John Green 187492 Royal Field Artillery & died under the alias, John Gavin 309926 Royal Air Force. Son of Martin & Mary Canavan. From Ballinasloe.
Buried: Creagh new cemetery – Ballinasloe – Ireland (C. 27).
Remembered: Roll of Honour – Killed in Action – 1914–1918 – Ballinasloe – Ireland.

CANAVAN, Joseph   Fisherman Trawler *Pretty Polly*   Mercantile Marines
Presumed Drowned: 31 May 1918. Age 20.
Supplementary Notes: Son of Joe & Barbara Canavan of Ard East, Carna, Connemara. The sinking of the *Pretty Polly* was recorded in *Galway and the Great War*, p. 98.
Remembered: Tower Hill Memorial – London – United Kingdom.

CANAVAN, Michael Private 14668 Thirteenth Royal Scots
  Died of Wounds: (France) 15 September 1915. Age 35.
  Supplementary Notes: Son of Peter & Margaret Canavan of Ardnagreevagh, Renvyle (Clifden).
  Buried: Noeux-le-Mines Communal Cemetery – Pas de Calais – France (I. A. 17).

CANAVAN, Mark Fisherman Trawler *Pretty Polly* Mercantile Marines
  Presumed Drowned: 31 May 1918. Age 37.
  Supplementary Notes: Brother of Michael Canavan, see above.
  Remembered: Tower Hill Memorial – London – United Kingdom.

CANAVAN, Mark Fisherman Trawler *Pretty Polly* Mercantile Marines
  Presumed Drowned: 31 May 1918. Age 26.
  Supplementary Notes: Son of Bridget Canavan of Ard East, Carna, Connemara.
  Remembered: Tower Hill Memorial – London – United Kingdom.

CANAVAN, Patrick Private 25044 Fifteenth Lancashire Fusiliers
  Killed in Action: (Somme, France) 1 July 1916. Age 40 or 43.
  Supplementary Notes: Husband of Bridget Canavan of Cellar, Rosmuck, Connemara.
  Buried: Connaught Cemetery, Thiepval – Somme – France (II. E. 4).

CANAVAN, Tom Fisherman Trawler *Pretty Polly* Mercantile Marines
  Presumed Drowned: 31 May 1918. Age 63.
  Supplementary Notes: Son of the late Tom & Bridget Canavan; husband of Bridget Canavan (*nee* McDonogh) of Ard East, Carna, Connemara.
  Remembered: Tower Hill Memorial – London – United Kingdom.

CANNY, Peter Rifleman 5531 Second King's Royal Rifle Corps
  Killed in Action: (France) 10 November 1914.
  Supplementary Notes: Born: Tuam.
  Remembered: Ypres (Menin Gate) Memorial – Ieper – West-Vlaanderen – Belgium (51 & 53).

CARMODY, Edward Private S/13 or 5113 Fifth Connaught Rangers
  Killed in Action: (Salonika) 25 March 1917. Age 22.
  Supplementary Notes: Enlisted: Galway. Son of Michael & Delia Carmody of 5 Montpelier Terrace, Galway (Craughwell).
  Remembered: Doiran Memorial – Greece.

CARNEY, Dennis   Sergeant   British Expeditionary Force
Death: 1914–1918.
Supplementary Notes: From Ballinasloe.
Remembered: Roll of Honour – Killed in Action – 1914–1918 – Ballinasloe – Ireland.

CARNEY, Francis   Lance Corporal 3088   Second Leinster Regiment
Died of Wounds: (Belgium) 28 September 1918.
Supplementary Notes: Formerly of the Connaught Rangers 753. Born: Creagh, Ballinasloe.
Buried: Vlamertinghe New Military Cemetery – Ieper – Belgium (XV. F. 1).

CAROLIN, Joseph James   Corporal 201916   Second & Tenth Manchester Regiment
Killed in Action: (France) 9 October 1917.
Supplementary Notes: Born: Clifden.
Remembered: Tyne Cot Memorial Zonnebeke – West-Vlaanderen – Belgium (162 to 163).

CARR, James   Sapper 136277   173rd Royal Engineers
Killed in Action: (France) 25 June 1916.
Supplementary Notes: (Tunnel Company). Born: Mountbellew.
Remembered: Arras Memorial – Pas de Calais – France (1).

CARR, John   Private 10124   Sixth Royal Irish Regiment
Killed in Action: (France) 21 November 1917. Age 23.
Supplementary Notes: Son of Michael & Margaret Carr of Abbeygate Street, Galway.
Buried: Croisilles British Cemetery – Pas de Calais – France (II. D. 9).

CARR, Patrick   Private 39876   Connaught Rangers
Killed in Action: (France) 11 August 1916. Age 30.
Supplementary Notes: Born: Galway.

CARR, Thomas   Sergeant 31413   Connaught Rangers
Died of Illness: (Galway) 19 February 1919. Age 35 or 37.
Supplementary Notes: Enlisted: Ballinasloe. Illness caused by the influenza pandemic that broke out in 1918. Husband of Mary Anne Carr of Jubilee Street, Ballinasloe.
Buried: Creagh new cemetery – Ballinasloe – Ireland (D2. 623).

CARR, William   Lance Corporal 1393   Sixth Connaught Rangers
Killed in Action or Died of Wounds: (Loos, France) 9 March 1916. Age 27 or 29.
Supplementary Notes: Enlisted: Cork. Son of Bartly & Kate Carr of Cartoor, Moycullen.
Remembered: Loos Memorial – Pas de Calais – Fraike (124).

CARRICK, Patrick   Private B/7630   First Cameronians (Scottish Rifles)
Killed in Action: (France) 24 October 1915.
Supplementary Notes: Enlisted: Glasgow. Born: Galway.
Buried: Cambrin Churchyard Cemetery – France (D. 19).

CARRICK, Patrick   Private 24159   First Royal Inniskilling Fusiliers
Killed in Action: (Somme, France) 1 July 1916.
Supplementary Notes: Enlisted: Lanark. Son of Michael & Mary Carrick (*nee* O'Farrell) of the Claddagh, Galway.
Buried: Y Ravine Cemetery – Beaumont-Hamel – Somme – France (D. 45).

CARROLL, J.   Private 6683   Third Connaught Rangers
Death: (Ballinasloe) 18 January 1919.
Supplementary Notes: Enlisted: Ballinasloe. Husband of C. Carroll of Haymarket Street, Ballinasloe.
Buried: Barrack Street Old Graveyard – Nenagh (north-west, near north wall) – Ireland.

CARROLL, James   Corporal 8744   Second Royal Munster Fusiliers
Killed in Action: (France) 24 August 1916.
Supplementary Notes: Enlisted: Tralee, Co. Kerry. Born: Galway.
Remembered: Thiepval Memorial – Somme – France (4 A & 40).

CARROLL, Joseph   Sapper WR/249319   Royal Engineers
Death: (France) 27 April 1918.
Supplementary Notes: Formerly of the London Regiment 5079. Born: Galway.
Buried: Abbeville Communal Cemetery Extension – Somme – France (IV. A. 16).

CARROLL, Patrick   Private G19390   Third Royal Irish Fusiliers
Death: (Galway) 3 April 1917.
Supplementary Notes: Born: Annaghdown.
Buried: Shorncliffe Military Cemetery – United Kingdom (C. 512).

CARROLL, T. Private 2873 Sixth Connaught Rangers
Killed in Action: 2 April 1916. Age 35.
Supplementary Notes: Son of Mary Carroll of Herald House, Dublin Road, Tuam &
of the late James Carroll (Annaghdown).
Buried: Noeux-les-Mines Communal Cemetery – Pas de Calais – France (I. H. 29).

CARTER, Jackson Private 21173 Connaught Rangers
Killed in Action: (France) Age 28.
Supplementary Notes: Born: Galway.

CARTER, John Private 757 Fifth Connaught Rangers
Died of Wounds: (Gallipoli) 12 August 1915. Age 32.
Supplementary Notes: Enlisted: Galway. Son of the late John & Mary Carter;
husband of Helen Carter (*nee* Flaherty) of Flood Street, Galway. Born: Galway.
Remembered: Helles Memorial – Turkey (181 to 183).

CARTY, John Sergeant Major 6683 (6083) First Connaught Rangers
Killed in Action: (Mesopotamia) 18 April 1916.
Supplementary Notes: Born: Galway.
Remembered: Basra Memorial – Iraq (40 & 64).

CASEY, James Private 15 Fifth Connaught Rangers
Died of Wounds: (Gallipoli) 9 September 1915.
Supplementary Notes: Enlisted: Galway. Born: St Nicholas' Parish, Galway.
Buried: Alexandria (Hadra) War Memorial Cemetery – Egypt (F. 120).

CASEY, John Private 4216 Second Connaught Rangers
Died of Wounds: (Galway) 11 March 1915. Age 21.
Supplementary Notes: Enlisted: Gort. Awarded Mons Star. Born: Loughrea.
Buried: Loughrea (Garrybreda) Cemetery – Loughrea – Ireland (near north
boundary).

CASEY, Martin Private 7754 Second Leinster Regiment
Killed in Action: (Belgium) 20 October 1914. Age 41.
Supplementary Notes: Son of Martin & Mary Casey of Main Street, Ballinasloe.
Remembered: Ploegsteert Memorial – Comines–Warneton – Hainaut – Belgium (10).

CASEY, Micheal   Private 8728   First Connaught Rangers
Died of Wounds: (France) 29 April 1915. Age 25.
Supplementary Notes: Enlisted: Ballinasloe. Awarded 1914 Star. Born: Ahascreagh, Ballinasloe.
Buried: Boulogne Eastern Cemetery – Pas de Calais – France (VIII. A. 43).

CASEY, Patrick   Private 4247   Third Connaught Rangers
Died of Wounds: (Kinsale) 2 February 1915. Age 19.
Supplementary Notes: Enlisted: Ballinasloe. Born: Kilclooney, Ballinasloe.
Buried: Kinsale (Old Cemetery) Graveyard – Kinsale (special memorial near entrance).

CAULEY, Timothy   Private or Corporal 3818   First Connaught Rangers
Killed in Action: (France) 1 June 1915.
Supplementary Notes: Enlisted: Ballinasloe. Born: Kilclooney, Ballinasloe.
Buried: Cabaret-Rouge British Cemetery – Souchez – France (XXVII. A. 25).

CAULFIELD, F.W.   Private M2/077318   Army Service Corps
Death: 1 October 1915. Age 53.
Supplementary Notes: Son of Francis William & Mary Caulfield of Clifden; husband of Harriet Martha Caulfield of 27 Chapel Grove, Somers Town, London. Born: Galway.
Buried: Kensal Green (St Mary's) Roman Catholic Cemetery – London – United Kingdom

CAULFIELD, James   Private   Royal Irish Fusiliers
Death: 1914–1918.
Supplementary Notes: From Ballinasloe.
Remembered: Roll of Honour – Killed in Action – 1914–1918 – Ballinasloe – Ireland.

CAULFIELD, Stephen   Private 11115   First Royal Irish Fusiliers
Killed in Action or Died of Wounds: (France) 11 or 13 April 1917. Age 22.
Supplementary Notes: Enlisted: Ballinasloe. Son of Maria Caulfield of Haymarket Street, Ballinasloe (Kilclooney).
Buried: Athies Communal Cemetery Extension – Pas de Calais – France (B.14).

CAVANAGH, John Henry   Private 10578   Second Irish Guards
Killed in Action: (France) 23 July 1917. Age 33.

Supplementary Notes: Son of Martin & Bridget Cavanagh of 3 New Docks. He emigrated to the United States and lived for some time in California, where he was secretary of the Burlingham Club. He returned home either shortly before, or just after, the war began. His brother, Mike, served with the royal navy during the Great War and survived.

Buried: Dozinghem Military Cemetery – Poperinge – West-Vlaanderen – Belgium. (I.I. 4).

CAWLEY, James   Private   British Expeditionary Force
Death: 1914–1918.
Supplementary Notes: From Ballinasloe.
Remembered: Roll of Honour – Killed in Action – 1914–1918 – Ballinasloe.

CAWLEY, John   Private 8838   First Connaught Rangers
Killed in Action: (France) 2 November 1914. Age 22 or 24.
Supplementary Notes: Enlisted: Ballinasloe. Son of John & Anne Cawley of Harbour Street, Ballinasloe (Kilclooney).
Buried: Royal Irish Rifles Graveyard – Laventie – Pas de Calais – France (V. A. 15).

CAWLEY, William   Private 17314   Second Royal Irish Fusiliers
Death: 15 March 1915. Age 30.
Supplementary Notes: Son of John & Anne Cawley of Harbour Street, Ballinasloe; husband of M. Cawley of 86 Raleigh Road, Shepherd's Bush, London.
Remembered: Ypres (Menin Gate) Memorial – Ieper – West-Vlaanderen – Belgium (42).

CHAPMAN, Alfred B.   Unknown   Royal Dublin Fusiliers
Death: 1914–1918.
Supplementary Notes: From Ballinasloe.
Remembered: Roll of Honour – Killed in Action – 1914–1918 – Ballinasloe; and St John's Church Roll of Honour – Ballinasloe – Ireland.

CHAPMAN, William   Private 11680   Second Irish Guards
Killed in Action: (France) 27 November 1917.
Supplementary Notes: Born: Eyrecourt.
Remembered: Cambrai Memorial – Lou Verval – Nord – France (2 & 3).

CHRISTIAN, Michael Joseph   Private 137086   Royal Army Medical Corps
Died of Wounds: (Blackpool) 5 November 1918. Age 20.
Supplementary Notes: Formerly of the Royal Warwickshire Regiment 32801. Son of John & Sarah Anne Christian of Cross Street, Loughrea.
Buried: Blackpool Cemetery – Lancashire – United Kingdom (Q. 123).

CLANCY, James   Lance Corporal 91965   Royal Medical Corps
Died of Wounds: (Galway) 3 November 1918.
Supplementary Notes: Born: Gurteen.
Buried: Kensal Green (St Mary's) Roman Catholic Cemetery – London – United Kingdom (3. 2759).

CLARE, Robert   Sapper 270887   Royal Engineers
Died of Wounds: (France) 16 October 1917. Age 42
Supplementary Notes: Enlisted: Maryborough. Formerly of the 327 Quarry Company. Son of Laurence & Louisa Clare of Galway.
Buried: Calais Southern Cemetery – Pas de Calais – France (D. LA. 2).

CLARKE, J.   Lieutenant   British Expeditionary Force
Death: 1914–1918.
Supplementary Notes: From Ballinasloe.
Remembered: Roll of Honour – Killed in Action – 1914–1918 – Ballinasloe – Ireland.

CLARKE, Jack   Corporal 608704   Eighteenth London Irish Rifles
Killed in Action: (France) 23 August 1918.
Supplementary Notes: Formerly of the 327th Quarry Company. Born: Woodford.
Buried: Bray Vale British Cemetery – Bray-Sur-Somme – France (II. A. 11).

CLARKE, John   Corporal 14198   First Royal Munster Fusiliers
Died of Wounds: (France) 12 September 1916. Age 39.
Supplementary Notes: Born: Kilkerrin.
Buried: Heilly Station Cemetery – Mericourt-L'Abbe – Somme – France (IV. C. 43).

CLARKE, John   Gunner 47263   Twenty-fifth (Siege) Royal Garrison Artillery
Killed in Action: (France) 5 April 1917. Age 29 or 31.
Supplementary Notes: Son of John & Honor Clarke of Addergoole Beg, Dunmore.
Buried: Agny Military Cemetery – Pas de Calais – France (G. 39).

CLARKE, William John   Private 11803   Second Royal Dublin Fusiliers
Killed in Action: (France) 25 April 1915.
Supplementary Notes: Enlisted: Carlow. Born: Galway.
Remembered: Ypres (Menin Gate) Memorial – Ieper – West-Vlaanderen – Belgium
(44 & 46).

CLOHERTY, Christopher   Private 40435   First Royal Dublin Fusiliers
Killed in Action: (France) 29 March 1918. Age 47.
Supplementary Notes: Formerly of the Connaught Rangers 7877. Son of Thadey &
Mary Cloherty of Knock, Clifden; husband of Anne Cloherty of Knock, Inishbofin,
Clifden.
Remembered: Pozieres Memorial – Somme – France (79 & 80).

CLOHERTY, Joseph   Private 114   Fifth Connaught Rangers
Killed in Action: (Mesopotamia) 12 January 1917. Age 35.
Supplementary Notes: Enlisted: Galway. Son of Thomas & Brigid Cloherty of
Mourneen, Cleggan, Clifden.
Buried: Baghdad (North Gate) War Cemetery – Iraq (Angora Mem. 46).

CLOHERTY, Michael   Private 4251   First Connaught Rangers
Killed in Action: (France or Mesopotamia) 17 April 1916. Age 22.
Supplementary Notes: Enlisted: Galway. Born: New Street West, Galway (Barna).
Remembered: Basra Memorial – Iraq (40 & 64).

CLORAN, Gerald J.   Lieutenant   Royal Navy
Death: (Royal Naval Hospital, Deal) 7 November 1917.
Supplementary Notes: Died following an accident on board ship. Son of the late
Michael Cloran of Fort Lorenzo, Galway and Tuam. Brother of Captain Michael
Cloran of the Royal Garrison Artillery.
Buried: Deal Cemetery – Kent – United Kingdom.

COEN, Martin   Unknown   British Expeditionary Force
Killed in Action: (France) 17 November 1915. Age 23.
Supplementary Notes: Born: Galway.

COEN, Martin   Driver 58187   Royal Field Artillery
Killed in Action: (France or Flanders) 2 May 1917.

Supplementary Notes: Enlisted: Galway. Born: Galway.
Buried: Wancourt Cemetery (III. E. 19).

COFFEY, Thomas   Private 25096   Seventh South Irish Horse
Died of Wounds: (France) 12 December 1917. Age 20.
Supplementary Notes: Enlisted: Ballinasloe. Formerly of the Seventh Royal Irish Regiment. Son of Patrick & Kate Coffey of Mackney, Ballinasloe.
Buried: Villers-Faucon Communal Cemetery Extension – Somme – France (I. C. 19).

COGHLAN, M.   Lance Corporal 7546   Second Irish Guards
Killed in Action: (France) 14 March 1917. Age 24.
Supplementary Notes: Son of Thomas & Mary Coghlan of Powerscross, Portumna.
Buried: Sailly-Saillisel British Cemetery – Somme – France (VI. I. 7).

COLEMAN, Joseph   Private 13111 (18111)   Third (West Riding) Duke of Wellington Reg
Death: (Galway) 1 December 1916. Age 44.
Supplementary Notes: Enlisted: Breary Banks. Son of Thomas & Mary Coleman of Kilkerrin.
Buried: Tynemouth (Preston) Cemetery – Northumberland – United Kingdom (F. R. C. 846).

COLLINS, Edward   Private 7836   Second Royal Dublin Fusiliers
Killed in Action: (France) 24 May 1915.
Supplementary Notes: Born: Glenamaddy.
Remembered: Ypres (Menin Gate) Memorial – Ieper – West-Vlaanderen – Belgium (44 & 46).

COLLINS, John   Private 3/7834   First Connaught Rangers
Death: (Mesopotamia) 21 July 1917.
Supplementary Notes: Born: Galway.
Buried: Baghdad (North Gate) War Cemetery – Iraq (XI. L. 5).

COLLINS, Frank   Lance Sergeant 74305   Twenty-eighth Canadian Infantry
Death: (France) 4 May 1917. Age 29.
Supplementary Notes: (Saskatchewan). Enlisted: Canada. Son of Thomas & Catherine Collins of Cogaula, Clonbern.
Remembered: Vimy Memorial – Pas de Calais – France.

COLLINS, John   Private 3/7824   First Connaught Rangers
Death: (Mesopotamia) 21 July 1917. Age 35.
Supplementary Notes: Enlisted: Bradford. Son of John & Celia Collins of Kilkeel, Headford.
Buried: Baghdad (North Gate) War Cemetery – Iraq (XI. L. 5).

COLLINS, Michael   Gunner 25188   Seventh (Siege) Royal Garrison Artillery
Died of Wounds: (Bristol) 6 July 1915. Age 35 or 37.
Supplementary Notes: Son of Patrick & Mary Collins of Leitra, Glenamaddy.
Buried: Bristol (Arnos Vale) Roman Catholic Cemetery – Gloucestershire – United Kingdom (C).

COLLINS, Michael   Private 12/3960   Second Auckland Regiment NZEF
Death: 15 September 1916. Age 39.
Supplementary Notes: Son of William & Mary Collins of Lisheenavalla, Claregalway.
Remembered: Caterpillar Valley (New Zealand) Memorial – Somme – France.

COLLINS, Patrick   Private 7653   Second Leinster Regiment
Killed in Action: (France) 20 October 1914.
Supplementary Notes: Born: Ballymore.
Remembered: Ploegsteert Memorial – Comines-Warneton, Hainaut – Belgium (10).

COLLINS, Thomas   Private 5421   Sixth Connaught Rangers
Killed in Action: (Bombay) 18 August 1917. Age 32.
Supplementary Notes: Born: Galway.

COLLINS, Thomas   Deck Hand 28775D   HMS *Prize*   Royal Navy Reserves.
Killed in Action: (Atlantic Ocean) 14 August 1917. Age 21.
Supplementary Notes: Killed during action with an enemy submarine. Son of Peter & Delia Collins of Fairhill Road, Claddagh, Galway.
Remembered: Portsmouth Naval Memorial – Hampshire – United Kingdom (27)

COLLINS, Thomas   Pioneer 105279   Royal Engineers
Died of Wounds: (France) 3 October 1917. Age 39 or 43.
Supplementary Notes: Enlisted: Doncaster, Yorkshire. Born: Galway.
Buried: Hooge Crater Cemetery – Ypres – Belgium (I. A. 19).

COLLINS, William   Private 365   Seventh Royal Munster Fusiliers
Killed in Action: (France) 28 June 1916. Age 28.
Supplementary Notes: Son of Patrick & Margaret Collins of Ballinastack (Glenamaddy).
Buried: St Patrick's Cemetery – Loos – Pas de Calais – France (I. D. I).

COLLINS, William   Gunner 29399   Seventh Royal Munster Fusiliers
Killed in Action: 28 June 1918. Age 46.
Supplementary Notes: Born: Glenamaddy.

COMBER, Patrick   Private 3177   First Leinster Regiment
Killed in Action: (France) 12 April 1916.
Supplementary Notes: Born: Clonfert.

COMBER, Thomas   Private 1077   First Lancashire Fusiliers
Killed in Action: (Gallipoli) 31 July 1915.
Supplementary Notes: Born: Glenamaddy.

COMMONS, Willie   Private   British Expeditionary Force
Death: 1914–1918.
Supplementary Notes: From Ballinasloe.
Remembered: Roll of Honour – Killed in Action – 1914–1918 – Ballinasloe - Ireland.

CONCANNON, J.   Driver T/312552   Eighth Royal Army Service Corps
Death: (France) 5 December 1918. Age 42.
Supplementary Notes: Son of Patrick & Margaret Concannon of Moylough; husband of Rose Concannon of 2 Corsewall Street, Webster Road, Liverpool.
Buried: Caudry British Cemetery – Nord – France (II. E. 18).

CONCANNON, Patrick   Private 4646   First Irish Guards
Died of Wounds: (France) 14 May 1915.
Supplementary Notes: Enlisted: Drogheda, Co. Louth. Born: Galway.
Buried: Aire Communal Cemetery – Pas de Calais – France (I. A. 1).

CONLEY, Michael   Private 13122   Ninth West Riding Regiment
Killed in Action: (France) 24 June 1917.
Supplementary Notes: Born: Milltown.

CONLON, Patrick W.   Private 5673   First Irish Guards
Killed in Action: (France) 15 September 1916. Age 22.
Supplementary Notes: Born: Creggs.
Remembered: Thiepval Memorial – Somme – France (7D).

CONNAIRE, John   Private 1331   Seventh Leinster Regiment
Died of Wounds: (France) 18 September 1916. Age 33.
Supplementary Notes: Son of Patrick & Julia Connaire (*nee* Fahy) of Cloncah, Wood-
lawn (Clonfert).
Buried: Grove Town Cemetery, Meaulte – Somme – France (I. D. 39).

CONNAUGHTON, John   Private 9861   First Connaught Rangers
Killed in Action: (France) 11 April 1915. Age 30.
Supplementary Notes: Enlisted: Galway. Born: Galway.
Buried: Rue–du–Bacquerot No. 1 Military Cemetery – Laventie – Pas de Calais –
France (I. B. 4).

CONNAUGHTON, John   Private 28769   Connaught Rangers
Killed in Action: (France) Age 21.
Supplementary Notes: Born: Galway.

CONNEALLY, Michael   Private 4498   Eighth King's Royal Irish Hussars
Death: (Belgium) 6 November 1914. Age 38.
Supplementary Notes: Son of John & Honor Conneally of Aghalative, Creggs;
husband of Mary Conneally (*nee* King) of 40 Hemdean Road, Caversham, Reading.
Buried: Railway Chateau Cemetery – Ieper – West-Vlaanderen – Belgium (C. 12).

CONNEELY, Michael Deck Hand 220SD HM Trawler *Eastern Dawn* Royal Navy Reserves
Death: 26 January 1918.
Supplementary Notes: Accidentally drowned. Son of the late Patrick & Mary Con-
neely; husband of Bridget Conneely of Long Walk, Galway.
Remembered: Portsmouth Naval Memorial – Hampshire – United Kingdom (31).

CONNEELY, Patrick   Seaman 5040A   HMS *Laurentic*   Royal Navy Reserves
Death: 25 January 1917. Age 24.
Supplementary Notes: Ship was struck by a mine and sank off Lough Swilly on the
northern coast of Donegal. Born: Long Walk or the Claddagh, Galway.
Remembered: Portsmouth Naval Memorial – Hampshire – United Kingdom (21).

CONNEELY, Peter　　　　Seaman 8257A　　　HMS *Ascot*　Royal Navy Reserves
Killed in Action: 10 November 1918. Age 20.
Supplementary Notes: Killed during action with an enemy submarine off the Farne Islands. Son of Patrick & Mary Ann Conneely of Fairhill Road, Claddagh, Galway.
Remembered: Portsmouth Naval Memorial – Hampshire – United Kingdom (31).

CONNEELY, Thomas　　　　Private 7389　　　　Fifth Connaught Rangers
Died of Jaundice: (Egypt) 31 July 1918. Age 28.
Supplementary Notes: Enlisted: Galway. Son of John & Barbara Conneely of Dinartha, Carraroe, Connemara.
Buried: Alexandria (Hadra) War Memorial Cemetery – Egypt (C. 86).

CONNELL, Claude　　　　Private 9469　　　　Second Leinster Regiment
Died of Wounds: (France) 14 August 1915.
Supplementary Notes: Born: Aughrim.
Buried: Lussenthoek Military Cemetery (III. D. 33).

CONNELL, Michael　　　　Private 5/3787　　　Fifth Connaught Rangers
Died of Wounds: (Gallipoli) 24 August 1915. Age 22 or 23.
Supplementary Notes: Born: Kilclooney, Ballinasloe.
Buried: Alexandria (Hadra) War Memorial Cemetery – Egypt (J. 71).

CONNELL, Michael　　　　Private 4475　　　　Second Connaught Rangers
Killed in Action: 8 November 1914. Age 19.
Supplementary Notes: Enlisted: Ballinasloe. Son of John & Mary Connell of Rigney's Row, Ballinasloe. Brother of Stephen Connell, listed below.
Remembered: Ypres (Menin Gate) Memorial – Ieper – West-Vlaanderen – Belgium (42).

CONNELL, Stephen　　　　Private 477 (4077)　　　Fifth Connaught Rangers
Killed in Action or Died of Sickness: (Salonika) 27 October 1915 or 15 December 1917. Age 27.
Supplementary Notes: Enlisted: Galway. Brother of Michael Connell, listed above.
Buried: Salonika (Lembet Road) Military Cemetery – Greece (1590).

CONNELL, William Patrick　　Captain　　　　Fifty-fifth Royal Field Artillery
Death: (Mesopotamia) 24 November 1918. Age 30.

Supplementary Notes: 'Mentioned in Despatches'. Son of George & Mary E. Connell of Powerscross, Portumna.

Buried: Baghdad (North Gate) War Cemetery – Iraq (XIX.E. 15).

CONNELLY, Murton   Private 67385   First Machine Gun Corps

Killed in Action: (France) 30 November 1917.

Supplementary Notes: Enlisted: Gateshead-on-Tyne. Born: Galway.

Remembered: Cambrai Memorial – Lou Verval – Nord – France (12 & 13).

CONNELLY, William   Private 7609   Second Royal Lancaster Regiment

Killed in Action: (France) 21 April 1915.

Supplementary Notes: Born: Ballinamore.

CONNISS, James William   Gunner 203586   Royal Garrison Artillery

Killed in Action: (France) 13 October 1918.

Supplementary Notes: Born: Galway.

Buried: St Aubert British Cemetery (III. A. 12).

CONNOLLY, James   Private 61965   101st (Twenty-sixth Brigade) US Infantry Division

Killed in Action: (France) 23 October 1918.

Supplementary Notes: Born: Rossaveal, Connemara. He had three sisters and five brothers, one of whom, Thomas, also served in the war, and survived.

Buried: Meuse-Argonne Cemetery – France (51. 10).

CONNOLLY, John   Private 41930   First Staffordshire Regiment

Killed in Action: (France) 17 April 1918.

Supplementary Notes: Born: Galway.

Remembered: Ploegsteert Memorial – Comines-Warneton, Hainaut – Belgium (8).

CONNOLLY, Leo   Private 3580   Sixth Connaught Rangers

Killed in Action or Died of Wounds: (France) 29 July 1916. Age 30.

Supplementary Notes: Enlisted: Ballinasloe. Son of Patrick & Maria Connolly of Ballinasloe (Kilclooney).

Buried: Bethune Town Cemetery – Pas de Calais – France (V. G. 52).

CONNOLLY, Michael   Private 6534   Sixth Connaught Rangers

Killed in Action: (France) 21 March 1918. Age 19.

Supplementary Notes: Enlisted: Galway. Son of Thomas & Barbara Connolly of Ballyconneely, Connemara.

Buried: St Emilie Valley Cemetery – Villers-Faucon – Somme – France (III. A. 1).

CONNOLLY, Peter   Private 5237   First Connaught Rangers
Died of Wounds: (France) 27 September 1915.
Supplementary Notes: Enlisted: Liverpool. Born: Galway.
Buried: Cabaret-Rouge British Cemetery – Souchez – France (XVII. B. 31).

CONNOR, Domnick   Private 6418   Second Connaught Rangers
Killed in Action: (France) September 1915. Age 23.
Supplementary Notes: Born: Galway.

CONNOR, John   Private 2987   Connaught Rangers
Killed in Action: (France) 21 August 1915. Age 37.
Supplementary Notes: Born: Galway.

CONNOR, Patrick   Private 5696   Sixth Connaught Rangers
Killed in Action: (France) 20 November 1917.
Supplementary Notes: Enlisted: Atherton. Born: Killcrain.

CONNOR, Peter   Private 4/6105   Fifth Connaught Rangers
Died of Tumour: (Malta) 31 March 1917. Age 45.
Supplementary Notes: Enlisted: Ballinasloe. Born: Galway.
Buried: Addolorata Cemetery – Malta (E. EA. A. 700).

CONNOR, Thomas   Private 5439   First Connaught Rangers
Died of Wounds: (France) 28 August 1915. Age 44.
Supplementary Notes: Enlisted: Galway. Son of Mary Anne Connor of 40 Marlborough Street, Dublin, and the late James Connor. Born: St Joseph's Parish, Galway.
Buried: Merville Communal Cemetery – Nord – France (III. U. 4).

CONNORS, Patrick   Private 6795   Second Connaught Rangers
Killed in Action: (France) 2 November 1914.
Supplementary Notes: Enlisted: Cork. Born: St Joseph's Parish, Galway.

CONROY, John   Private 9238   First Irish Guards
Died of Wounds: (France) 26 September 1916.

Supplementary Notes: Son of Matt & Anne Conroy of Aileback, Ballyconneely, Connemara.

Buried: Bronfay Farm Military Cemetery – Bray-Sur-Somme – Somme – France (II. D. 39).

CONROY, John Michael   Private 371515   Labour Corps
Death: (France) 4 March 1918.
Supplementary Notes: Enlisted: Sheffield. Formerly of the York & Lancaster Regiment 4006. Born: Galway.
Buried: Louvencourt Military Cemetery – Somme – France (1. E. 2).

CONROY, Joseph   Deck Hand 21826/DA   HMS *Vivid*   Royal Navy Reserves.
Died of Wounds: (Co. Galway) 17 September 1918.
Supplementary Notes: Son of Honor Conroy of Roundstone, Connemara.
Buried: Gorteen Graveyard – Co. Galway (about nine yards from east boundary).

CONROY, Michael   Private 5331   Fifth Connaught Rangers
Died of Wounds: (Salonika) 27 December 1915.
Supplementary Notes: Enlisted: Newcastle-on-Tyne. Born: New Village.

CONWAY, Patrick   Private 59364   Fourteenth Welsh Regiment
Killed in Action: (France) 26 July 1917. Age 24.
Supplementary Notes: Born: Clunbar.
Buried: Bard Cottage Cemetery – Ypres – West-Vlaanderen – Belgium (III. F. 5).

CONWAY, Peter   Private 12219   First Cheshire Regiment
Killed in Action: (France) 25 July 1916.
Supplementary Notes: Born: Dunmore.
Remembered: Caterpillar Valley (New Zealand) Memorial – Somme – France (X. H. 30).

COOKE, Joseph   Corporal 8317   First Leinster Regiment
Died of Wounds: (Salonika) 10 March 1917.
Supplementary Notes: Born: Ballinasloe.

COOKE, Thomas   Private 6310   Sixth Connaught Rangers
Killed in Action: (France) 21 March 1918.
Supplementary Notes: Enlisted: Northwich. Born: Galway.

Remembered: Pozieres Memorial – Somme – France (77).

COONEY, Michael   Private 6958   Second Royal Irish Fusiliers (Regiment)
Killed in Action: (France) 14 May 1915.
Supplementary Notes: Born: Portumna.
Remembered: Ypres (Menin Gate) Memorial – Ieper – West-Vlaanderen – Belgium (42).

CORBETT, James   Private 10386   Second Irish Guards
Killed in Action: (France) 31 July 1917. Age 36 or 38.
Supplementary Notes: Born: Caran.
Remembered: Ypres (Menin Gate) Memorial – Ieper – West-Vlaanderen – Belgium (11).

CORBETT, Thomas   Second Lieutenant 8/336   Otago Regiment NZEF
Death: (New Zealand) 10 March 1920.
Supplementary Notes: Died as a result of the war. Son of Peter Corbett of Athenry, Galway.
Buried: Invercargill (Eastern) Cemetery – Invercargill City – New Zealand (Soldiers' Avenue. BIk. 10. End of Row).

CORBETT, Seamus   Private   British Expeditionary Force
Killed in Action: (France) 1914–1918.
Supplementary Notes: Ard West, Carna, Connemara.

CORCORAN, Thomas   Lance Corporal 10189   Second Irish Guards
Killed in Action: (Bourlon Wood, France) 28 November 1917. Age 26.
Supplementary Notes: Son of James & Bridget Corcoran of Eyrecourt (Meelick).
Buried: Rocquigny-Equancourt Road British Cemetery – Manancourt – Somme – France (III. A. 28).

CORLESS, James   Private 8072   First Leinster Regiment
Died of Wounds: (France) 4 June 1915. Age 30.
Supplementary Notes: Son of John Corless of Kinvara.
Buried: Boulogne Eastern Cemetery – Pas de Calais – France (VIII. A. 67).

CORLEY, John   Private 5361   Fifth Connaught Rangers
Killed in Action: (Salonika) 7 December 1915. Age 28.
Supplementary Notes: Enlisted: Galway. Son of John & Bridget Corley of Mount-

bellew; husband of Catherine Corley of New Castle, Mountbellew.
Remembered: Doiran Memorial – Greece.

CORR, John   Sergeant 25470   Second Royal Dublin Fusiliers
Killed in Action: (France) 3 October 1918.
Supplementary Notes: Born: Glenamaddy.
Buried: Unicorn Cemetery – Vend'Huile – France (IV. E. 24).

COSGROVE, Peter   Private 18616   Sixth South Lancaster Regiment
Killed in Action: (Mesopotamia) 12 February 1917. Age 28.
Supplementary Notes: Born: Ballyglooney.
Buried: Basra Memorial – Iraq (23).

COSTELLO, Gabriel Patrick   Second Lieutenant   Fifth Royal Irish Regiment
Killed in Action: (Gallipoli) 16 August 1915. Age 27.
Supplementary Notes: Son of Thomas A. & Mary Costello of Vicars Croft, Tuam.
Remembered: Helles Memorial – Turkey (55).

COSTELLO, James   Private 317517 (7515)   First Connaught Rangers
Killed in Action: (Mesopotamia) 15 November 1917. Age 26.
Supplementary Notes: Enlisted: Aston-on-Lyne (Huddersfield). Born: Milltown.
Buried: Baghdad (North Gate) War Cemetery – Iraq (XII. B. 2).

COSTELLO, Joseph   Private 6941   Second Leinster Regiment
Died of Wounds: (France) 14 March 1915.
Supplementary Notes: Born: Whitegate. Same military number recorded for Sammy Stokes, p. 215.
Buried: Cite Bonjean Military Cemetery – Armentieres – Nord – France (IX. C. 38).

COSTELLO, M.   Sergeant 4442   Fourth Connaught Rangers
Died of Wounds: 6 February 1916.
Supplementary Notes: Born: Ballinasloe.
Buried: Alternative Commemoration – Creagh new cemetery – Ballinasloe – Ireland (screen wall).
Remembered: Grangegorman Memorial – Dublin – Ireland.

COSTELLO, Patrick   Private 16694   Eighth East Lancaster Regiment
Killed in Action: (France) 29 June 1916.
Supplementary Notes: Born: Tuam.

Buried: Hannescamps New Military Cemetery – Pas de Calais – France (A. 20).

COSTELLO, Patrick   Private 411152   Canadian Light Infantry
Death: (France or Flanders) 1914–1918.
Supplementary Notes: (Princess Patricia Regiment) Enlisted: Canada. Born: Galway.

COUGHLAN, Michael   Lance Corporal 7546   Second Irish Guards
Killed in Action: (France) 4 March 1917.
Supplementary Notes: Son of Thomas & Mary Coughlan of Powerscross, Portumna. Brother of Thomas Coughlan, listed below.
Buried: Sailly-Sallisel British Cemetery – Somme – France.

COUGHLAN, Thomas   Able Seaman   Royal Navy
Death: (North Sea) 1914–1918.
Supplementary Notes: Son of Thomas & Mary Coughlan of Powerscross, Portumna. Brother of Michael Coughlan, listed above.

COX, George   Rifleman 6629   Ninth Royal Irish Rifles
Killed in Action: (France) 7 June 1917.
Supplementary Notes: Born: Abbert.
Remembered: Ypres (Menin Gate) Memorial – Ieper – West-Vlaanderen – Belgium (40).

COY, Charles   Officer   Grenadier Guards
Killed in Action: (France) 10 March 1915. Age 24.
Supplementary Notes: Enlisted: April 1915. Son of Hugh Coy of Galway. Brother of Tom Coy, listed below.
Buried: Calais – France.
Remembered: Great War monument – St Nicholas' Collegiate Church – Galway – Ireland.

COY, Tom   Leading Telegraphist J/4768   *E49*   Royal Navy
Death: 12 March 1917. Age 21.
Supplementary Notes: Lost his life on board a submarine. Son of Hugh Coy of Galway. Brother of Charles Coy, listed above.
Remembered: Plymouth Naval Memorial – Devon – United Kingdom (22) & Great War monument – St Nicholas' Collegiate Church – Galway – Ireland.

COYNE, John   Private 2779   Second Connaught Rangers
Died of Wounds: (Boulogne, France) 11 November 1914 or 4 November 1915. Age 41.

Supplementary Notes: Enlisted: Oranmore. Awarded Mons Star. Born: Loughrea.
Buried: Wimereux Communal Cemetery – Pas de Calais – France (I. A. 26).

COYNE, John   Private 638667 (7138)   Royal Munster Fusiliers
Death: (Irish Sea) 10 October 1918.
Supplementary Notes: Labour Corps. Drowned following the sinking of SS *Leinster* by a German submarine. The sinking of the SS *Leinster* is recorded in *Galway and the Great War*, p. 98, 99, 100, 101. Born: Carran.
Remembered: Hollybrook Memorial – Southampton – Hampshire – United Kingdom.

COYNE, Martin   Lance Corporal 14034   First Royal Munster Fusiliers
Killed in Action: (France) 9 September 1916.
Supplementary Notes: Enlisted: Liverpool. Formerly of the Connaught Rangers 5596. Born: Galway.
Remembered: Thiepval Memorial – Somme – France (16 C).

COYNE, M.   Private 2360   Ninth Australian Infantry
Death: 18 May 1917. Age 20.
Supplementary Notes: Son of Philip Coyne of Knock Brack, Cleggan, Connemara.
Buried: Grevillers British Cemetery – Pas de Calais – France (III. A. II).

CRADDOCK, Michael   Private 43139   Seventh Royal Irish Fusiliers
Died of Wounds: (France) 7 September 1916. Age 39.
Supplementary Notes: Enlisted: Ballinasloe. Formerly of the Connaught Rangers 5239. Son of Michael & Catherine Craddock of Derrymullen, Ballinasloe.
Buried: La Neuville British Cemetery – Corbie – Somme – France (II. C. 36).

CRAHAN, Michael   Private 169362   Yorkshire Light Infantry
Died of Wounds: (France) 27 March 1918.
Supplementary Notes: Labour Corps. Born: Galway.
Remembered: Pozieres Memorial – Somme – France (94).

CRAIG, William   Rifleman 17489   Eleventh Royal Irish Rifles
Killed in Action: (Somme, France) 1 July 1916.
Supplementary Notes: Born: Roxborough.
Remembered: Thiepval Memorial – Somme – France (15A & 15B).

CRANE, John   Private 9062   First Connaught Rangers
Died of Wounds: (Galway) 3 February 1915.
Supplementary Notes: Enlisted: Galway. Formerly of the Grenadier Guards. Born: Raheen, Athenry.

CREHAN, M.   Private 30009   Twenty-fifth Works Battalion
Died of Wounds: (France) 27 March 1918. Age 43.
Supplementary Notes: Formerly of the Durham Light Infantry 169362, and the One hundred and fifty-fourth Labour Corps. Son of William & Margret Crehan of Castlegar, Galway (Mountbellew).
Buried: Etaples Military Cemetery – Pas de Calais – France (XXXI. J. 24).

CREHAN, Mark   Private 5825   Sixth Connaught Rangers
Killed in Action: (France) 30 July 1916. Age 28.
Supplementary Notes: Born: Ballygare.

CREHAN, Thomas   Private 6022   Sixth Connaught Rangers
Killed in Action: (France) 3 June 1917.
Supplementary Notes: Enlisted: St Helens, Lancashire. Born: Mountbellew.
Buried: Kemmel Chateau Cemetery – Belgium (M. 41).

CROSBY, J.J.   Private 202714 Ninth York & Lancaster Regiment
Killed in Action: 15 June 1918. Age 19.
Supplementary Notes: Son of Sarah Crosby of St Vincent, Solly Street, Sheffield and Co. Galway.
Buried: Granezza British Cemetery – Italy (I. D. 14).

CUMMINS, John   Private 3558   Fifth Connaught Rangers
Killed in Action: (France) 10 October 1918. Age 30.
Supplementary Notes: Enlisted: Oranmore. Son of Michael & Mary Cummins of Kilclooney, Ballinasloe.
Buried: Montay-Neuvilly Road Cemetery – Montay – France (I. F. 19).

CUNNIFFE, Pat Private 260200 Second & Sixth Royal Warwickshire Regiment
Killed in Action: (France) 24 September 1917.
Supplementary Notes: Born: Galway.
Buried: Douchy-les-Ayette British Cemetery – Pas de Calais – France (I. J. 2).

CUNNIFFE, Michael   Sapper 72593   Cable Section Royal Engineers
Killed in Action: (Palestine or Egypt) 11 October 1918. Age 30 or 31.
Supplementary Notes: Enlisted: Bradford. Son of John & Honor Cunniffe of Adder-goolemore, Dunmore. Following his death his comrades wrote a letter of condolence to his parents and raised finance to have a memorable tablet erected.
Buried: Haifa War Cemetery – Israel (B. 6).

CUNNINGHAM, John   Private 1651   First Irish Guards
Killed in Action: (France) 3 November 1914. Age 22.
Supplementary Notes: Born: Kilconly.
Remembered: Ypres (Menin Gate) Memorial – Ieper – West-Vlaanderen – Belgium (42).

CUNNINGHAM, Richard   Private 5774   First Connaught Rangers
Killed in Action: (Mesopotamia) 8 March 1916.
Supplementary Notes: Born: Galway.
Buried: Basra Memorial – Iraq (40 & 64).

CUNNINGHAM, William   Private 2/10917   Second Irish Guards
Killed in Action: (France) 23 March 1918. Age 25.
Supplementary Notes: Born: Kilmore.
Remembered: Arras Memorial – Pas de Calais – France (1).

CURLEY, Daniel S.   Private 43814   Sixth Royal Scots Lothian Regiment
Killed in Action: (France) 17 June 1917.
Supplementary Notes: Enlisted: Glasgow. Born: Galway.
Buried: Cabaret-Rouge British Cemetery – Souchez – France (XVII. AA. 22).

CURLEY, Patrick   Private   British Expeditionary Force
Death: 1914–1918.
Supplementary Notes: From Ballinasloe.
Remembered: Roll of Honour – Killed in Action – 1914–1918 – Ballinasloe – Ireland.

CURLEY, Patrick   Seaman 4265A   HMS *Monmouth*   Royal Navy Reserves
Killed in Action: (Coronel) 1 November 1914. Age 21.
Supplementary Notes: Son of Julia Curley of Quay Street, Galway, and the late John Curley.
Remembered: Portsmouth Naval Memorial – Hampshire – United Kingdom (6).

CURRAN, Thomas   Gunner 73362   Royal Field Artillery
Died of Wounds: (Galway) 17 December 1915. Age 21 or 31.
Supplementary Notes: Enlisted: Galway. Son of Kate Curran of Raleigh Row, Galway.
Buried: Barna Old Graveyard – Co. Galway – Ireland (13 yards from the north boundary).

CURTIN, William   Private 195904   Twenty-first Canadian Infantry
Died of Wounds: (France) 12 October 1918. Age 30.
Supplementary Notes: (Eastern Ontario Regiment). Enlisted: Canada. Son of David & Ellen Curtin of Peterborough, Ontario. Born: Galway.
Buried: Bucquoy Road Cemetery – Ficheux – Pas de Calais – France (III. G. 24).

CUSTY, Edward   Private 5203   First Irish Guards
Killed in Action: (France) 19 May 1915.
Supplementary Notes: Born: Tuam.
Buried: Guards' Cemetery Windy Corner – Cuinchy – Pas de Calais – France (IV. K. 38).

CUSTY, Frank   Private 2562   First Royal North Lancaster Regiment
Killed in Action: (France) 26 January 1915.
Supplementary Notes: Born: Tuam.
Buried: Lievin Communal Cemetery Extension – Pas de Calais – France (III. G. 18).

D'ARCY, Lionel George   Second Lieutenant   Eighteenth Royal Flying Corps
Death: (France) 20 December 1916. Age 28.
Supplementary Notes: Formerly of the Connaught Rangers. Son of Hyacinth D.L. & Louisa Alicia D'Arcy of New Forest, Ballinamore Bridge. Brother of Captain James D'Arcy of the Connaught Rangers.
Remembered: Arras Flying Services Memorial – Pas de Calais – France.

DALTON, Thomas   Private 5747   Sixth Connaught Rangers
Killed in Action: (Kemmel, France) 21 January 1916 or 31 January 1917. Age 19 or 21.
Supplementary Notes: Enlisted: Galway. Son of Henry & Bridget Dalton of Lavally, Gort.
Buried: Kemmel Chateau Military Cemetery – Heuvelland – West-Vlaanderen – Belgium (M. 51).

DALY, Edward   Private 6543   First Connaught Rangers
Killed in Action: (Mesopotamia) 11 March 1916. Age 38.
Supplementary Notes: Enlisted: Ashton-on-Makerfield. Son of Patrick & Ellen Daly.
Born: Monivea.
Buried: Basra Memorial – Iraq (40 & 64).

DALY, Richard George   Corporal 3121   Eleventh Prince Albert's Own Hussars
Died of Wounds: (Messines) 31 October or 1 November 1914. Age 27
Supplementary Notes: Awarded 1914 Star. Son of Henry V. Daly (Archdeacon of
Clonfert) & Elizabeth Alice Daly (*nee* St George) of Deanery, Gort.
Buried: La Brique Military Cemetery No. 2 – Ieper – West-Vlaanderen – Belgium (I.
D. 7).

DALY, Thomas   Private 17417   Second Royal Irish Fusiliers
Killed in Action: (France) 14 March 1915.
Supplementary Notes: Enlisted: Devizes, Wilts. Born: Galway.
Remembered: Ypres (Menin Gate) Memorial – Ieper – West-Vlaanderen – Belgium
(42).

DALY, William Cecil Thomas   Second Lieutenant   Third Rifle Brigade
Killed in Action: (Somme, France) 18 August 1916. Age 19.
Supplementary Notes: Son of William, J.P., D.L. & Julia C.A. Daly (*nee* Burke,
daughter of Sir Thomas Burke of Marble Hill) of Dunsandle. Second Lieutenant Daly
died having been struck by a German bullet while leading his men into battle.
Buried: Bernafay Wood British Cemetery – Somme – France (N. 32).

DAVENPORT, Francis John   Private 245088   Second London Regiment
Killed in Action: (France) 7 August 1917.
Supplementary Notes: Born: Kinvara.
Remembered: Ypres (Menin Gate) Memorial – Ieper – West-Vlaanderen – Belgium
(52).

DAVIDSON, James John   Private 15877   Seventh Royal Dublin Fusiliers
Killed in Action: (Suvla Bay, Gallipoli) 16 August 1915. Age 19.
Supplementary Notes: Enlisted: Dublin. Son of Hutchinson & Nellie Davidson of
Ballinasloe (Creagh).
Buried: Azmak Cemetery – Suvla – Turkey (special memorial 37).

DAVITT, Charles   Rifleman 20486   First Royal Irish Rifles
Killed in Action: 7 September 1918. Age 25.
Supplementary Notes: Son of John & Bridget Davitt of Ballinafad, Toombeola.
Remembered: Ploegsteert Memorial – Comines-Warneton, Hainaut – Belgium (9).

DEELY, Edward   Acting Bombardier 30621   Seventy-sixth Royal Field Artillery
Died of Wounds: (France) 1 June 1917. Age 30 or 36.
Supplementary Notes: Son of Thomas & Celia Clarke Deely of Cregg, Craughwell (Loughrea).
Buried: Boulogne Eastern Cemetery – Pas de Calais – France (IV. B. 46).

DELANEY, John   Private 4072   Second Connaught Rangers
Killed in Action: (France) 2 November 1914.
Supplementary Notes: Enlisted: Oranmore. Born: Loughrea. Upon hearing the news of his death, his mother became ill and died of 'heart failure'.
Buried: Sanctuary Wood Cemetery – Belgium (IV. E 4/6).

DELANEY, John   Private 8750   Second Royal Irish Regiment
Killed in Action: (France) 14 July 1916.
Supplementary Notes: Enlisted: Cashel, Co. Tipperary. Born: Galway.
Remembered: Thiepval Memorial – Somme – France (3. A).

DELANEY, Michael   Lance Corporal 1/10623   First Irish Guards
Killed in Action: (France) 22 May 1918. Age 30.
Supplementary Notes: Born: Killyan.
Buried: Douchy-les-Ayette British Cemetery – Pas de Calais – France (C. 5).

DEMPSEY, John   Private 362369   107th Area Company Labour Corps
Death: (Egypt) 26 August 1918. Age 23 or 27.
Supplementary Notes: Enlisted: Ballinasloe. Formerly of the Fifth Connaught Rangers 10534. Son of Kate Dempsey of Brackernagh, Ballinasloe (Kilclooney).
Remembered: War Memorial Cemetery – Cairo – Egypt (M. 175).

DEMPSEY, Peter   Private 2217   Second South Lancashire Regiment
Killed in Action: (France) 3 July 1916.
Supplementary Notes: Born: Tuam.
Buried: Lonsdale Cemetery – Authuile – Somme – France (IV. P. 6).

DERRAINE, J.   Fireman   SS *Artist*   Mercantile Marines
Death: 27 January 1917. Age 32.
Supplementary Notes: Drowned as a result of an attack by an enemy submarine. Born: Galway.
Remembered: Tower Hill Memorial – London – United Kingdom.

DERRICK, John   Driver 101045   Fifty-ninth Royal Field Artillery
Died of Wounds: (France) 21 August 1917. Age 24.
Supplementary Notes: Enlisted: Athlone. Son of Michael Derrick of College Road, Galway.
Buried: Bard Cottage Cemetery – Ieper – West-Vlaanderen – Belgium (IV. D. 22).

DERRICK, Peter   Rifleman 9963   Seventh Royal Irish Rifles
Killed in Action: (France) 12 November 1914.
Supplementary Notes: Born: Derrypark.

DERRICK, Thomas   Able Seaman 60965   Royal Navy Reserves
Death: (France) 1914–1918. Age 21.
Supplementary Notes: Born: Galway.

DE STACPOOLE, Robert   Second Lieutenant   Connaught Rangers.
Killed in Action: (Marne or Aisne, France) 20 September 1914. Age 22.
Supplementary Notes: Son of the Duke & Duchess de Stacpoole of Mount Hazel, Woodlawn. Brother of Roderick de Stacpoole, listed below.
Remembered: La Ferten-Sous-Jouarre Memorial – Seine-et-Marne – France.

DE STACPOOLE, Roderick   Second Lieutenant   Royal Field Artillery
Killed in Action: (Neuve Chapelle, France) 11 March 1915. Age 19.
Supplementary Notes: 'Mentioned in Despatches'. On 7 May 1915, a solemn requiem mass was held for him at the Church of Saints Peter and Paul in Ballymacward. It was presided over by the Most Rev. Dr Gilmartin. Brother of Robert de Stacpoole, listed above, both are remembered on a memorial plaque in the church. Another brother, Hubert, served with the Leinster regiment, and was recovering from wounds when his brother was killed. A fourth brother, George, served with the Connaught Rangers, and survived.
Buried: Pont-du-Hem Military Cemetery, La Gorgue – Nord – France (VI. A. 10).

DEVANE, John   Private 1747   Sixth Connaught Rangers
Killed in Action: (France) 26 February 1918. Age 28.

Supplementary Notes: Enlisted: Newcastle-on-Tyne. Son of Bridget Devane of Imanebeg, Barnaderg (Tuam).

Buried: Villers-Faucon Communal Cemetery Extension – Somme – France (III. F. I).

DEVANEY, Patrick   Sailor   SS *Royal Edward*   Mercantile Marines
Presumed Drowned: 13 August 1915. Age 34.
Supplementary Notes: Son of Bridget Devaney (*nee* Reaney) of Chapel Lane, Claddagh, Galway, and the late Patrick Devaney. Born: Fairhill, Claddagh, Galway. The sinking of the SS *Royal Edward* was recorded in *Galway and the Great War*, pp. 92, 93.
Remembered: Tower Hill Memorial – London – United Kingdom.

DISHELL, Thomas   Private 40552   Second & Fourth Royal Dublin Fusiliers
Died of Wounds: 6 May 1918. Age 30.
Supplementary Notes: Son of Thomas & Catherine Dishell of Ballyconneely, Connemara. According to one source, his brother was also killed, but there are no details available about him.
Buried: Cologne Southern Cemetery – Koln (Cologne) – Nordrhein-Westfal – Germany (II. A. 15.).

DISKIN, John   Private 44555   Lancaster Fusiliers
Died of Wounds: (France) 12 September 1917. Age 30.
Supplementary Notes: (Labour Corps). Born: Tuam.

DOHERTY, John Charles   Seaman   SS *Eupion*   Mercantile Marines
Death: 3 October 1918. Age 23.
Supplementary Notes: Drowned as a result of an attack by an enemy submarine. Son of Mary Doherty and the late Patrick Doherty; husband of Catherine Doherty (*nee* Maguire) of 67 Regent Street, Liverpool. Born: Galway.
Remembered: Tower Hill Memorial – London – United Kingdom.

DOHERTY, William   Sergeant 11466   Leinster Regiment
Died of Illness: (Galway) 1919.
Supplementary Notes: Formerly of the Machine Gun Corps. Illness caused through active service during the war. Born: Galway.
Buried: St Mary's – (new cemetery) – Bohermore – Galway – Ireland (R.C. B. 10. 9).

DOLAN, John   Private 5632   First Connaught Rangers
Death: (Mesopotamia) 15 August 1916. Age 22.

Supplementary Notes: Enlisted: Ballinasloe. Son of Michael & Mary Dolan of Ardna-lug, Ballinasloe.
Buried: Basra War Cemetery – Iraq (V. P. 10).

DOLAN, John   Private 8638   Second Munster Regiment
Killed in Action: (France) 20 October 1914.
Supplementary Notes: Born: Dunmore.
Remembered: Le Touret Memorial – Pas de Calais – France (34 & 35).

DOLAN, Michael   Lance Corporal P/5623   Military Police
Death: (Egypt) 31 October 1918.
Supplementary Notes: Enlisted: Ballinasloe. Formerly of the Connaught Rangers, 6285. Born: Creagh, Ballinasloe.
Buried: Ramleh War Cemetery – Ramla – Israel (BB. 24).

DONAGHEY, Alexander Stewart   Gunner 101081   Twenty-second &
105th Royal Field Artillery
Killed in Action: (France) 20 August 1916. Age 22.
Supplementary Notes: Son of John Donaghey of Headford.
Remembered: Thiepval Memorial – Somme – France (1. A & 8. A).

DONELAN, John Arthur   Private 23570   Seventh Royal Irish Fusiliers
Killed in Action: (France) 24 August 1916.
Supplementary Notes: Enlisted: Athlone. Son of James & Kate Donelan of Woods Avenue, Main Street, Ballinasloe (St Michael's, Galway). Brother of Patrick Donelan, Private 16786 [see below].
Buried: Bois-Carre Military Cemetery – Haisnes – France (Sp. Men. 18).

DONELAN, Michael   Private 543   First Irish Guards
Died of Wounds: 20 January 1915.
Supplementary Notes: Born: Dunmore.
Buried: Le Touret Military Cemetery – Richebourg-L'Avoue – Pas de Calais – France (II. A. 5).

DONELAN, Patrick   Private 4529   Second Connaught Rangers
Killed in Action: (France) 23 October 1914. Age 19.
Supplementary Notes: Enlisted: Ballinasloe. Son of Michael & Mary Donelan of Main Street, Ballinasloe.

Remembered: Ypres (Menin Gate) Memorial – Ieper – West-Vlaanderen – Belgium (42).

DONELAN, Patrick   Private 16786   Sixth Royal Irish Fusiliers
Killed in Action: (Gallipoli) 15 August 1915. Age 28.
Supplementary Notes: Enlisted: Ballinasloe, shot by a sniper at 4 a.m. while on sentry duty. Formerly of the Connaught Rangers 821. Brother of John Arthur Donelan, above.
Remembered: Helles Memorial – Turkey (178 to 180).

DONELAN, Thomas   Private 92751   The King's Liverpool Regiment
Died of Wounds: (Ballinasloe) 8 December 1919.
Supplementary Notes: Son of Mrs K. Donelan of Main Street, Ballinasloe.
Buried: Creagh new cemetery – Ballinasloe – Ireland (D. 7).

DONOGHUE, Michael   Private 12213   First Irish Guards
Killed in Action: (France) 10 October 1918. Age 30.
Supplementary Notes: Born: Moylough.
Buried: St Hilaire-les-Cambrai British Cemetery – Nord – France (A. 6).

DONOGHUE, Patrick   Private 8193   First Irish Guards
Killed in Action: (France) 3 August 1917. Age 33.
Supplementary Notes: Brother of Thomas O'Donoghue of Shrull, Galway.
Buried: Artillery Wood Cemetery – Ieper – West-Vlaanderen – Belgium (X. E. 15).

DONOHUE, Patrick   Private 2745   Third South Lancaster Regiment
Death: (Home) 1 September 1915.
Supplementary Notes: Born: Loughrea.
Buried: Liverpool (Kirkdale) Cemetery – Liverpool – United Kingdom (screen wall II. R.C. 90). Recorded in Commonwealth War Graves Commission Records.

DONOHOE, Thomas   Private 11353   Second Irish Guards
Died of Wounds: (France) 7 August 1917. Age 22.
Supplementary Notes: Son of Mr & Mrs Thomas Donohoe. Born: Moylough, Ballinasloe.
Buried: Etaples Military Cemetery – Pas de Calais – France (XXII. 0. 12).

DONOHUE, Thomas   Rifleman 373540 (372540 & 5188)   Eighth London Regiment
Died of Wounds: (London) 12 June 1917. Age 33.
Supplementary Notes: (Post Office Rifles). Husband of Bridget Donohue of Esker, Athenry. His name is spelled 'Donohoe' on his headstone.
Buried: Kilconierin Catholic Churchyard – Co. Galway (north-east section).

DONOVAN, Patrick John   Lieutenant   HM Trawler *Lotus* Royal Navy Reserves
Died of Wounds: 23 June 1916. Age 40.
Supplementary Notes: Son of William & Bridget Donovan of Rock Ferry, Cheshire; husband of Catherine Donovan of Parkmore, Galway.
Buried: Haslar Royal Naval Cemetery – Hampshire – United Kingdom (B. 40. 16).

DONOVAN, William   Private 9949   First Connaught Rangers
Killed in Action: (France) 23 November 1914. Age 27.
Supplementary Notes: Son of Patrick Donovan of 2 Parkmore Terrace, Tuam.
Remembered: Le Touret Memorial – Pas de Calais – France (43).

DORAN, John   Private 307344   Eighth King's Liverpool Regiment
Killed in Action: (France) 11 September 1916.
Supplementary Notes: Enlisted: Liverpool. Born: Galway.
Remembered: Thiepval Memorial – Somme – France (1 D. 8 B. & 8C).

DOWD, James   Private 1/5101   First Irish Guards
Killed in Action: (France) 8 October 1915. Age 19 or 21.
Supplementary Notes: Born: Tuam. Brother of Patrick Joseph Dowd, listed below.
Buried: St Mary's Cemetery – Haisnes – Pas de Calais – France (II. F. 8).

DOWD, John   Private   Connaught Rangers
Killed in Action: (France) December 1916. Age 26.
Supplementary Notes: Born: Galway.

DOWD, Patrick Joseph   Lance Corporal 1/5102   Second Irish Guards
Killed in Action: (France) 29 July 1916. Age 32.
Supplementary Notes: Born: Tuam. Brother of James Dowd, listed above.
Buried: St Peter-in-Thanet Churchyard – Kent – United Kingdom (19. 3).

DOYLE, Dominick   Private 6834   Irish Guard Reserves
Died of Wounds: (London) 9 January 1916. Age 28.

Supplementary Notes: Killed in a bomb explosion. Born: Galway.

Buried: Great Warley (Christ Church) Cemetery – Essex – United Kingdom (L. 71).

DOYLE, John   Corporal 824   Fifth Connaught Rangers

Died of Wounds: (Gallipoli) 23 August or 28 September 1915. Age 30.

Supplementary Notes: Enlisted: Sheffield. Son of John & Bridget Doyle of Banavane, Ahascragh.

Remembered: Helles Memorial – Turkey (181 to 183).

DUANE, Joseph Patrick   Private G/3971   Second Royal Sussex Regiment

Killed in Action: (France) 9 August 1915.

Supplementary Notes: Born: Woodford.

Buried: Cambrin Churchyard Extension – Pas de Calais – France (F. 21).

DUANE, Michael   Private 3421   Sixth Connaught Rangers

Killed in Action: (France) 27 April 1916. Age 38.

Supplementary Notes: Enlisted: Galway. Son of Thomas & Mary Duane of Ballymacward (Whitepark, Woodlawn).

Buried: Mazingarbe Communal Cemetery Extension – Pas de Calais – France (I. A. 7).

DUGGAN, Michael   Private SS/19442   Royal Army Service Corps

Death: (Egypt) 8 January 1916. Age 41.

Supplementary Notes: Born: Headford.

Remembered: Cairo War Memorial Cemetery – Egypt (M. 90).

DUGGAN, Michael   Able Seaman 220784   HMS *Sandhurst*   Royal Navy

Died of Wounds: 1 December 1917. Age 33.

Supplementary Notes: Son of Peter & Mary Duggan of 56 Fairhill Road, Claddagh, Galway.

Buried: Lyness Royal Naval Cemetery – Orkney – United Kingdom (0. 19).

DUGGAN, Patrick   Private 19357   Labour Corps

Died of Wounds: (France) 29 October 1917.

Supplementary Notes: Born: Milltown.

DUGGAN, Thomas   Private 19283   Fifteenth Hampshire Regiment

Death: 15 September 1916. Age 41.

Supplementary Notes: Son of the late Mr & Mrs P. Duggan of the Claddagh, Galway; husband of Mary Duggan of 36 Cross Street, Portsea, Portsmouth.
Remembered: Thiepval Memorial – Somme – France (7 C & 7 B).

DWYER, Michael Private 3/5329 Fifth Connaught Rangers
Died of Wounds: (Egypt) 7 January 1918. Age 32.
Supplementary Notes: Enlisted: Ballinasloe. Born: Cappa, Aughrim.
Buried: Commonwealth War Cemetery – Damascus – Syria (A. 65).

EASTWOOD, Bernard Gunner 38093 Royal Field Artillery
Killed in Action: (Gallipoli) 7 August 1915.
Supplementary Notes: Born: Ballinakill.
Buried: Pink Farm Cemetery – Helles – Turkey (Sp. Mem. 27).

EASTWOOD, Frank Private 32789 Second Highland Light Infantry
Killed in Action: (France) 28 April 1917.
Supplementary Notes: Born: Letterfrack, Connemara.
Remembered: Arras Memorial – Pas de Calais – France (8).

EASTWOOD, William Private 12754 Eleventh Royal Scots
Died of Wounds: (France) 23 October 1916.
Supplementary Notes: Born: Clifden.

EGAN, James Gerard Lance Sergeant I/4161 First Irish Guards
Killed in Action: (Ginchy, France) 22 February 1915. Age 21.
Supplementary Notes: Son of John & Margaret Egan of Elerton, Loughrea.
Buried: Cuinchy Communal Cemetery – Pas de Calais – France (II. D. 3).

EGAN, John Private 1950 Second Leinster Regiment
Killed in Action: (France) 27 March 1918. Age 27.
Supplementary Notes: Born: Loughrea.
Remembered: Pozieres Memorial – Somme – France (78).

EVANS, Thomas Albert Colour Sergeant 21938 First Yorkshire Regiment
Died of Wounds: (Home) 8 January 1918.
Supplementary Notes: Enlisted: Bradford. Formerly of the East Yorkshire Regiment 9992. Born: Galway.
Buried: Bradford (Undercliffe) Cemetery – United Kingdom (F. "C" 81).

EYRE, Patrick   Private 9127   First Connaught Rangers
Killed in Action: 26 April 1915. Age 30.
Supplementary Notes: Enlisted: Galway. Son of Helen Eyre of Derry Cottage, Eyrecourt (Laurencetown).
Remembered: Ypres (Menin Gate) Memorial – Ieper – West-Vlaanderen – Belgium (42).

FAGAN, Christopher   Private 8992   Second Connaught Rangers
Killed in Action: (France) 19 September 1914. Age 22 or 27.
Supplementary Notes: Son of the late William & Ellen M. Fagan (former RIC sergeant of Barna) of 18 Nuns' Island, Galway; husband of the late Ann Fagan (Oughterard).
Remembered: La Ferten-Sous-Jouarre Memorial – Seine-et-Marne – France.

FAGAN, John   Private 2992   First Irish Guards
Died of Wounds: (France) 6 November 1914. Age 30 or 38.
Supplementary Notes: Son of John & Sara Fagan of Barna; husband of Maria Fagan of Truskey East, Barna.
Remembered: Ypres (Menin Gate) Memorial – Ieper – West-Vlaanderen – Belgium (11).

FAHEY, Michael   Private 7155   Second Connaught Rangers
Killed in Action: (France) 21 September 1914. Age 26.
Supplementary Notes: Enlisted: Cork. Awarded 1914 Star. Born: Killooley, Ballinasloe.
Buried: Vailly British Cemetery – Aisne – France (III. A. 49).

FAHY, Bernie Lance Corporal 4/1423 New Zealand Engineering Tunnelling Company
Killed in Action: (France) 20 April 1917.
Supplementary Notes: Enlisted: New Zealand. Born: Cregboy, Claregalway. A collection of his letters are held by the family. Some were included in *Galway and the Great War*, pp. 161, 162.
Buried: Faubourg D'Amiens Cemetery – Arras – France (V. A. 30).

FAHY, John   Private   Royal Field Artillery
Killed in Action: (France) May 1918.
Supplementary Notes: Enlisted: 1914. Described as 'only a boy' upon enlistment. Born: Portumna.

FAHY, Michael   Private 3851   First Connaught Rangers
Died of Wounds: (Mesopotamia) 7 June 1916. Age 32.
Supplementary Notes: Enlisted: Manchester. Son of Patrick Fahy of Cartimore, Athenry and the late Bridget Fahy.
Buried: Amara War Cemetery – Iraq (VII. E. 9).

FAHY, Michael   Private   British Expeditionary Force
Death: 1914–1918.
Supplementary Notes: From Ballinasloe. Believed to have been a Connaught Ranger. One of his brothers was later killed at Monte Cassino during the Second World War.
Remembered: Roll of Honour – Killed in Action – 1914–1918 – Ballinasloe – Ireland.

FAIR, David Hedley   Trooper 2025   First Household Cavalry
Killed in Action: (France) 30 October 1914.
Supplementary Notes: (Life Guards). Enlisted: Galway. Born: Ballinasloe.
Remembered: Ypres (Menin Gate) Memorial – Ieper – West-Vlaanderen – Belgium (3).

FALLON, William   Private   British Expeditionary Force
Death: 1914–1918.
Supplementary Notes: From Ballinasloe.
Remembered: Roll of Honour – Killed in Action – 1914–1918 – Ballinasloe – Ireland.

FARRAN, Francis Baker   Private 16640   Seventh Canadian Infantry
Death: 24 April 1915.
Supplementary Notes: (British Columbia Regiment). Enlisted: Canada. Son of William J. & Emmeline S. Farran of Toorleitra, Woodford. Brother of Edmond Farran, see below.
Remembered: Ypres (Menin Gate) Memorial – Ieper – West-Vlaanderen – Belgium (18. 28. 30).

FARRAN, Edmond Baker   Second Lieutenant   Fifth Black Watch
Death: 18 August 1915. Age 26.
Supplementary Notes: Brother of Francis Farran, see above.
Buried: Forgan (Vicarsford) Cemetery – Fifeshire – United Kingdom (E. 33).

FARRELL, James   Private   British Expeditionary Force
Death: (Gallipoli) 1915.

Supplementary Notes: From Ballinasloe.

Remembered: Roll of Honour – Killed in Action – 1914–1918 – Ballinasloe – Ireland.

FARRELL, John Private 1000 Fifth Connaught Rangers
Killed in Action: (Gallipoli) 28 August 1915.
Supplementary Notes: Enlisted: Boyle, Co. Roscommon. Born: Ballinasloe.
Remembered: Helles Memorial – Gallipoli – Turkey (181 & 183).

FARRELL, Matthew Private 901 South Irish Horse
Killed in Action: (France) 12 July 1916.
Supplementary Notes: Born: Galway.
Remembered: Thiepval Memorial – Somme – France (1 A).

FEATHERSTON, John Private 6028 Seventh Leinster Regiment
Died of Wounds: (France) 24 November 1917. Age 34.
Supplementary Notes: Born: Ballygar.
Buried: Croisilles Railway Cemetery – Pas de Calais – France (I. D. 1).

FEENEY, Michael Private 18086 Second Royal Irish Regiment
Killed in Action: (Guillemont, France) 3 September 1916.
Supplementary Notes: Born: Lettermore, Connemara.
Buried: Delville Wood Cemetery – Longueval (V. K. 5).

FEENEY, Peter Private 6756 Second Royal Irish Regiment
Killed in Action: (Aisne, France) 20 October 1914. Age 33.
Supplementary Notes: Awarded Mons Star. Born: Laanie.
Remembered: Ploegsteert Memorial – Comines-Warneton – Hainaut – Belgium (10).

FENOUGHTY, Michael Private 11029 Sixth Connaught Rangers
Killed in Action: (Guillemont, France) 3 September 1916.
Supplementary Notes: Enlisted: Coventry. Born: Mountbellow.
Remembered: Thiepval Memorial – Somme – France (15 A).

FFRENCH-COMYN, David Charles Edward Major Tenth Lancashire Fusiliers
Death: 12 May 1917. Age 41.
Supplementary Notes: Son of the late Francis & Cecilia Comyn Ffrench of Woodstock. (Fellow of the Royal Geographical Society & Order of St John of Jerusalem in England.) Also served in the South African campaign.

Remembered: Arras Memorial – Pas de Calais – France (5).

FINLAY, Michael   Private 9705   Second Leinster Regiment
Died of Wounds: (France) 19 August 1916.
Supplementary Notes: Born: Portumna.

FINNERTY, M.   Sergeant 27070   Second Royal Dublin Fusiliers
Killed in Action: (Belgium) 27 May 1917.
Supplementary Notes: Enlisted: Dublin. Born: Ballinasloe.
Buried: Kemmel Chateau Military Cemetery – Heuvelland – Belgium (N. 68).

FINNERTY, Mark   Private 6/13435   Sixth Royal Dublin Fusiliers
Death: (Gallipoli) 10 August 1915. Age 34 or 36.
Supplementary Notes: Son of Mark & Bridget Finnerty of Cranagh, Castleblakeney,
Ballinasloe.
Remembered: Helles Memorial – Turkey (190 to 196).

FINNERTY, Matthew   Private 13434   Sixth Royal Dublin Fusiliers
Died of Wounds: (Balkans) 3 or 27 April 1916.
Supplementary Notes: Enlisted: Warrington. Born: Galway.
Buried: Plovdiv Central Cemetery – Bulgaria (G. 5).

FINNERTY, Patrick   Private 10031   First & Fifth Connaught Rangers
Killed in Action: (Kustirino, Bulgaria) 7 December 1915. Age 21 or 22.
Supplementary Notes: Enlisted: Ballinasloe. Son of Patrick Finnerty of Harbour
Street, Ballinasloe.
Remembered: Doiran Memorial – Greece.

FINNERTY, Patrick Stephen   Private 307599   Eighth King's Liverpool Regiment
Killed in Action: (France) 7 June 1918. Age 41 or 48.
Supplementary Notes: Enlisted: Liverpool. Son of Redmond & Rose Finnerty of
Doone, Ahascragh, Ballinasloe.
Buried: Couin New British Cemetery – Pas de Calais – France (F. 58).

FINNIGAN, Joseph   Lance Sergeant 16522   Seventh Royal Enniskilling Fusiliers
Died of Wounds: (France) 28 April 1916.
Supplementary Notes: Born: Woodlawn.

FINNIGAN, Thomas   Private 3102   Sixth Royal Lancaster Regiment
    Death: (Mesopotamia) 25 April 1916. Age 36.
    Supplementary Notes: Born: Tuam.
    Remembered: Basra Memorial – Iraq (7).

FISHER, Hubert Patrick   Second Lieutenant   Shropshire Light Infantry
    Killed in Action: (Somme, France) 9 July 1916. Age 21.
    Supplementary Notes: Enlisted: May 1915. Attached to the Gloucester Regiment.
    Son of Harry Fisher (editor of *The Galway Express*) of Taylor's Hill House, Galway.
    Remembered: Great War monument – St Nicholas' Collegiate Church – Galway
    – Ireland.

FITZGERALD, John   Lance Sergeant 19216   Twentieth Northumberland Fusiliers
    Died of Wounds: (France) 10 September 1917.
    Supplementary Notes: Born: Galway.
    Buried: Tincourt New British Cemetery – Somme – France (II. A. 13).

FITZMAURICE, John   Private 9951   First Irish Guards
    Killed in Action: (France) 30 March 1918. Age 28.
    Supplementary Notes: Born: Galway.
    Remembered: Arras Memorial – Pas de Calais – France (1).

FLAHERTY, Arthur   Private 3896   First Connaught Rangers
    Died of Wounds: (France) Age 20.
    Supplementary Notes: Born: Galway.

FLAHERTY, Colman   Seaman 8605A   SS *Basil*   Royal Navy Reserves
    Death: 11 November 1917. Age 23.
    Supplementary Notes: Drowned after a collision. Son of Myles & Margaret Flaherty
    of Dynish, Lettermullen, Connemara.
    Remembered: Portsmouth Naval Memorial – Hampshire – United Kingdom (27).

FLAHERTY, Dominick   Private 3711   First Connaught Rangers
    Killed in Action: (France) 28 April 1916. Age 30.
    Supplementary Notes: Born: Galway.

FLAHERTY, Dominick   Fireman 933175   HMS *Eagle*   Mercantile Marines
    Death: 6 November 1917. Age 28.

Supplementary Notes: Son of Morgan & Bridget Flaherty of Grattan Road, Galway.
Buried: Liverpool (Anfield) Cemetery – Lancashire – United Kingdom (V. R. C. 1796).

FLAHERTY, John   Private 2347   Connaught Rangers
Killed in Action: (France) 19 July 1917. Age 24.
Supplementary Notes: Born: Galway.

FLAHERTY, Joseph   Leading Seaman 2281A   SS *Maloja*   Royal Navy Reserves.
Death: 27 February 1916. Age 21.
Supplementary Notes: Killed by a mine explosion off Dover. Son of Michael & Mary
Flaherty of Lower Fairhill Road, Claddagh, Galway.
Remembered: Portsmouth Naval Memorial – Hampshire – United Kingdom (23).

FLAHERTY, Joseph   Private 39871   Connaught Rangers
Killed in Action: (France) 17 February 1916. Age 28.
Supplementary Notes: Born: Galway.

FLAHERTY, Martin   Private 6040   First Irish Guards
Death: (Irish Sea) 10 October 1918. Age 24.
Supplementary Notes: Drowned following the sinking of the SS *Leinster* by a
German submarine. Son of Kate Flaherty of Castleboy, Ardrahan (Kilcreest). The
sinking of the SS *Leinster* was recorded in *Galway and the Great War*, pp. 98–101.
Buried: Grangegorman Military Cemetery – Dublin – Ireland (RC. 610).

FLAHERTY, Michael   Private 4971   First Connaught Rangers
Killed in Action: (Mesopotamia) 13 April 1916.
Supplementary Notes: Enlisted: Earlstown. Born: Ballysker, Athenry.
Remembered: Basra Memorial – Iraq (40 & 64).

FLAHERTY, Michael   Private 4978   First Connaught Rangers
Killed in Action: (France) 21 April 1916. Age 31.
Supplementary Notes: Born: Galway.

FLAHERTY, Patrick   Private 4195   Second Connaught Rangers
Killed in Action: (France) 11 November 1914 or 19 August 1917. Age 25.
Supplementary Notes: Enlisted: Galway. Born: Joseph's Parish, Galway.
Remembered: Ypres (Menin Gate) Memorial – Ieper – West-Vlaanderen – Belgium
(42).

FLAHERTY, Patrick   Seaman 4864B   HMS *Bulwark*   Royal Navy Reserve
Death: 26 November 1914. Age 40.
Supplementary Notes: Killed by an internal explosion on board ship off Sheerness.
Son of Michael & Margaret Flaherty of Galway; husband of Sabina Flaherty of Lower
Fairhill, Claddagh, Galway.
Remembered: Portsmouth Naval Memorial – Hampshire – United Kingdom (6).

FLAHERTY, Peter   Chief Stoker 283876   HMS *Marmion*   Royal Navy
Death: 21 October 1917. Age 40.
Supplementary Notes: Drowned after a collision in the North Sea. Husband of Annie
Flaherty of Seapoint, Barna.
Remembered: Plymouth Naval Memorial – Devon – United Kingdom (22).

FLAHERTY, Thomas   Sergeant 9347   Second Leinster Regiment
Death: (Belgium) 28 January 1916.
Supplementary Notes: Son of Mary Flaherty of Middle Street, Galway.
Buried: Lijssenthoek Military Cemetery Poperinge West-Vlaanderen – Belgium (II.
B. 37A).

FLAHERTY, Thomas   Staff Officer 32118   Royal Irish Rifles
Killed in Action: (France) 17 February 1916.
Supplementary Notes: Born: Galway.

FLANEGAN, Lionel Christopher   Officer   Tank Corps
Killed in Action: 20 November 1917. Age 21.
Supplementary Notes: Only son of Dr & Mrs Flanegan of Clacton-on-Sea and
Eyrecourt.
Remembered: Cambrai Memorial – Lou Verval – Nord – France (13).

FLANNERY, Thomas   Private 24205   Lancashire Fusiliers
Death: 28 August 1919. Age 28.
Supplementary Notes: Transferred to 410th Agricultural Company Labour Corps
584202. Son of Thomas Flannery of Galway; husband of Grace Flannery of 20 Camden
Road, London.
Buried: Forest of Dean (Christ Church) Churchyard – Gloucestershire – United
Kingdom.

FLEMING, Thomas   Lance Corporal 19830   First Royal Dublin Fusiliers
Killed in Action: (France) 29 March 1918.

Supplementary Notes: Born: Williamstown.

Buried: Epehy Wood Farm Cemetery – Epehy – Somme – France (III. D. 4).

FLOOD, Freeman Oscar　　　　Gunner 35560　　　　Royal Garrison Artillery

Death: (Home) 10 February 1917.

Supplementary Notes: Born: Gort.

Buried: Parkhurst Military Cemetery – United Kingdom (IV. B. 101). Recorded in Commonwealth War Graves Commission Records.

FLOOD, Michael　　　　Private 8472　　　　Sixth Connaught Rangers

Killed in Action: (Guillemont, France) 3 September 1916. Age 27 or 32.

Supplementary Notes: Enlisted: Galway. Born: Clifden.

Buried: Serre Road Cemetery No. 2 – Somme – France (IX. D. 15).

FLYNN, James　　　　Private 11257　　　　Second Irish Guards

Died of Wounds: (France) 4 December 1917. Age 27.

Supplementary Notes: Born: Templetoher.

Buried: St Sever Cemetery Extension – Rouen – Seine-Maritime – France (P. VI. C. 11A).

FLYNN, John　　　　Private 9692　　　　First Leinster Regiment

Died of Wounds: (France) 14 February 1915.

Supplementary Notes: Born: Portumna.

Remembered: Ypres (Menin Gate) Memorial – Ieper – West-Vlaanderen – Belgium (44).

FLYNN, Martin　　　　Private 19477　　　　Tenth Lancashire Fusiliers

Death: 27 June 1916. Age 33.

Supplementary Notes: Son of John & Mary Flynn of Milltown; husband of Ellen Flynn (*nee* McLoughlin) of 11 Jones Street, Shaw Road, Oldham, Lancashire.

Remembered: Thiepval Memorial – Somme – France (3 C & 3-D).

FLYNN, Patrick　　　　Gunner 31211　　　　Royal Field Artillery

Died of Wounds: (France) 10 July 1917. Age 23

Supplementary Notes: Born: Galway.

Buried: Mendinghem Military Cemetery – West-Vlaanderen – Belgium (I. F. 19).

FLYNN, Thomas　　　　Private 6870　　　　Second Royal Irish Regiment

Killed in Action: (France) 19 October 1914. Age 30.

Supplementary Notes: Born: St Patrick's Parish, Galway.
Remembered: La Touret Memorial – Pas de Calais – France (11 & 12).

FOLAN, John   Private 5890   Fifth Connaught Rangers
Killed in Action: (France) 9 October 1918. Age 26.
Supplementary Notes: Enlisted: Dumbarton. Son of Thomas & Mrs A. Folan of Derrygimla, Ballyconneely, Clifden. Brother of Patrick Folan, (below). Another brother, Thomas, also served in the war, and survived.
Buried: Busigny Communal Cemetery Extension – Nord – France (Ill. A. 35).

FOLAN, Joseph   Private 6163   First Connaught Rangers
Died of Appendicitis: (Mesopotamia) 4 May or 23 July 1918. Age 22 or 23.
Supplementary Notes: Enlisted: Aran. Son of Michael & Agnes Folan of Kilronan, Aran Islands.
Buried: Ramleh War Cemetery – Ramla – Israel (AA. 31).

FOLAN, Patrick   Private 890   Fifth Connaught Rangers
Killed in Action: (Gallipoli) 27 August 1915.
Supplementary Notes: Enlisted: Clydebank. Brother of John Folan, above.
Remembered: Helles Memorial – Turkey (181 to 183).

FOLAN, Peter   Seaman   Royal Navy
Death: 19 December 1919. Age 41.
Supplementary Notes: Born: Galway.

FOLEY, J   Gunner 76555   Nineteeth Royal Field Artillery
Death: (Belgium) 19 April 1918. Age 22.
Supplementary Notes: Son of Patrick & Cecilia Foley of Old Street, Portumna.
Buried: Reninghelst New Military Cemetery – Poperinge – West-Vlaanderen – Belgium (V. C. 8).

FOLEY, Michael   Trimmer 1470/ST   HMS Zaria   Royal Navy
Death: 26 October 1915. Age 48.
Supplementary Notes: Son of Michael & Mary Foley (*nee* Donohue) of Kilkerrin, Carna, Connemara; husband of the late Anne Foley.
Buried: Osmond Wall Cemetery – Orkney – United Kingdom (E.93).

FORDE, John   Private 4954   First Connaught Rangers
Death: (Egypt) 24 October 1918. Age 37.

Supplementary Notes: Enlisted: Warrington. Born: Ballybane, Galway. Brother of James Forde of Kiniskia, Claregalway.

Buried: Alexandria (Hadra) War Memorial Cemetery – Egypt (C. 102).

FORDE, John Patrick   Second Lieutenant   Ninth Royal Dublin Fusiliers
Died of Wounds: (France) 16 August 1917. Age 23 or 24.
Supplementary Notes: Son of the late James & Norah Forde of Wood Quay, Galway.
Remembered: Tyne Cot Memorial Zonnebeke – West-Vlaanderen – Belgium (144 to 145).

FORDE, Patrick   Corporal 2671   Second Household Cavalry
Killed in Action: (Ypres, Belgium) 31 October 1914.
Supplementary Notes: (Lifeguards). Formerly of the First Irish Guards. Born: Beagh.
Remembered: Ypres (Menin Gate) Memorial – Ieper – West-Vlaanderen – Belgium (3).

FOSTER, Francis   Sergeant 3241   Second Connaught Rangers
Killed in Action: (France) 14 September 1914. Age 36
Supplementary Notes: Enlisted: Burnmore. Awarded Mons Star. Born: Tuam.
Buried: Vailly British Cemetery – Aisne – France (SP. Mem. 3).

FOUNDS, James Laurance   Able Seaman J/7618   HMS *Indefatigable*   Royal Navy
Killed in Action: (Jutland) 31 May 1916. Age 25.
Supplementary Notes: Son of J. Founds (Coastguardsman) of Co. Galway.
Remembered: Portsmouth Naval Memorial – Hampshire – United Kingdom (12).

FOYNES, Michael   Private 11723   Eighth Welsh Regiment
Killed in Action: (Gallipoli) 8 August 1915.
Supplementary Notes: Enlisted: Cardiff. Son of Patrick Foynes of Co. Galway.
Remembered: Helles Memorial – Turkey (140 to 144).

FRENCH, John   Private 881   Fifth Connaught Rangers
Killed in Action: (Gallipoli) 28 August 1915. Age 36.
Supplementary Notes: Enlisted: Leigh. Son of Henry & Norah French of Galway Road, Tuam.
Remembered: Helles Memorial – Turkey (181 to 183).

FUREY, Alick   Private 4240   First Connaught Rangers
Killed in Action: (France) 7 April 1915. Age 18.

Supplementary Notes: Enlisted: Ballinasloe. Son of William & Mary Furey of Bride Street, Loughrea.

Buried: Rue-du-Bacquerot No. 1 Military Cemetery – Laventie – Pas de Calais – France (I. A. 10).

FUREY, Francis   Private 4236   Sixth Connaught Rangers
Killed in Action: (France) 3 August 1917. Age 24 or 26.
Supplementary Notes: Enlisted: Ballinasloe. Son of the late Thomas & Mary Furey of Mountbellew.
Remembered: Ypres (Menin Gate) Memorial – Ieper – West-Vlaanderen – Belgium (42).

FUREY, John   Private 61907   First Machine Gun Corps
Killed in Action: (France) 11 July 1917.
Supplementary Notes: (Infantry). Formerly of the Connaught Rangers. Born: Oranmore.
Remembered: Basra Memorial – Iraq (41).

FUREY, Patrick   Private 2132   Sixth Connaught Rangers
Killed in Action: (France) 26 June 1916. Age 34.
Supplementary Notes: Enlisted: Galway. Born: Mountbellew.

GALLAGHER, Michael   Private 4394   First Irish Guards
Died of Influenza: (Cologne, France) 21 February 1919. Age 27.
Supplementary Notes: Born: Ross.
Buried: Cologne Southern Cemetery – Germany (II. F. 7).

GALLAGHER, Thomas   Private 11624   Second Royal Irish Regiment
Killed in Action: (Guillemont, France) 3 September 1916.
Supplementary Notes: Born: Ballinasloe.
Remembered: Thiepval Memorial – Somme – France (3 A).

GALLAGHER, Thomas   Sergeant Major 6388   Fifth Connaught Rangers
Died of Wounds: (France) 10 October 1918.
Supplementary Notes: Enlisted: Clifden. Born: Omey, Clifden.
Buried: Serain Communal Cemetery Entension – France (A. 1).

GALLAGHER, Thomas   Private 26450   Second Oxfordshire & Buckinghamshire Regiment

Died of Wounds: (France) 8 September 1917.

Supplementary Notes: (Light Infantry). Formerly of the Wilts Regiment 10901. Born: Galway.

GALVIN, Michael   Private 18504   British Expeditionary Force

Death: 12 December 1915.

Supplementary Notes: Born: Mountbellew.

Buried: Moston (St Joseph's) Roman Catholic Cemetery – Lancashire – United Kingdom (P. 169).

GANNON, John   Private 5640   Fifth Connaught Rangers

Killed in Action: (Salonika) 7 December 1915. Age 34.

Supplementary Notes: Enlisted: Warrington. Born: Galway.

Remembered: Doiran Memorial – Greece.

GARRITY, George   Private 15153   First Royal Munster Fusiliers

Killed in Action: (France) 20 November 1917. Age 48.

Supplementary Notes: Son of Martin & Bridget Garrity of Cloondine, Gort.

Remembered: Arras Memorial – Pas de Calais – France (9).

GARVEY, David   Private 917   First Irish Guards

Killed in Action: (France) 1 November 1914.

Supplementary Notes: Born: Dunmore.

Remembered: Ypres (Menin Gate) Memorial – Ieper – West-Vlaanderen – Belgium (11).

GARVEY, Michael   Private 1540   Sixth Connaught Rangers

Killed in Action: (Guillemont, France) 3 September 1916. Age 22.

Supplementary Notes: Enlisted: Galway. Husband of Sabina Garvey of Grattan Road, Galway.

Remembered: Thiepval Memorial – Somme – France (15 A).

GARVEY, Thomas   Private G/33268   Seventeenth Middlesex Regiment

Killed in Action: (France) 30 November 1917.

Supplementary Notes: Born: Headford.

Remembered: Cambrai Memorial – Lou Verval – Nord – France (9).

GARVEY, William   Guardsman 23873   Third Grenadier Guards

Killed in Action: (France) 27 November 1917.

Supplementary Notes: Born: Errismore.

Remembered: Cambrai Memorial – Lou Verval – Nord – France (2).

GAUCKWIN, John   Private 17024   Second & Fourth South Lancaster Regiments

Died of Wounds: (France) 29 August 1918. Age 26.

Supplementary Notes: Enlisted: St Helens, Lancashire. Awarded Military Medal. Born: Ballinasloe.

Buried: Cabaret-Rouge British Cemetery – Souchez – France (VIII. N. 42).

GEAREY, Michael   Private 415807   First Connaught Rangers

Died of Wounds: (Mesopotamia) 6 April 1917. Age 20.

Supplementary Notes: Enlisted: Galway. Son of John & Margaret Gearey of Clifden.

Buried: Baghdad (North Gate) War Cemetery – Iraq (IX. D. 13).

GEARY, Martin   Private 3812A   Forty-ninthth Australian Infantry

Killed in Action: (Guillemont, France) 3 September 1916. Age 22.

Supplementary Notes: Born: on 3 September 1894, the son of Patrick & Honor Geary of Carna, Connemara, and later 21 Long Walk, Galway.

Remembered: Villers-Bretonneux Memorial – Somme – France.

GEARY, Michael   Private 5807   First Connaught Rangers

Died of Wounds: (Mesopotamia) 6 April 1917. Age 22.

Supplementary Notes: Born: Clifden.

GEARY, Patrick   Private 31191   Second Royal Irish Rifles

Killed in Action: (France) 21 April 1916. Age 21.

Supplementary Notes: Born: Galway.

GERAGHTY, Patrick   Private 12098   Second Royal Irish Regiment

Death: (France) 22 September 1918. Age 40.

Supplementary Notes: (Labour Corps). Son of Michael & Catherine Geraghty (*nee* Murray); husband of Mary A. Geraghty of Dalystown, Loughrea.

Buried: Beaumetz Cross Roads Cemetery – Beaumetz-les-Cambraj – Pas de Calais – France (E. 16).

GIBSON, Thomas   Private 16384   Eighth Royal Dublin Fusiliers

Killed in Action: (France) 12 August 1917. Age 30.

Supplementary Notes: Enlisted: St Helens, Lancashire. Born: Ballinasloe.
Buried: Vlamertinghe New Military Cemetery – Ieper – Belgium (V.C. 4).

GILBANY, Michael   Private 19530   Second East Lancashire Regiment
Killed in Action: (France) 9 May 1915. Age 36.
Supplementary Notes: Born: Galway.
Remembered: Ploegsteert Memorial – Comines-Warneton – Hainaut – Belgium.

GILL, Bartly   Deck Hand   Trawler *Neptune*   Mercantile Marines
Death: (Galway Bay) 17 December 1917. Age 47.
Supplementary Notes: Drowned as a result of enemy action. Son of the late Patrick
& Mary Gill; husband of Winifred Gill (*nee* Carrick) of 3 Quay Street, Galway. The
sinking of the *Neptune* was recorded in *Galway and the Great War*, pp. 95, 96.
Remembered: Tower Hill Memorial – London – United Kingdom.

GILL, Michael   Private 24899   First Royal Dublin Fusiliers
Killed in Action: (France) 21 March 1918.
Supplementary Notes: Born: Loughrea.
Remembered: Pozieres Memorial – Somme – France (78 / 80).

GILMORE, Michael   Rifleman 1787   Second Royal Irish Rifles
Killed in Action: (France) 24 May 1915.
Supplementary Notes: Born: Caltra.
Buried: Dickebusch New Military Cemetery Extension – Ieper – West-Vlaanderen
– Belgium (L. 26).

GLYNN, John   Private 14/1252   Fourteenth York & Lancaster Regiment
Killed in Action: (Somme, France) 1 July 1916.
Supplementary Notes: Born: Tuam.
Buried: Euston Road Cemetery – Colincamps – Somme – France (II. S. 4).

GLYNN, John   Lance Corporal 202952   Second Lancashire Fusiliers
Killed in Action: (France) 31 July 1917. Age 33.
Supplementary Notes: Son of Patrick & Bridget Glynn of Ahane, Kilkerrin, Ballina-
sloe.
Remembered: Ypres (Menin Gate) Memorial – Ieper – West-Vlaanderen – Belgium
(33).

Maxin gun section of Second Connaught Rangers
(Courtesy of Ray Duke)

Shooting team of Second Connaught Rangers
(Courtesy of Ray Duke)

EILEEN ALANNAH (1)

EILEEN Alannah, Eileen Asthore,
Light of my soul and its queen evermore,
It seems years have lingered since last we did part,
Eileen Alannah, the pride of my heart.

BAMFORTH COPYRIGHT — WORDS BY PERMISSION OF EVANS & CO., 95, CASTLE STREET, LONDON

EILEEN ALANNAH (2)

OH! darling loved one, your dear smile I miss,
My lips seem to cling to that sweet parting kiss;
Mavourneen, thy dear face I see at the door,
Eileen Alannah, Angus Asthore.

(REFRAIN)

Soon I'll be back to the Colleen I adore,
Eileen Alannah, Angus Asthore.

BAMFORTH COPYRIGHT — WORDS BY PERMISSION OF EVANS & CO., 95, CASTLE STREET, LONDON, W.

EILEEN ALANNAH (4).

GOD bless you, darling, I know you are true,
True to the boy who would now die for you;
My heart is now bleeding to its innermost core,
Eileen Alannah, Angus Asthore.

(REFRAIN)

Soon I'll be back to the Colleen I adore,
Eileen Alannah, Angus Asthore.

BAMFORTH COPYRIGHT — WORDS BY PERMISSION OF EVANS & CO., 95, CASTLE STREET, LONDON, W.

EILEEN ALANNAH (3)

EILEEN Alannah, Eileen Asthore,
The ocean's blue waters wash by the shore
Of that dear land of shamrock where thou doth abide
Waiting the day when I'll call thee my bride.

BAMFORTH COPYRIGHT — WORDS BY PERMISSION OF EVANS & CO., 95, CASTLE STREET, LONDON, W.

Four postcards sent home from the western front
(Courtesy of Tony Finnerty)

Somme offensive, Guillemont railway station after the attack
(Courtesy of the Irish Guards)

Destroyed German aircraft behind Monchy le Preux
(Courtesy of the Irish Guards)

Ypres canal after the attack of 31 July 1917 during the third battle of Ypres, or 'Passchendaele' *(Courtesy of the Irish Guards)*

Royal Field Artillery gun crew. Gunner Malachy Goode from Aughrim is standing to the extreme right of the photograph. The photograph was taken on 11 November 1918, after they had received their rations *(Courtesy of Mary & Paul McLoughlin)*

The remains of Montauban church 1916
(Courtesy of the Irish Guards)

Wounded soldiers and hospital staff outside Almondsbury subsidiary hospital, England, 1915
(Courtesy of Helen Spelman)

Soldiers of the Royal Irish Rifles. Two of the men in the front of the row have been identified; Jackie Condell is on the extreme left, and Richard Pepper is on the extreme right. Both men were from Ballinasloe *(Courtesy of Douglas Rafter)*

Soldiers of the Royal Field Artillery. Standing on the extreme right is William Griffin, killed in action in France or Flanders *(Courtesy of Paddy Monaghan)*

Action during the campaign in Palestine *(Courtesy of the Smith Collection)*

Photograph believed to be of the allies shortly after entering Jerusalem in December 1917
(Courtesy of the Smith Collection)

Allied troops setting up camp during the campaign in Palestine
(Courtesy of the Smith Collection)

Watering the horses during the campaign in Palestine
(Courtesy of the Smith Collection)

Allied troops relaxing during the campaign in Palestine
(Courtesy of the Smith Collection)

Victory parade in Palestine
(Courtesy of the Smith Collection)

Above: Captured German train,
11 November 1918
(Courtesy of the Irish Guards)

RMS Martin Rhattagin, Con-
naught Ranger, 21 Beattystown
(Ex-service-man's houses),
Claddagh
(Courtesy of Chris Costello)

The last Connaught Rangers veterans parade held on Sunday 4 June 1972, on the fiftieth anniversary of the handing in of the colours *(Courtesy of Ray Duke)*

Connaught Rangers reunion dinner on 12 June 1959. Lieutenant Colonel Henry Jourdain is seated second from the right. Second Lieutenant Alan McPeake is standing fourth from the left of the photograph. War notes from Lieutenant McPeake were included in *Galway and the Great War*, p. 249 *(Courtesy of Ray Duke)*

Connaught Rangers reunion dinner on 16 June 1961. The rangers' banner in the background. Note on the extreme left of the photograph, also in the background, is the replica of the famous Jingling Johnny. The original 'war trophy' was captured from the French by the rangers during the peninsular wars *(Courtesy of Ray Duke)*

Collection of Great War memorabilia belonging to Victor Smith of the Royal Field Artillery. They include his photograph, a sowing set, officer's whistle, trench spade, shell, cap badge and a small make-up case from Ypres *(Courtesy of the Smith Collection)*

Great War, Boer War & Indian Campaign medals of warrant officer Richard E. Byrne
(Courtesy of Dickie Byrne)

Connaught Rangers badges of warrant officer Richard E. Byrne
(Courtesy of Dickie Byrne)

Medals of Private James Quinn 6501, who served with the 2nd Connaught Rangers
at Mons and the first battle of Ypres. They include the Great War Medal, Victory Medal
and the 1914 Star
(Courtesy of Margaret 'Dillie' Thornton)

US troops march through the streets of Boston in 1919, shortly after disembarking from
France. Private Mark Kelly of Ballykeaghra, Tuam is fourth from the left of the photograph
(Courtesy of Maureen Kelly)

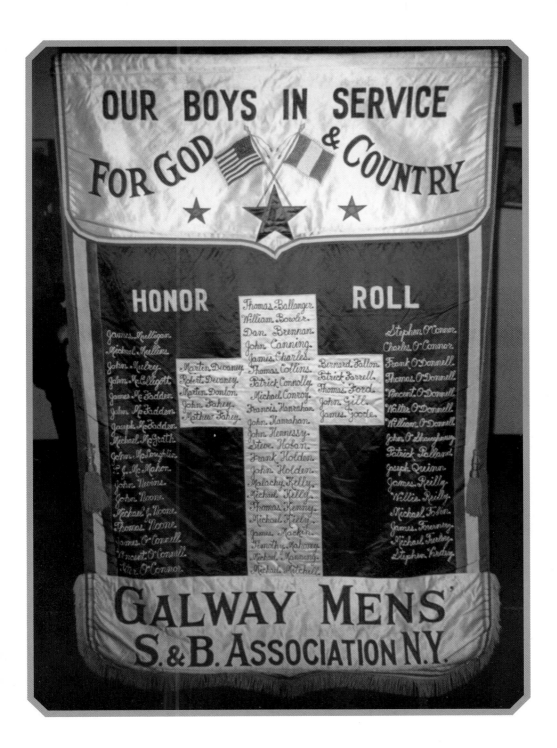

Galway Men's S & B Association New York US army banner, Renmore barracks museum, Galway. The banner records the names of men of Galway origin who were killed and served with the US army in the Great War. The names on the cross indicate those who died, surrounded by those who served (*Author's collection*)

Connaught Rangers Great War graves in St Mary's (new cemetery), Bohermore, Galway
(Author's collection)

GLYNN, Martin (Mattie) Second Lieutenant Tenth & Second Worcestershire Regiment
  Killed in Action: (France) 29 September 1918. Age 24 or 26.
  Supplementary Notes: Formerly of the Irish Guards. Son of Mary Glynn of Clough, Gurteen.
  Buried: Pigeon Ravine Cemetery – Epehy – Somme – France (I. A. 6).

GLYNN, Martin Private 37477 First Connaught Rangers
  Death: (Mesopotamia) 3 February 1917.
  Supplementary Notes: Enlisted: Manchester. Born: Ballyglunin.
  Buried: Amara War Cemetery – Amara – Iraq (XIV. G. 27).

GLYNN, Michael Private 3162 First Irish Guards
  Killed in Action: (Ypres, Belgium) 6 November 1914. Age 26 or 28.
  Supplementary Notes: Awarded Mons Star & Distinguished Conduct Medal. Son of William & Mary Glynn of Glenamaddy.
  Remembered: Ypres (Menin Gate) Memorial – Ieper – West-Vlaanderen – Belgium (11).

GLYNN, Patrick Private 14708 Seventh East Lancashire Regiment
  Death: (France) 12 December 1915.
  Supplementary Notes: Enlisted: Darwen, Lancashire. Born: Ballinasloe.
  Buried: Merville Communal Cemetery – Nord – France (IV. P. 1).

GODFREY, Michael Private 16250 Second South Lancashire Regiment
  Killed in Action: (France) 13 July 1916.
  Supplementary Notes: Born: Timmard.
  Buried: Bapaume Post Military Cemetery – Albert – France (I. F. 1).

GOLDEN, Dennis Private 922 Sixth Connaught Rangers
  Killed in Action: (Guillemont, France) 3 September 1916. Age 22.
  Supplementary Notes: Son of John & Bridget Golden of 19 Hanover Street, Bolton; husband of Mary Golden of 21 Beatty's Town, Galway.
  Remembered: Thiepval Memorial – Somme – France (15 A).

GOLDING, Joseph Private 2498 Connaught Rangers
  Killed in Action: (France) 21 October 1914.
  Supplementary Notes: Awarded 1914 Star. Born: Galway.

GOLDRICK, Patrick   Private 5790   Fifth Connaught Rangers
Died of Wounds: (France) 9 November 1918. Age 20.
Supplementary Notes: Enlisted: Ballinasloe. Son of Mr T. Goldrick of Cappercha, Kilconnell, Ballinasloe (Tuam).
Buried: Le Cateau Military Cemetery – Nord – France (V. H. 15).

GOODE, Benjamin   Private 49493   Northumberland Fusiliers
Died at Sea: 25 May 1918.
Supplementary Notes: Formerly of the Connaught Rangers. Born: Dunmore.
Remembered: Chatby Memorial – Egypt.

GOODWIN, Thomas   Private 26606   Tenth Royal Dublin Fusiliers
Died of Wounds: (France) 9 February 1917.
Supplementary Notes: Born: Milltown.
Buried: Varennes Military Cemetery – Somme – France (I. H. 85).

GOOLEY, James   Private 14501   Eighth Royal Dublin Fusiliers
Killed in Action: (France) 29 April 1916.
Supplementary Notes: Born: Scragg, Killivie.
Remembered: Loos Memorial – Pas de Calais – France (127 - 129).

GORDON, William   Private 112196   Twelfth Tank Corps
Death: (France or Flanders) 29 August 1918. Age 24.
Supplementary Notes: Son of James G. Gordon of Kilclooney, Ballinasloe.
Buried: Mory Abbey Military Cemetery – Mory – Pas de Calais – France (V. D. 29).

GORHAM, John   Sergeant 10056   Tenth Cameronians (Scottish Rifles)
Killed in Action: (France) 15 September 1916. Age 45.
Supplementary Notes: Son of Patrick & Anne Gorham of Drinagh, Errislannan, Clifden.
Remembered: Thiepval Memorial – Somme – France (4 D).

GORHAM, Joseph   Private   Connaught Rangers
Death: (France or Flanders) 1914–1918.
Supplementary Notes: Born: Inishnee, Roundstone, Connemara. Possibly related to Private Owen Gorham, below.

GORHAM, Martin   Private 18123   Second Leinster Regiment
Killed in Action: (France) 18 June 1918. Age 21.
Supplementary Notes: Son of Val & Mary Gorham of Roundstone, Connemara. (Arrismore).
Remembered: Ploegsteert Memorial – Comines-Warneton – Hainaut – Belgium (10).

GORHAM, Owen   Private 2/10387   Second Irish Guards
Killed in Action: (Ypres, France) 31 July 1917. Age 23 or 24.
Supplementary Notes: Son of John & Annie Gorham of Inishnee, Roundstone, Connemara.
Buried: Artillery Wood Cemetery – Ieper – West-Vlaanderen – Belgium. (I. A. II).

GOULDING, Joseph   Private 2842   Second Connaught Rangers
Killed in Action: (France) 14 September 1914. Age 32.
Supplementary Notes: Son of the late Michael & Julia Goulding of New Road, Galway; husband of Mary Goulding (*nee* Walsh); father of Paddy, Martin, Elle and Bensin Goulding. Family home was at Lower Fairhill, Claddagh, Galway. Brother of William Goulding, below (Rahoon).
Buried: Vailly British Cemetery – Aisne – France (II.E. 11).

GOULDING, William   Private 10946   Second Irish Guards
Died of Wounds: (Somme, France) 27 March 1918. Age 28.
Supplementary Notes: Just before his death he wrote a letter to his mother asking her to pray for him. Brother of Joseph Goulding, above.
Buried: Doullens Communal Cemetery Extension No. 1 – Somme – France.

GRADY, William   Private 10936   Second Connaught Rangers
Died of Wounds: (France) 19 November 1914. Age 23 or 28.
Supplementary Notes: Enlisted: Ballinasloe. Awarded 1914 Star. Son of Patrick & Bridget Grady of Ballydaragh, Kiltormer.
Buried: St Sever Cemetery – Rouen – Seine-Maritime – France (A. 1. 10).
Remembered: Roll of Honour – Killed in Action – 1914–1918 – Ballinasloe – Ireland.

GRAHAM, Byron John (Squire) Second Mate   SS *Saint Ronald* Mercantile Marines.
Death: 19 September 1917. Age 28.
Supplementary Notes: Drowned as a result of an attack by an enemy submarine. Son of the late John & Mary Eleanor Graham (*nee* Squire) of 35 Carfrae Terrace, Lipson, Plymouth. Born: Cleggan, Connemara.

Remembered: Tower Hill Memorial – London – United Kingdom.

GRAHAM, Augustine   Private 23056   Fifth Royal Berkshire Regiment
Killed in Action: (France) 29 April 1917.
Supplementary Notes: Born: Galway.
Remembered: Arras Memorial – Pas de Calais – France (7).

GRAHAM, Joseph   Sergeant 2488   Second Connaught Rangers
Killed in Action: (France) 13 November 1914.
Supplementary Notes: Enlisted: Oranmore. Born: Annaghdown.
Remembered: Ypres (Menin Gate) Memorial – Ieper – West-Vlaanderen – Belgium
(42).

GRAHAM, Patrick   Corporal 8532   First Royal Irish Regiment
Died of Wounds: (Galway) 22 January 1915.
Supplementary Notes: Born: Dunmore.

GRAHAM, Thomas   Private 4332   Second Connaught Rangers
Killed in Action: (France) 15 November 1914. Age 39.
Supplementary Notes: Enlisted: Galway. Son of the late Mrs Annie Graham; husband
of Annie Graham of 24 Henry Street, Galway (Rahoon).
Remembered: Ypres (Menin Gate) Memorial – Ieper – West-Vlaanderen – Belgium
(42).

GREHAN, Thomas   Private 43323   Third Connaught Rangers
Killed in Action: (Dardanelles) 21 October 1914. Age 31.
Supplementary Notes: Born: Galway. Because of the date and location of Private Thomas
Grehan's death, it is necessary to explain that this is the official recorded information.

GRATTAN–BELLEW, W.A.M.C.   Major   Twenty-ninth Royal Flying Corps
Death: (France or Flanders) 24 March 1917. Age 23.
Supplementary Notes: Formerly of the Connaught Rangers. 'Mentioned in Despatches'.
Awarded Military Cross. Son of Sir Henry & Lady Sophia Grattan-Bellew of Mountbellew.
Brother of Captain William Arthur Grattan-Bellew of the Connaught Rangers & Royal
Flying Corps.
Buried: Avesnes-le-Comte Communal Cemetery Extension – Pas de Calais – France
(III. C. 3).

GREGORY, Robert   Major   Sixty-sixth Royal Flying Corps
Killed in Action: 23 January 1918. Age 37.
Supplementary Notes: Formerly of the Connaught Rangers. Awarded Military Cross & Chevalier of the Legion of Honour. Son of the late Rt Hon. Sir William Gregory, KCMG, of Coole Park & Lady Augusta Gregory (*nee* Persse, daughter of the late Dudley Persse of Roxburgh House); husband of Graham Parry; father of Richard, Anne and Catherine Gregory. The Italian Air Force shot down his aircraft in error. William Butler Yeats wrote the poem *An Irish Airman Foresees His Death* in memory of Robert Gregory.
Buried: Padua Main Cemetery – Italy (A. 12).

GREY, William   Private 16166   First Royal Irish Fusiliers
Killed in Action: (France) 9 April 1918. Age 21.
Supplementary Notes: Enlisted: Ballinasloe. Son of Emily Grey of Colley Street, Wicklow, and the late Thomas Grey. Born: Ballinasloe.
Remembered: Tyne Cot Memorial – Zonnebeke – West-Vlaanderen – Belgium (140 & 141).

GREY, William   Private 11691   Second Irish Guards
Killed in Action: (France) 9 October 1917.
Supplementary Notes: Born: Clifden.

GRIFFIN, John   Private 3866   Second Connaught Rangers
Killed in Action: 7 November 1914. Age 30.
Supplementary Notes: Enlisted: Oranmore. Son of Thomas & Maria Griffin of Ballinasloe; husband of Ellen Griffin of Haymarket Street, Ballinasloe.
Remembered: Ypres (Menin Gate) Memorial – Ieper – West-Vlaanderen – Belgium (42).

GRIFFIN, John Joseph   Gunner   Royal Navy
Death: 15 January 1921. Age 36.
Supplementary Notes: Son of Patrick & Mary Anne Griffin; husband of Teresa Griffin of 5 Upper Merchants Road, Galway.
Buried: Haslar Royal Naval Cemetery – Hampshire – United Kingdom (B. 38. 1).

GRIFFIN, Michael   Private 26066   Second South Lancashire Regiment
Died of Wounds: (France) 27 December 1916. Age 42.
Supplementary Notes: Born: Glenamaddy.

Buried: Lapugnoy Military Cemetery – Pas de Calais – France (II. G. 3).

GRIFFIN, William   Private 5684   Fifth Connaught Rangers
Died of Fever: (Salonika) 18 December 1915.
Supplementary Notes: Enlisted: Dublin. Born: Barna.
Buried: Salonika (Lembet Road) Military Cemetery – Greece (21).

GRIFFIN, William   Private   Royal Field Artillery
Death: (France or Flanders) 1914–1918.
Supplementary Notes: He had three brothers, Paddy, Jack and Eddie Griffin. Born: Galway, lived at 4 St Bridget's Terrace, Galway.

GUY, William   Private 11641   Second Irish Guards
Killed in Action: (France) 9 October 1917. Age 24.
Supplementary Notes: Son of Martin & Mary Guy of Bunowen, Ballyconneely, Clifden.
Buried: Hagle Dump Cemetery – Ieper – West-Vlaanderen – Belgium (III. D. 14).

GWYNN, Rev. John S.J.   Chaplain   Irish Guards
Died of Wounds: (Gallipoli) 12 October 1915. Age 47.
Supplementary Notes: It was reported during the war that a memorial plaque was erected to Fr Gwynn in St Ignatius Church, Sea Road, Galway. Born: Galway.
Buried: Boulogne Eastern Cemetery – Pas de Calais – France (II. K. 6).

HAGARTY, Thomas   Private 4003   Tenth Lancaster Fusiliers
Killed in Action: (France) 10 November 1916.
Supplementary Notes: Born: Craig.
Remembered: Thiepval Memorial – Somme – France (P & F 3. C & 3D).

HALL, Arthur Henry   Captain M C   Second & Eighth Somerset Light Infantry
Killed in Action: 19 November 1916. Age 25.
Supplementary Notes: Son of Louie J. Bradshaw of Athenry and the late Arthur F. Hall.
Buried: Ancre British Cemetery – Beaumont-Hamel – Somme – France (VII. E. 7).

HAMILTON, Frederick C.   Private 509   First Irish Guards
Killed in Action: (France) 1 September 1914. Age 27.
Supplementary Notes: Born: Athenry.

Remembered: La Ferte-Sous-Jouarre Memorial – Seine-et-Marne – France.

HANCOCK, John   Private 4930   Sixth Connaught Rangers
    Killed in Action: (France) 15 May 1916. Age 33.
    Supplementary Notes: Enlisted: Inverkeithing. Born: Fairhill, Claddagh, Galway.
    Buried: Dud Corner Cemetery – Loos – Pas de Calais – France (I. H. 19).

HANLEY, Patrick   Rifleman 64926.   First & Third NZ Rifle Brigade
    Death: (France) 30 August 1918. Age 40.
    Supplementary Notes: Son of John & Ellen Hanley (*nee* Fahy) of Carnmore, Clare-
galway.
    Buried: Bancourt British Cemetery – Pas de Calais – France (I. C. 12.4).

HARDIMAN, James   Sapper 6441   Third Royal Engineers
    Died of Wounds: (France) 15 December 1916. Age 36.
    Supplementary Notes: Son of Michael & Julia Hardiman of Kilchreest, Loughrea.
    Buried: Etaples Military Cemetery – Pas de Calais – France (XX. H. 1).

HARNEY, Thomas   Private 29165   New Zealand Regiment
    Killed in Action: (France) 13 June 1917.
    Supplementary Notes: Son of Michael Harney of Moore, Ballydangan, Ballinasloe.
    Remembered: Messines Ridge (NZ) Memorial – Belgium

HARRISON, Joseph   Private 16811   Eighth Royal Irish Fusiliers
    Died of Wounds: (Somme, France) 26 September 1916. Age 16.
    Supplementary Notes: Enlisted: Ballinasloe. Son of James & Mary Harrison of
Ballinasloe.
    Buried: Abbeyville Communal Cemetery Extension – Somme – France.

HATTE, Alfred Henry   Private 23/1413   Third Auckland Regiment NZEF
    Killed in Action: 19 October 1917.
    Supplementary Notes: Son of the late James Rayson Hatte & Anne Hatte (*nee*
Kirkwood) of Ballygar. Born: Galway.
    Remembered: Tyne Cot Memorial – Zonnebeke – West-Vlaanderen – Belgium (1).

HAY, Arthur S.L.   Lance Corporal 265490   Sixth Seaforth Highlanders
    Died of Wounds: (France) 4 April 1918. Age 32.
    Supplementary Notes: Enlisted: Elgin, Morays. Born: Galway.
    Buried: Etaples Military Cemetery – Pas de Calais – France (XXXIII. D. 16).

HAY, James Lyle   Second Lieutenant   Twelfth Northumberland Fusiliers
Death: 3 July 1916. Age 20.
Supplementary Notes: Enlisted: Galway 1914. Son of William & Mary Hay of Clonbrock, Ballinasloe. Educated at the Grammar School, College Road and studied engineering at University College Galway.
Buried: Gordon Dump Cemetery – Ovillers-la Boisselle – France (II. F. 3).

HAYES, Francis   Private 3819   Second Royal Munster Fusiliers
Death: 10 November 1917. Age 23
Supplementary Notes: Son of Michael & Amy Annie Hayes of Killimore, Ballinasloe.
Remembered: Tyne Cot Memorial – Zonnebeke – West-Vlaanderen – Belgium (143 to 144).

HAYES, John   Private 10117   First Connaught Rangers
Death: (Mesopotamia) 12 May 1916. Age 31.
Supplementary Notes: Enlisted: Galway. Born: St Nicholas' Parish, Galway.
Buried: Baghdad (North Gate) War Cemetery – Iraq (XXI. L. 14).

HAYES, John   Private 6987   Second South Lancashire Regiment
Killed in Action: (France) 24 October 1914.
Supplementary Notes: Enlisted: Liverpool. Born: Galway.
Remembered: La Touret Memorial – Pas de Calais – France (23).

HAYES, Richard   Private 6487   First King's Liverpool Regiment
Died of Wounds: (France) 15 February 1915.
Supplementary Notes: Enlisted: Warrington. Born: Galway.
Buried: Bethune Town Cemetery – Pas de Calais – France (IV. A. 19).

HAYES, Thomas   Private 13914   Second Otago Regiment NZEF
Killed in Action: (France or Flanders) 16 June 1917. Age 33.
Supplementary Notes: Son of Edward & Margaret Hayes (*nee* Cleary) of Derrygoolin, Whitegate.
Remembered: Messines Ridge (NZ) Memorial – Mesen – West-Vlaanderen – Belgium.

HAYWARD, Charles Henry   Rifleman 3067   Second Rifle Brigade
Death: 9 May 1915. Age 21.
Supplementary Notes: Son of Cecelia Hayward of Sea View, Clifden and the late Henry Hayward.

Remembered: Ploegsteert Memorial – Comines-Warneton – Hainaut – Belgium (10).

HEALEY, (Healy) Thomas   Private 5195   Coldstream Guards
  Killed in Action: (France) 1 November 1914. Age 38.
  Supplementary Notes: Born: Milltown.
  Remembered: Ypres (Menin Gate) Memorial – Ieper – West-Vlaanderen – Belgium (11).

HEALEY, John   Lance Corporal 2919   First Connaught Rangers
  Death: (Mesopotamia) 2 June 1916.
  Supplementary Notes: Enlisted: Oranmore. Born: Creagh, Ballinasloe.
  Buried: Amara War Cemetery – Amara – Iraq (VII. E. 12).

HEALY, Joseph   Lance Corporal 3317   First Irish Guards
  Died of Wounds: (France) 18 May 1915. Age 24.
  Supplementary Notes: Born: Lickmolassy.
  Buried: Bethune Town Cemetery – Pas de Calais – France (IV. C. 8).

HEALY, Michael   Private 17029   Eighth South Lancaster Regiment
  Killed in Action: (France) 29 August 1916.
  Supplementary Notes: Born: Headford.
  Remembered: Thiepval Memorial – Somme – France (P & F 7. A & 7B).

HEALY, Patrick   Private 932   Second Lancaster Fusiliers
  Died of Wounds: (France) 17 October 1916.
  Supplementary Notes: Born: Tuam.
  Buried: Etaples Military Cemetery – Pas de Calais – France (VIII. B. 6).

HEALY, Thomas   Private 18147   Second Leinster Regiment
  Died of Wounds: (France) 3 June 1918.
  Supplementary Notes: Born: Ballygar.
  Buried: Ebblinghem Military Cemetery – Nord – France.

HEALY, Timothy   Private 4179   Sixth Connaught Rangers
  Killed in Action: (France) 2 September 1916. Age 31.
  Supplementary Notes: Born: Galway.

HEGARTY, John   Quarter Master Sergeant 7982   Fifth Connaught Rangers
  Killed in Action: (Gallipoli) 21 or 22 August 1915.

Supplementary Notes: Enlisted: Dublin. Born: Athenry.

Remembered: Helles Memorial – Turkey (181 to 183).

HENAGHAN, Simon   Lance Corporal 8306   Second Irish Guards

Killed in Action: (France) 9 October 1917. Age 25 or 30.

Supplementary Notes: Son of James & Mary Henaghan of Kilcoghans, Tuam; husband of Annie Henaghan of Marley, Tuam.

Remembered: Tyne Cot Memorial – Zonnebeke – West-Vlaanderen – Belgium (10 to 11).

HENDERSON, George   Lance Sergeant 266   Fifth Connaught Rangers

Killed in Action: (Gallipoli) 21 August 1915.

Supplementary Notes: Enlisted: Galway. Born: Portumna.

Remembered: Helles Memorial – Turkey.

HENIHAN, Michael   Private 3191   Fifth Connaught Rangers

Death: (Salonika) 4 December 1915.

Supplementary Notes: Enlisted: Rotherham. Born: Annaghdown.

HENSHALL, William   Private 6991   Sixth Connaught Rangers

Killed in Action: (France) 8 September 1916.

Supplementary Notes: Enlisted: Galway. Born: Clifden.

Remembered: Thiepval Memorial – Somme – France (P & F 15. A).

HESSIDY, Patrick   Private 6318   Eighth Royal Munster Fusiliers

Killed in Action: (France) 23 June 1918.

Supplementary Notes: Born: Galway. The same military number is recorded for Patrick Hession, listed below.

HESSION, John   Sapper 36776   Corps of Royal Engineers

Died of Wounds: (Home) 23 July 1916.

Supplementary Notes: Formerly of the Royal Lancaster Regiment 5570 & 157th Field Company 14762. Enlisted: Manchester. Born: Galway.

Buried: Moston (St Joseph's) Roman Catholic Cemetery – Lancashire (St Anthony's section 1015).

HESSION, Patrick   Private 6318   Second Royal Munster Fusiliers

Death: (France) 17 February 1916. Age 40.

Supplementary Notes: Enlisted: Huddersfield. Born: Galway.
Buried: St Marie Cemetery – Le Havre – France (D. 19. R. 5).

HIGGINS, James   Private 7899   Second Connaught Rangers
Killed in Action: (France) 26 August 1914. Age 32.
Supplementary Notes: Enlisted: Ballinasloe. Awarded 1914 Star. Born: Ballymacward, Kilconnell.
Remembered: La Ferte-Sous-Jouarre Memorial – Seine-et-Marne – France.

HIGGINS, John   Private 8052   First Connaught Rangers
Died of Cholera: (Mesopotamia) 9 May 1916. Age 34.
Supplementary Notes: Enlisted: Ballinasloe. Awarded 1914 Star. Born: Ballymacward, Kilconnell (Castleblakeney).
Buried: Amara War Cemetery – Amara – Iraq (VII. F. 2).

HIGGINS, Lawrence   Private 61207   Sixth Royal Munster Fusiliers
Killed in Action: (France) 5 September 1915. Age 21 or 29.
Supplementary Notes: Son of Patrick & Kate Higgins of Shantalla, Galway.
Buried: Kensal Green (St Mary's) Roman Catholic Cemetery – London – United Kingdom (2. Screen Wall).

HIGGINS, Martin   Private 474   Fifth Connaught Rangers
Killed in Action: (Gallipoli) 11 August 1915.
Supplementary Notes: Enlisted: Clydebank. Born: Ballinasloe.

HIGGINS, Michael   Private 3650   First Connaught Rangers
Killed in Action: (France) 26 April 1915.
Supplementary Notes: Son of John & Margaret Higgins of Porridgetown, Oughterard (Kilcannon, Ross).
Remembered: Ypres (Menin Gate) Memorial – Ieper – West-Vlaanderen – Belgium (42).

HIGGINS, Patrick   Private 4358 (4658)   Fifth York & Lancaster Regiment
Died of Wounds: (Home) 21 June 1916.
Supplementary Notes: Born: Kilkerin.
Buried: Whinney Hill (St Gerard's) Roman Catholic Cemetery (B. 13).

HILLARY, Francis   Private 8790   First Connaught Rangers
Killed in Action or Died of Wounds: (Mesopotamia) 1 February 1916. Age 18 or 21.

Supplementary Notes: Enlisted: Ballinasloe. Son of John & Mary Anne Hillary of Haymarket Street, Ballinasloe (Kilclooney). Brother of Michael Hillary, below.
Buried: Amara War Cemetery – Amara – Iraq (VII. H. 4).

HILLERY, Michael   Private 8009   Fifth Connaught Rangers
Killed in Action or Died of Wounds:(France) 10 October 1918. Age 28 or 30.
Supplementary Notes: Enlisted: Ballinasloe; husband of Mary Hillery of Brackernagh, Ballinasloe (Kilclooney). Brother of Francis Hillery, above.
Buried: Roisel Communal Cemetery Extension – Somme – France (I. A. 5).

HOAR, Frederick   Private 15298   Connaught Rangers
Died of Wounds: (France) 21 January 1917. Age 39
Supplementary Notes: Born: Galway.

HOARE, Frederick   Private 5571   First Connaught Rangers
Death: (Mesopotamia) 13 July 1916.
Supplementary Notes: Enlisted: Galway. Born: Woodquay, Galway. Husband of Bridget Hoare (*nee* Derrick, sister of Driver John Derrick 101045, p. 108). They had twelve children, two of whom, Fred and John, also fought in the war. Both sons survived the war.
Buried: Amara War Cemetery – Iraq (VII. C. 10).

HOAREY, Edward   Private 4745   First Irish Guards
Killed in Action: (France) 18 May 1915. Age 21.
Supplementary Notes: Born: Laurencetown 15 October 1894.
Remembered: La Touret Memorial – Pas de Calais – France.

HOGAN, Joseph   Private 4888   Fifth Royal Irish Regiment
Death: 18 September 1915. Age 24.
Supplementary Notes: Son of Thomas & Mary Hogan of Killimore.
Remembered: Doiran Memorial – Greece.

HOLIAN, Anthony   Private 10446   First Connaught Rangers
Killed in Action: (France) 23 November 1914. Age 18.
Supplementary Notes: Enlisted: Tuam. Awarded Mons Star. Born: Tuam.
Remembered: La Touret Memorial – Pas de Calais – France (43).

HOLIAN, Stephen   Private 3968   First Connaught Rangers
Killed in Action or Died of Wounds: (France) 24 June 1915. Age 26.

Supplementary Notes: Enlisted: Tuam. Born: Tuam.

HOLLAND, Craiell   Private 8253   Fifteenth York & Lancaster Regiment
Died of Wounds: (France) 22 March 1915. Age 25.
Supplementary Notes: Born: Gort.
Buried: Dranouter Churchyard.

HOLMES, Cecil Crampton   Captain   First Lincolnshire Regiment
Killed in Action: (Mons, Belgium) 26 August 1914. Age 26.
Supplementary Notes: Awarded 1914 Star. 'Mentioned in Despatches'. Son of Captain Harry William & Anna Holmes of Rockwood, Galway. Brother of Edmond Holmes, below.
Buried: Frameries Communal Cemetery – Frameries – Hainaut – Belgium (III. A. 8).
Remembered: Great War monument – St Nicholas' Collegiate Church – Galway – Ireland.

HOLMES, Edmond Concannon   Lieutenant   HMS *Astraea*   Royal Navy
Death: (Cape of Good Hope) 11 October 1918. Age 32.
Supplementary Notes: Brother of Cecil Holmes, above.
Buried: Simon's Town (Dido Valley) Cemetery – Cape Town – South Africa.
Remembered: Great War monument – St Nicholas' Collegiate Church – Galway – Ireland.

HOLMES, Reginald R.J.   Captain   Royal Army Medical Corps
Death: (Military Hospital, Malta) April 1916.
Supplementary Notes: Only son of the late Robert Galway Holmes of Cloncagh, Woodlawn.
Buried: Pieta Military Cemetery – Malta.

HOWARD, William   Driver 75297   Fourteenth & Fifty-seventh Royal Field Artillery
Died of Wounds: (Mesopotamia) 8 April 1916. Age 24.
Supplementary Notes: Enlisted: Galway. Son of Mary Howard of Water Lane, Galway, and the late Michael Howard. Worked in Dowler's Coach Factory, Victoria Place before the war (Prospect Hill & Ballinasloe).
Remembered: Basra Memorial – Iraq (3 & 60).

HOWLEY, Patrick   Rifleman 242093   First & Fifth South Lancashire Regiment
Killed in Action: (Ypres, Belgium) 31 July 1917. Age 28.

Supplementary Notes: Son of Martin & Mary Howley of Cloghroak, Ardrahan. There were nine children in the family.

Remembered: Ypres (Menin Gate) Memorial – Ieper – West-Vlaanderen – Belgium (37).

HUGHES, John Joseph   Private G/12833   First the Buffs (East Kent Regiment)

Killed in Action: (France) 15 April 1917. Age 27.

Supplementary Notes: Son of Mr & Mrs Michael Hughes of Mountbellew.

Remembered: Loos Memorial – Pas de Calais – France (15 to 19).

HUGHES, Martin James   Private 40216   Second Canterbury Regiment NZEF

Died of Wounds: 19 August 1917. Age 25.

Supplementary Notes: Son of Mr F. Hughes of Gardenham, Drumgriffin.

Buried: Etaples Military Cemetery – Pas de Calais – France (XXII. Q. 20A).

HUGHES, Patrick   Lance Corporal 6555   Second Irish Guards

Killed in Action: (France) 19 October 1915.

Supplementary Notes: Born: Tuam.

Buried: Vermelles British Cemetery – Pas de Calais – France (I. K. 10).

HUGHES, Thomas   Gunner 464 (454)   Royal Garrison Artillery

Killed in Action: (France) 26 September 1916.

Supplementary Notes: Born: Milltown.

Buried: Dantzig Alley British Cemetery – Mametz – Somme – France (VIII. E. 9).

HURLEY, James   Private 5497   Fifth Connaught Rangers

Death: (Salonika) 30 October 1915.

Supplementary Notes: Enlisted: Chesterfield. Born: Buggauns.

Remembered: Doiran Memorial – Greece.

HUXFORD, Edward   Leading Boatman 204643 PO   HMS *President* IV   Mercantile Marines.

Death: (Galway) 12 February 1919.

Supplementary Notes: Husband of Catherine Huxford. Born: Galway.

Buried: Cleggan Graveyard – Co. Galway (screen wall).

Remembered: Grangegorman Memorial – Dublin – Ireland (Alternative Commemoration).

HYLAND, James   Private 7720   Sixth Connaught Rangers
Killed in Action: (France) 4 June 1917. Age 22.
Supplementary Notes: Enlisted: Galway. Son of Mr & Mrs Michael Hyland of Cloonluane, Renvyle.
Remembered: Ypres (Menin Gate) Memorial – Ieper – West-Vlaanderen – Belgium (42).

HYNES, Martin   Private 432   First Royal Munster Fusiliers
Killed in Action: (Somme, France) 1 July 1916.
Supplementary Notes: Son of Mary Hynes of Mountross, Headford.
Buried: Bethune Town Cemetery – Pas de Calais – France (V. F. 21).

HYNES, Michael   Lance Corporal 9098   First Connaught Rangers
Killed in Action: (France) 19 March 1915.
Supplementary Notes: Enlisted: Gort. Born: Gort. Same military number is recorded for Peter McKeown, p.179.
Remembered: Le Touret Memorial – Pas de Calais – France (43).

HYNES, P.   Private 4602   Sixth Connaught Rangers
Death: (France) 4 May 1916. Age 33.
Supplementary Notes: Son of James & Honora Hynes of Headford; husband of Alice Hynes of 6 Rafters Road, Crumlin, Dublin.
Buried: Dud Corner Cemetery – Loos – Pas de Calais – France (I. G. 20).

ICKLAM, Edward   Private 9876   First Royal Munster Fusiliers
Killed in Action: (France) 19 February 1918.
Supplementary Notes: Born: Gort.
Buried: Villers-Faucon Communal Cemetery Extension – Somme – France (I. B. 12).

IGOE, John   Private 4696   Connaught Rangers
Killed in Action: (Egypt) 19 July 1917. Age 31.
Supplementary Notes: Born: Galway. Same military number is recorded for Michael McDonagh, p. 174.

IGOE, Patrick   Private 3119   First Connaught Rangers
Death: (Egypt) 21 October 1917 or 1918. Age 28.
Supplementary Notes: Son of Annie Igoe of Bowling Green, Galway.
Buried: Haifa War Cemetery – Israel (B. 1).

JENINGS, George Pierce (Creagh)   Lieutenant First King's Shropshire Light Infantry
   Death: 6 November 1914. Age 27 or 29.
   Supplementary Notes: Son of the late Lieutenant Colonel Ulick Jenings of Ironpool.
   Educated at Royal Military College, Sandhurst (lived in Mervue & Tuam).
   Remembered: Ploegsteert Memorial – Comines-Warneton – Hainaut – Belgium (8).

JOHNS, John   Lance Corporal 8151   Second Royal Irish Rifles
   Died of Wounds: (France) 14 October 1914.
   Supplementary Notes: Born: Gort.
   Remembered: Le Touret Memorial – Pas de Calais – France (43).

JOHNSTONE, Hugh Stanley   Private 9878   Second Scots Guards
   Died of Wounds: (France) 7 October 1915. Age 26.
   Supplementary Notes: Enlisted: Liverpool. Son of Thomas H. & Mary A. Johnstone
   of Galway Road, Tuam.
   Buried: Longuenesse (St Omer) Souvenir Cemetery – Pas de Calais – France (II. A.
   51).

JOISE (JOYCE), John   Private 3198   Connaught Rangers
   Killed in Action: (France) 19 August 1915. Age 32.
   Supplementary Notes: Born: Galway.

JONES, George E.   Lance Corporal 197   Seventh South African Infantry
   Killed in Action: (German East Africa) 12 February 1916. Age 39.
   Supplementary Notes: Son of the late George Jones. Born: Galway. Three other
   brothers also served, Harry and Percy, Royal Engineers; Fred, Irish Guards and survived
   the war. All were former pupils of the grammar school.
   Buried: Taveta Military Cemetery – Kenya (IX. B. 1).
   Remembered: Great War monument – St Nicholas' Collegiate Church – Galway
   – Ireland.

JORDAN, Patrick   Private 9435   First Connaught Rangers
   Killed in Action: (France) 26 April 1915.
   Supplementary Notes: Enlisted: Galway. Born: Gort.
   Remembered: Ypres (Menin Gate) Memorial – Ieper – West-Vlaanderen – Belgium
   (32).

JORDAN, Patrick Frank   Private S/475   Second Royal Fusiliers
  Killed in Action: (Gallipoli) 6 June 1915.
  Supplementary Notes: City of London Regiment. Enlisted: Sheffield. Born: Galway.
  Remembered: Helles Memorial – Turkey (37 to 41 or 328).

JORDAN, Stephen   Private 8248   Second Irish Guards
  Killed in Action: (France) 31 July 1917.
  Supplementary Notes: Enlisted: Galway. Born: Galway.
  Buried: Artillery Wood Cemetery – Ieper – West-Vlaanderen – Belgium (I. B. 3).

JOYCE, Festus   Private 9151   Fifth Connaught Rangers
  Killed in Action: (Salonika) 7 December 1915 or 1916. Age 34.
  Supplementary Notes: Enlisted: Galway. Awarded Mons Star. Son of Michael & Mary Joyce of Market Street, Clifden.
  Remembered: Doiran Memorial – Greece.

JOYCE, Henry Arthur   Private (Bandsman) 19697   Second Dragoon Guards
  Killed in Action: (France) 31 October 1914. Age 32.
  Supplementary Notes: Born: Castlegar, Galway.
  Remembered: Ypres (Menin Gate) Memorial – Ieper – West-Vlaanderen – Belgium (3).

JOYCE, Patrick   Lance Sergeant 6176   Second Leinster Regiment
  Killed in Action: (France) 28 September 1918. Age 28.
  Supplementary Notes: Awarded Mons Star. Born: Tuam.
  Buried: Hooge Crater Cemetery – Ieper – West-Vlaanderen – Belgium (XIX. J. 7).

JOYCE, Patrick   Private 10376   Second Cameronians (Scottish Rifles)
  Death: 9 May 1915.
  Supplementary Notes: Son of Martin & Mary Joyce of Leenane, Connemara.
  Remembered: Ploegsteert Memorial – Comines-Warneton – Hainaut – Belgium (5).

JOYCE, Stephen   Private 3905   Fifth Connaught Rangers
  Killed in Action: (Gallipoli) 21 August 1915. Age 21.
  Supplementary Notes: Enlisted: Galway. Son of Stephen & Catherine Joyce of Maam, Connemara (Ross).
  Remembered: Helles Memorial – Turkey (181 to 183).

JOYCE, Stephen Anthony   Lance Corporal 6636   First Irish Guards
   Killed in Action: (Loos, France) 30 September 1915. Age 21 or 23.
   Supplementary Notes: Son of Patrick & Bridget Joyce of Fahy, Eyrecourt.
   Buried: Dud Corner Cemetery – Loos – Pas de Calais – France (III. K. 7).

JOYCE, Thomas   Private 7026   Second Durham Light Infantry
   Killed in Action: 22 August 1915. Age 29.
   Supplementary Notes: Son of John & Mary Joyce of Albion Street, Jarrow-on-Tyne, Durham. Born: Galway.
   Buried: Hop Store Cemetery – Ieper – West-Vlaanderen – Belgium (I. E. 29).

JOYCE, W.   Lance Corporal 23040   Seventh Royal Inniskilling Fusiliers
   Death: 28 December 1918. Age 21.
   Supplementary Notes: Transferred to the Labour Corps 336822. Son of Margaret Joyce of Cashel, Recess, Connemara.
   Buried: Deansgrange Cemetery – Co. Dublin – Ireland (W. W2. 38).

KAVANAGH, Joseph   Lance Corporal 7004   Second Connaught Rangers
   Died of Wounds: (France) 14 September 1914.
   Supplementary Notes: Enlisted: Ballinasloe. Born: Kilmacduagh, Gort.
   Buried: Vailly British Cemetery – Aisne – France (II. C. 19).

KAVANAGH, Thomas   Private 6220   Fifth Connaught Rangers
   Death: (Salonika) 30 November 1915.
   Supplementary Notes: Enlisted: Ballinasloe. Born: Killimore.
   Buried: Chichester Cemetery – West Sussex – United Kingdom (1 26. 34).

KAVENEY, Malachy   Private 1501   Second Royal Munster Fusiliers
   Killed in Action: (France) 20 August 1916.
   Supplementary Notes: Born: Glenamaddy.
   Remembered: Thiepval Memorial – Somme – France (P & F16 C).

KAYLL, Hugh Oswald   Lieutenant   Royal Navy Reserves
   Died of Pneumonia: (Galway) 11 December 1918. Age 33.
   Supplementary Notes: Died of pneumonia during the influenza pandemic that broke out in 1918. Born: Galway.
   Buried: St Mary's – (new cemetery) – Bohermore – Galway – Ireland.

KEADY, James   Sergeant   US army
  Killed in Action: (France) July 1918.
  Supplementary Notes: Son of Martin & Julia Keady. Born: Clunmore, Moycullen.

KEANE, Barthely   Chief Stoker 153201   Motor Lighter HM *X6*   Royal Navy
  Killed in Action: (North Sea) 24 January 1918.
  Supplementary Notes: (RFR/DEV/A/3582). Killed during action with an enemy submarine. Son of Anthony & Nora Keane of Barna; husband of Sarah Keane of Knocknaraddy Furbo, Barna.
  Remembered: Plymouth Naval Memorial – Devon – United Kingdom (27).

KEANE, John Joseph   Corporal R1263   Fifth Canadian Mounted Rifles
  Death: (France) 2 October 1916. Age 32.
  Supplementary Notes: (Quebec Regiment). Enlisted: Canada. Son of John & Norah Keane of Galway.
  Buried: Regina Trench Cemetery – Grandcourt – Somme – France (II. C. 13).

KEANE, Michael   Private 2510   First & Fifteenth Yorkshire Light Infantry
  Killed in Action: (France) 27 May 1915.
  Supplementary Notes: Son of Thomas & Catherine Keane of Cappagh, Toomard. (New Bridge).
  Buried: White City Cemetery – Bois-Grenier – Nord – France (D. 3).

KEANE, Michael   Private   British Expeditionary Force
  Death: 1914–1918.
  Supplementary Notes: From Derrymullen, Ballinasloe.
  Remembered: Roll of Honour – Killed in Action – 1914–1918 – Ballinasloe – Ireland.

KEANE, Patrick   Private 5283   Second Royal Munster Fusiliers
  Killed in Action: (France) 21 December 1914.
  Supplementary Notes: Born: Lisbrine.
  Remembered: Le Touret Memorial – Pas de Calais – France (43 & 44).

KEANE, Patrick Albert   Private 29777   First Royal Dublin Fusiliers
  Killed in Action: (France or Flanders) 21 or 28 March 1918. Age 22.
  Supplementary Notes: Son of John & Celia Keane (*nee* Fahy) of Moyleen, Loughrea.
  Buried: Heath Cemetery – Harbonnieres – Somme – France (X. D. 3).

KEANE, William Mary Augustine   Second Lieutenant   Third & Eighth Royal Irish Fusiliers.

Killed in Action: (France) 4 November 1916.

Supplementary Notes: Formerly of the Tenth Royal Dublin Fusiliers. Son of Thomas Keane of 34 Shop Street, Galway. Shot by sniper. Correspondence regarding his death was included in *Galway and the Great War*, pp. 243, 244.

Buried: Kemmel Chateau Military Cemetery – Heuvelland – West-Vlaanderen – Belgium (X. 37).

KEARNEY, Martin   Lance Corporal 8/238   Otago Regiment NZEF

Killed in Action: (Gallipoli) 29 April 1915. Age 22.

Supplementary Notes: Son of Peter & Anne Kearney of Ballinacourty, Oranmore.

Remembered: Lone Pine Memorial – Turkey (75).

KEARNEY, Michael   Rifleman 53788   Third & Fourth New Zealand Rifle Brigade

Killed in Action: (France) 5 April 1918.

Supplementary Notes: Son of Francis Kearney of Ballinacourty, Oranmore. Emigrated to New Zealand before the war. Shortly after the family was informed of his death, a letter arrived from Michael saying that he would be home soon.

Buried: Euston Road Cemetery – Colincamps – Somme – France (II. B. 4).

KEARNEY, Richard   Private 10/1868   First Wellington Regiment NZEF

Died of Wounds: (France) 19 September 1916. Age 23.

Supplementary Notes: Brother of Thomas Kearney of Knockdoe.

Buried: Heilly Station Cemetery – Mericourt-L'Abbe – Somme – France (IV. H. 21).

KEARNEY, Thomas   Acting Corporal 8838   First Royal North Lancaster Regiment

Killed in Action: (France) 31 October 1914.

Supplementary Notes: Born: St Nicholas' Parish, Galway.

Remembered: Ypres (Menin Gate) Memorial – Ieper – West-Vlaanderen – Belgium (41 & 43).

KEARNEY, William   Private 7164   First Canadian Infantry

Death: (France or Flanders) 1914–1918.

Supplementary Notes: Enlisted: Canada. Born: Galway.

KEATING, Patrick   Private 7571   Sixth Connaught Rangers
  Killed in Action: (France) 6 January 1917.
  Supplementary Notes: Lived at 64 West Worsley Street, Salford. Born: Tynagh.
  Buried: Pond Farm Cemetery – West-Vlaanderen – Belgium (H. 14).

KEAVENEY, Malachy   Private 3063   Fifth Connaught Rangers
  Killed in Action: (Gallipoli) 21 August 1915. Age 42 or 48.
  Supplementary Notes: Enlisted: Doncaster. Born: Glenamaddy.
  Remembered: Helles Memorial – Turkey (181 to 183).

KEAVENY, Patrick   Private 11495   Second Irish Guards
  Killed in Action: (France) 27 November 1917.
  Supplementary Notes: Born: Ballymoe.
  Remembered: Cambrai Memorial – Lou Verval – Nord – France (2 & 3).

KEDDY, John   Private 19925   First Royal Dublin Fusiliers
  Killed in Action: (France) 28 February 1917.
  Supplementary Notes: Enlisted: Bray, Co. Wicklow. Born: Galway.
  Remembered: Thiepval Memorial – Somme – France (P 5. 16 C).

KEEGAN, Michael   Corporal 6994   First Leinster Regiment
  Died of Wounds: (France) 24 April 1915.
  Supplementary Notes: Enlisted: Athlone. Born: Kilclooney, Ballinasloe. Same military
  number is recorded for John Small, p.212.
  Buried: Boulogne Eastern Cemetery – Pas de Calais – France (VIII. A. 20).

KEEGAN, William John   Bombardier 707247   331st Royal Field Artillery
  Killed in Action: (France or Flanders) 31 July 1917. Age 20.
  Supplementary Notes: Second son of John & Mary Keegan of Ballyglass, Ballymoe
  (Kilronan).
  Buried: Coxyde Military Cemetery – Koksijde – West-Vlaanderen – Belgium (II. B.
  11).

KEELEY, Martin   Private 6652   First Connaught Rangers
  Death: (India) 17 August 1914.
  Supplementary Notes: Enlisted: Ballinasloe. Born: Kilclooney, Ballinasloe.
  Remembered: 1914–1918 War Memorial – Karachi – Pakistan.

KEIGHREY, John   Private 3087   First Connaught Rangers
Killed in Action: (Mesopotamia) 21 January 1916. Age 23.
Supplementary Notes: Enlisted: Oranmore. Son of Patrick & Bridget Keighrey (*nee* Griffin) of Boulgers Lane, Ballinasloe. His brother, Peter, also served with the Connaught Rangers and survived the war.
Remembered: Basra Memorial – Iraq (40 & 64) & Roll of Honour – Killed in Action – 1914–1918 – Ballinasloe – Ireland.

KEIGHREY, Michael   Private 3205   Third Connaught Rangers
Died of Illness: (Ballinasloe) 12 November 1918. Age 20.
Supplementary Notes: Enlisted: Ballinasloe. Son of Peter Keighrey of Brackernagh, Ballinasloe.
Buried: Creagh new cemetery – Ballinasloe – Ireland (D2. 622).
Remembered: Roll of Honour – Killed in Action – 1914–1918 – Ballinasloe – Ireland.

KELLEHER, Joseph   Private 310   Second Leinster Regiment
Killed in Action: (France) 28 September 1918. Age 25.
Supplementary Notes: Son of John & Ellen Kelleher of Bolands Street, Gort.
Remembered: Tyne Cot Memorial Zonnebeke – West-Vlaanderen – Belgium (143).

KELLEHER, Patrick   Private 7182   First Connaught Rangers
Death: (Mesopotamia) 11 June 1916.
Supplementary Notes: Enlisted: Boyle, Co. Roscommon. Born: Loughrea.
Buried: Basra War Cemetery – Iraq (III. L. 16).

KELLY, Hubert   Sergeant   British Expeditionary Force
Death: 1914–1918.
Supplementary Notes: From Ballinasloe.
Remembered: Roll of Honour – Killed in Action – 1914–1918 – Ballinasloe – Ireland.

KELLY, J.D.   Private 035758   Eighteenth Royal Army Ordnance Corps
Death: (Salonika) 12 December 1918. Age 30.
Supplementary Notes: Attached to GHQ. Husband of Mary Kelly of Milleen, College Road, Galway. Born: Galway.
Buried: Mikra British Cemetery – Kalamaria – Greece (900).

KELLY, James   Lance Corporal 9929 (19925)   Eighth York & Lancaster Regiment
Killed in Action: (Somme, France) 1 July 1916.
Supplementary Notes: Born: Creggs.
Buried: Blighty Valley Cemetery – Authuile Wood – Somme – France (V. B. 27).

KELLY, John   Private 10311   First Connaught Rangers
Died of Wounds: (France) 25 May 1915. Age 21.
Supplementary Notes: Enlisted: Galway. Born: Cummer, Tuam (Ballyglunin).
Buried: Cabaret-Rouge British Cemetery – Souchez – France (XVII. E. 9).

KELLY, John   Private 11460   2 Company, First Irish Guards
Killed in Action: (Ypres, Belgium) 2 August 1917. Age 35.
Supplementary Notes: Son of Martin & Ellen Kelly of Derrybrien, Gort.
Remembered: Ypres (Menin Gate) Memorial – Ieper – West-Vlaanderen – Belgium (II).

KELLY, Joseph   Private 38079   Seventeenth Lancaster Fusiliers
Killed in Action: (France) 14 April 1918.
Supplementary Notes: Born: Galway.

KELLY, Joseph   Private 43227   Seventh Royal Inniskilling Fusiliers
Killed in Action: (France) 16 August 1917. Age 19.
Supplementary Notes: Born: Ballinasloe.
Buried: Tyne Cot Cemetery – Belgium (XVII. C. 4).

KELLY, Joseph   Private 2/11522.   Second Irish Guards
Killed in Action: (Doullens, France) 31 March 1918. Age 32.
Supplementary Notes: Son of Michael & Anne Kelly. Born: Moylough, Ballinasloe.
Buried: Doullens Communal Cemetery Extension No. 1 – Somme – France (VI. F. 5).

KELLY, Martin   Private 4312   Second Connaught Rangers
Killed in Action: (France) 23 October 1914. Age 24 or 25.
Supplementary Notes: Enlisted: Ballinasloe. Awarded Mons Star. Son of Mr & Mrs Andrew Kelly of Harbour Street, Ballinasloe. Same military number is recorded for John Monaghan, p. 184.
Remembered: Ypres (Menin Gate) Memorial – Ieper – West-Vlaanderen –Belgium (42).

KELLY, Martin   Private 16667   Eighth Royal Irish Fusiliers
    Killed in Action: (France) 6 September 1916.
    Supplementary Notes: Born: Moylough.
    Remembered: Thiepval Memorial – Somme – France (P & F 15 A).

KELLY, Michael   Private G/5569   Second Royal Sussex Regiment
    Killed in Action: (France) 9 September 1916. Age 24.
    Supplementary Notes: Born: Tuam.
    Buried: Serre Road Cemetery No. 2 (B. RC. 520).

KELLY, Michael James   Sergeant 21483   First Royal Dublin Fusiliers
    Killed in Action: (France) 1 March 1917. Age 24 or 26.
    Supplementary Notes: Enlisted: Galway. Son of Redmond & Margaret Kelly of Arch
House, Spanish Parade, Galway. He had also served in Gallipoli.
    Remembered: Thiepval Memorial – Somme – France (16 C).

KELLY, P.   Private 1176   Sixth Connaught Rangers
    Death: (France) 9 September 1916. Age 34.
    Supplementary Notes: Son of John & Bridget Kelly of Cleggan, Connemara.
    Buried: Guillemont Road Cemetery – Guillemont – Somme – France (IV. A. 8).

KELLY, Patrick   Private 1476   Sixth Connaught Rangers
    Killed in Action: 9 September 1916. Age 39.
    Supplementary Notes: Enlisted: Galway. Born: Cleggan, Connemara.

KELLY, Patrick   Private 4305   Second Connaught Rangers
    Died of Wounds: (Belgium) 3 November 1914.
    Supplementary Notes: Enlisted: Ballinasloe. Born: Kilclooney, Ballinasloe.
    Buried: Poperinge Old Military Cemetery – West-Vlaanderen – Belgium (I.L.45).

KELLY, Patrick   Private 6341   Sixth Connaught Rangers
    Killed in Action: 9 December 1916.
    Supplementary Notes: Enlisted: Atherton. Born: Brownsgrove, Tuam.

KELLY, Patrick (Paddy)   Rifleman 5/831   Eleventh Rifle Brigade
    Died of Wounds: 10 September 1916. Age 26.
    Supplementary Notes: Son of Bridget Kelly of Lettera, Williamstown, and the late
Stephen Kelly.

Buried: St Sever Cemetery – Rouen – Seine-Maritime – France (B. 25. 19).

KELLY, Peter   Private 7864   First Connaught Rangers
Death: (Egypt) 15 November 1918. Age 35.
Supplementary Notes: Son of Patrick & Mary Kelly of Clifden; husband of Barbara Kelly of 25 High Street, Dumbarton (Mories).
Buried: Alexandria (Hadra) War Memorial Cemetery – Egypt (C. 123).

KELLY, Peter   Sergeant 9304   Second East Lancaster Regiment
Killed in Action: (France) 17 August 1917. Age 29 or 35.
Supplementary Notes: Enlisted: Mullingar. Awarded Mons Star. Son of Hugh & Julia Kelly (*nee* Quinn) of Kinclare, Caltra, Ballinasloe.
Remembered: Tyne Cot Memorial – Zonnebeke – West-Vlaanderen – Belgium (77 to 79 & 163A).

KELLY, Thomas   Private 3571   Eleventh Manchester Regiment
Killed in Action: (France) 26 September 1916.
Supplementary Notes: Enlisted: Oldham, Lancashire. Born: Galway.
Remembered: Thiepval Memorial – Somme – France (P & F 13. A & 14 C).

KELLY, Thomas   Sergeant 3096   Third Connaught Rangers
Died of Wounds: (Ballinasloe, Co. Galway) 25 December 1914. Age 37.
Supplementary Notes: Enlisted: Oranmore. Formerly of the Royal Dublin Fusiliers. Awarded 1914 Star. Born: Kilclooney, Ballinasloe.
Buried: Creagh new cemetery – Ballinasloe – Ireland (D. 20).

KELLY, Thomas   Private 147572   First Machine Gun Corps
Died of Wounds: (France) 17 October 1918. Age 30 or 44.
Supplementary Notes: Born: Caltra.
Remembered: Vis-En-Artois Memorial – Pas de Calais – France (10).

KENDALL, Edward Hazell   Private PS/9591   Eighth Royal Irish Fusiliers
Died of Wounds: (France) 8 August 1916. Age 21.
Supplementary Notes: Son of Elizabeth Mary Kendall of Ardagh Lodge, Clifden, and the late Edward Kendall.
Buried: Varennes Military Cemetery – Somme – France (I. A. 10).

KENEAVY, Martin   Private 3868   Fifth Connaught Rangers
Killed in Action: (Salonika) 7 December 1915. Age 21.
Supplementary Notes: Enlisted: Galway. Son of Martin & Margaret Keneavey of Main Street, Oughterard.
Remembered: Doiran Memorial – Greece

KENNEDY, Andrew William   Rifleman 2373   Second Royal Irish Rifles
Killed in Action: (France) 7 May 1915.
Supplementary Notes: Born: Roundstone, Connemara.
Remembered: Ypres (Menin Gate) Memorial – Ieper – West-Vlaanderen – Belgium (40).

KENNEDY-LYDON, Patrick   Rifleman 77133   Third New Zealand Rifle Brigade
Died of Wounds: (France or England) 6 November 1918. Age 28.
Supplementary Notes: Son of John & Honora Lydon Kennedy (*nee* Cunniffe) of Cahercrin, Athenry. One of eight children, he emigrated to New Zealand as a young man. His brother, John, took part in the 1916 Easter Rebellion.
Buried: Cannock Chase War Cemetery – Staffordshire – United Kingdom (4. A. 8).

KENNEDY, Robert Thomas   Private 2610   First Irish Guards
Killed in Action: (Soupir, France) 14 September 1914.
Supplementary Notes: Enlisted: Dublin 6 June 1906. Born in 1886, the son of Thomas Kennedy of North Gate Street, Athenry, he had three brothers, Michael, Patrick and William. Although *Ireland's Memorial Records 1914–1918* record his death as occurring on 17 October 1914, the military casualty form records 14 September 1914.
Remembered: Ypres (Menin Gate) Memorial – Ieper – West-Vlaanderen – Belgium (11).

KENNY, John   Lance Corporal 530   Fifth Connaught Rangers
Died of Wounds: (Gallipoli) 22 August 1915. Age 22.
Supplementary Notes: Enlisted: Galway. Son of Michael & Kate Kenny (*nee* Foran) of Church Street, Gort (Kilmacduagh).
Remembered: Helles Memorial – Turkey (181 to 183).

KENNY, John   Private 10114   Fourteenth Northumberland Fusiliers
Died of Wounds: (France) 19 September 1916.
Supplementary Notes: Enlisted: Dewsbury, Yorkshire. Born: Galway.

KENNY, John Francis   Sergeant 10127   Second Leinster Regiment
Killed in Action: (France) 10 June 1917. Age 21.
Supplementary Notes: Son of Mary E. Kenny of Letterfrack, Connemara.
Remembered: Ypres (Menin Gate) Memorial – Ieper – West-Vlaanderen – Belgium (44).

KENNY, Joseph   Private 11329   Sixth Border Regiment
Killed in Action: (Gallipoli) 21 August 1915.
Supplementary Notes: Born: Gort.
Remembered: Helles Memorial – Turkey (119 to 125 or 222 & 223).

KENNY, Michael   Acting Corporal 515   Fifth Connaught Rangers
Died of Wounds: (Gallipoli) 21 August 1915. Age 21.
Supplementary Notes: Enlisted: Galway. Born: St Bridget's, Portumna.
Buried: Seventh Field Ambulance Cemetery – Gallipoli – Turkey (Sp. Mem. A. 89).

KENNY, Michael   Private 10243   First Connaught Rangers
Died of Wounds: (Mesopotamia) 21 January 1917. Age 24.
Supplementary Notes: Enlisted: Ballinasloe. Born: Kilclooney, Ballinasloe.
Buried: Amara War Cemetery – Amara – Iraq (XXVII. C. 4).

KEOGH, James   Private 6542   Second Irish Guards
Killed in Action: (France) 20 May 1916.
Supplementary Notes: Enlisted: Ballina, Co. Mayo. Born: Galway.
Remembered: Ypres (Menin Gate) Memorial – Ieper – West-Vlaanderen – Belgium (11).

KEOGH, Michael   Private 3894   Second Connaught Rangers
Killed in Action: 23 November 1914. Age 35.
Supplementary Notes: Enlisted: Ballinasloe. Awarded 1914 Star. Born: Kilclooney, Ballinasloe.
Buried: Poelcapelle British Cemetery – West-Vlaanderen – Belgium (LII. F. 1).

KERRIGAN, Mark   Trimmer 596/ST   HMS *Europa*   Royal Navy Reserve
Death: 21 December 1915. Age 23.
Supplementary Notes: Son of Mark Kerrigan of Cloghbrack, Clonbur.
Buried: Portianos Military Cemetery – Lemnos – Greece (III. B. 303).

KIERNAN, John Joseph   Seaman   SS *Beacon Light*   Mercantile Marines
Death: 19 February 1918. Age 16.
Supplementary Notes: Drowned as a result of an attack by an enemy submarine. Son of Bridget Kiernan (*nee* McDonagh) of St Elizabeth Street, Liverpool, and the late Brian Kiernan. Born: Ryehill, Galway.
Remembered: Tower Hill Memorial – London – United Kingdom.

KILKELLY, Edward Charles Randolph, M.C.   Major   186th Royal Field Artillery
Killed in Action: (Ypres, Belgium) 26 June 1917. Age 21.
Supplementary Notes: Son of Lieutenant Colonel C.R. (Grenadier Guards, retired) & Florence Kilkelly (*nee* Petre) of Drimcong, Moycullen.
Buried: Poperinge New Military Cemetery – Poperinge – West-Vlaanderen – Belgium (II. E. 13).

KILLELEA, Thomas   Private   Australian Imperial Force
Killed in Action: (France) 11 April 1917. Age 26.
Supplementary Notes: Son of James Killelea of 5 Upper Bohermore, Galway.

KILLIAN, Patrick   Gunner 15386   120th (Siege) Royal Garrison Artillery
Killed in Action: (France) 28 July 1917. Age 35.
Supplementary Notes: Enlisted: London. Son of Mr B. Killian of New Docks, Galway.
Buried: Dickebusch New Military Cemetery Extension – Ieper – West-Vlaanderen – Belgium (I. B. 2).

KILLILEA, Mark   Private 5992   First Royal Munster Fusiliers
Killed in Action: (France) 4 April 1917. Age 28.
Supplementary Notes: Enlisted: Stockport. Formerly of the Royal Field Artillery 74620. Son of Andrew & Catherine Killilea (*nee* Gordon) of Sloehill, Ballinamore Bridge.
Buried: La Laiterie Military Cemetery – Heuvelland – West-Vlaanderen – Belgium (IX. B. 9).

KILRANE, Richard Joseph   Private 3686   Eighth Royal Munster Fusiliers
Died of Wounds: (France) 27 October 1916.
Supplementary Notes: Born: Spiddal.
Buried: Bailleul Communal Cemetery Extension – Nord – France (III. A. 246).

KILROY, Bernard   Lance Sergeant 110   Fifth Connaught Rangers
Killed in Action: (Salonika) 7 December 1915.
Supplementary Notes: Born: Galway.
Remembered: Doiran Memorial – Greece.

KING, Edward   Deck Hand   HMS *Prize*   Royal Navy Reserve
Killed in Action: (Atlantic Ocean) 14 August 1917.
Supplementary Notes: Killed during action with an enemy submarine. Born: Grattan Road, Galway.

KING, Festus   Private 6608   Sixth Connaught Rangers
Killed in Action: (France) 21 March 1918. Age 21 or 22.
Supplementary Notes: Son of Thomas & Anne King (*nee* O'Donnell) of Bunahown, Cashel. Born: Galway.
Remembered: Pozieres Memorial – Somme – France (77).

KING, Jack   Private 28860   Seventh South Lancaster Regiment
Died of Wounds: (France) 2 June 1917.
Supplementary Notes: Born: Galway.
Buried: La Clytte Military Cemetery – West-Vlaanderen – Belgium (I. E. 2).

KING, John   Private 6109   Sixth Connaught Rangers
Killed in Action: (France) 7 June 1917.
Supplementary Notes: Enlisted: Galway. Born: Galway.

KING, Joseph   Private 49491   Royal Munster Fusiliers
Died of Wounds: (France) 28 January 1916. Age 42.
Supplementary Notes: Born: Galway.

KING, Martin   Private 17981   Second Royal Munster Fusiliers
Killed in Action: (France) Age 32.
Supplementary Notes: Born: Galway.

KING, Martin   Private 3671   Sixth Connaught Rangers
Died of Wounds: (France) 23 May 1918. Age 24.
Supplementary Notes: Enlisted: Galway. Son of Bryan King & Mary King of Fairhill Road, Claddagh, Galway.
Buried: Boisguillaume Communal Cemetery extension – Seine-Maritime – France (D. 12B).

KING, Michael　　　　　　　Private 4432　　　　　Sixth Leinster Regiment
　Died of Malaria: (Salonika) 15 October 1917. Age 30 or 34.
　Supplementary Notes: Born: Dunmore.
　Buried: Mikra British Cemetery – Kalamaria – Greece (1678).

KING, Nicholas　　　　Seaman 6829A　　HMS *Prize*　　Royal Navy Reserves
　Killed in Action: (Atlantic Ocean) 14 August 1917. Age 22.
　Supplementary Notes: Killed during action with an enemy submarine. Son of Delia King, of Claddagh Parade, Galway, and the late Nicholas King.
　Remembered: Portsmouth Naval Memorial – Hampshire – United Kingdom (27).

KING, Peter　　　　　　　Private 10429　　　　　Second Irish Guards
　Killed in Action: (France) 13 April 1918. Age 27
　Supplementary Notes: Born: Aughamore.
　Remembered: Ploegsteert Memorial – Comines-Warneton – Hainaut – Belgium (1).

KING, Stephen (Sonny)　Petty Officer Stoker 283056　HMS *Warrior*　Royal Navy
　Killed in Action: (Jutland) 31 May 1916.
　Supplementary Notes: Enlisted: August 1896. Served in the Boxer Rebellion. He had four brothers and one sister. Two of his brothers also served with the Royal Navy, and both survived. Born: Claddagh, Galway.
　Remembered: Plymouth Naval Memorial – Devon – United Kindom (14).

KING, Stephen　　　　　　Private 5169　　　　　First Connaught Rangers
　Killed in Action: (France) September 1916. Age 28.
　Supplementary Notes: Born: Galway.

KING, Stephen　　　　　　Private 8137　　　Second Royal Munster Fusiliers
　Killed in Action: (France) 23 August 1915. Age 38.
　Supplementary Notes: Born: Galway.

KING, Thomas　　　　　　S/S/Corporal 31205　　　Royal Field Artillery
　Died of Wounds: (France) 21 September 1918.
　Supplementary Notes: Enlisted: Galway. Born: Galway.
　Buried: Brie British Cemetery – Somme – France (II. F. 4).

KINKEAD, Richard Crofton, G.M.　　Captain　　Royal Army Medical Corps
　Killed in Action: (Ypres, Belgium) 30 October 1914. Age 31.

Supplementary Notes: Attached to the Tenth Prince of Wales Own Royal Hussars. Son of Professor R.J. & Emily Kinkead of Forster House, Galway. Correspondence regarding this man was included in *Galway and the Great War*, pp. 168, 169.
Buried: Ypres Town Cemetery – Ieper – West-Vlaanderen – Belgium (E2. 5).
Remembered: Great War monument – St Nicholas' Collegiate Church – Galway – Ireland.

KINSELLA, Vincent James   Private 128652   First Machine Gun Corps
   Killed in Action: (France) 28 March 1918.
   Supplementary Notes: Formerly of the London Regiment. Born: Dalystown.
   Remembered: Arras Memorial – Pas de Calais – France (10).

KISKELL, Patrick   Private 874   Second Royal Irish Regiment
   Killed in Action: (France) 27 September 1918.
   Supplementary Notes: Born: Mucklin.

KNIGHT, Martin Thomas   Gunner 21518   Royal Garrison Artillery
   Death: (Home) 1 March 1917.
   Supplementary Notes: Born: Dunmore.
   Buried: Aldershot Military Cemetery – Hampshire – United Kingdom (R. 344).

LAFFEY, Brian Bernard   Lance Corporal 4304.   First Irish Guards
   Killed in Action: (Villers Cotterets, France) 1 September 1914. Age 20.
   Supplementary Notes: Awarded Mons Star. Son of Michael & Catherine Laffey of Clooncah, Woodlawn (Killimara).
   Buried: Guards Grave – Villers Cotterets Forest – Aisne – France (24).

LAFFEY, Joseph   Private 67473   Royal Engineers
   Died of Wounds: 16 November 1918. Age 30.
   Buried: Kilmoylan Cemetery – Ireland (north east part).

LAFFEY, Luke   Private 16827   Sixth Royal Irish Fusiliers
   Killed in Action: (Salonika) 12 October 1916. Age 26 or 28.
   Supplementary Notes: Enlisted: Galway. Formerly of the Connaught Rangers 79. Son of Roger & Bridget Laffey of Ropewalk, Claddagh, Galway.
   Buried: Salonika (Lembet Road) Military Cemetery – Greece (568).

LALLY, Michael   Wireless Operator   SS *Bristol City*   Mercantile Marines
Death: 16 December 1917. Age 21.
Supplementary Notes: Drowned as a result of an attack by an enemy submarine. Son of James & Maria Lally (*nee* Bugler) of Ballyconnell, Gort. Brother of Thomas Lally, below.
Remembered: Tower Hill Memorial – London – United Kingdom.

LALLY, Peter   Private 3281   First Irish Guards
Killed in Action: (France) 18 May 1915. Age 36.
Supplementary Notes: Born: Roundstone, Connemara.
Remembered: Le Touret Memorial – Pas de Calais – France (4).

LALLY, Thomas   Sergeant 9455   Second Irish Guards
Death: (France) 27 October 1918. Age 30.
Supplementary Notes: Son of James & Maria Lally (*nee* Bugler) of Ballyconnell, Gort. Brother of Michael Lally, above.
Buried: Abbeville Communal Cemetery Extension – Somme – France (IV. K. 3).

LANE, Patrick   Private 5656   Fifth Connaught Rangers
Killed in Action: (Salonika) 7 December 1915.
Supplementary Notes: Enlisted: Warrington. Born: Abbey.
Remembered: Doiran Memorial – Greece.

LARKIN, James   Private 27668   Twelfth Manchester Regiment
Killed in Action: (France) 7 July 1916.
Supplementary Notes: Born: Kilmacslane.
Remembered: Thiepval Memorial – Somme – France (13 A & 14 C).

LARKIN, Michael   Private 15717   Ninth West Yorkshire Regiment
Killed in Action: (Gallipoli) 22 August 1915. Age 34.
Supplementary Notes: Son of Michael & Catherine Larkin of Emanelon, Barnaderg, Tuam.
Remembered: Helles Memorial – Turkey (47 to 51).

LARKIN, Patrick   Private 2/6971   Second & Seventh Irish Guards
Killed in Action: (France) 26 September 1916. Age 21.
Supplementary Notes: Enlisted: Loughrea March 1915. Wounded at Loos and Ypres. Son of James & Kate Larkin (*nee* Fahy) of Ballydaly.

Buried: A.I.F. Burial Ground – Flers – Somme – France (I. F. 15).

LAVELLE, Michael   Private 41276   Thirteenth Royal Scots (Lothian Regiment)
Killed in Action: (France) 1 August 1917
Supplementary Notes: Enlisted: Alexandria, Dumbartonshire. Born: Galway.
Remembered: Ypres (Menin Gate) Memorial – Ieper – West-Vlaanderen – Belgium
(11).

LAVERY, Michael   Private 6501   Sixth Connaught Rangers.
Death: (England) 11 January 1918. Age 19 or 20.
Supplementary Notes: Enlisted: Clifden. Died as a result of poison gas. Son of Mark
& Mary Lavery (*nee* Burke) of Ballyconneely, Connemara.
Buried: Newcastle-Upon-Tyne – St Andrew's & Jesmond Cemetery – Northumberland
– United Kingdom (Q. U. 368).

LAWS, Henry Alexander Engineer Sub-Lieutenant HMS *Egmont* Royal Navy Reserves.
Death: 19 October 1918. Age 36.
Supplementary Notes: Son of Henry Joseph & Isabel Laws of 6 Wetherby Road,
Boroughbridge, Yorks. Born: Galway.
Buried: Wivenhoe (Belle Vue Road) Cemetery – Essex – United Kingdom (D. 1).

LEE, Francis M.   Sapper 95960   Ninety-fifth Field Royal Engineers.
Killed in Action: (France) 3 December 1916. Age 21.
Supplementary Notes: Enlisted: Longford. Son of James & Sarah Anne Lee of 13
Wards Terrace, Longford. Born: Ballinasloe.
Buried: Serre Road Cemetery No.1 – Pas de Calais – France (Sp. Mem. 10).

LEECH, Martin   Private 8683   First Connaught Rangers
Killed in Action: (France) 10 December 1914. Age 25.
Supplementary Notes: Enlisted: Gort. Son of John & Ellen Leech of Church Street,
Gort (Kilmacduagh).
Remembered: Le Touret Memorial – Pas de Calais – France (43).

LEECH, Patrick   Private 544   Sixth Connaught Rangers
Killed in Action: (France) 20 November 1917.
Supplementary Notes: Enlisted: Galway. Born: Kilmacduagh, Gort.
Buried: Croisilles Railway Cemetery – Pas de Calais – France (I. D. 15).

LEFFEY, Patrick   Private 14467   Second Bedfordshire Regiment
     Killed in Action: (France) 30 July 1916.
     Supplementary Notes: Enlisted: Hertford. Born: Galway.
     Buried: Serre Road Cemetery No. 2 – Pas de Calais – France (IX. L. 8).

LEONARD, James   Private 9567   First Connaught Rangers
     Killed in Action: (Mesopotamia) 17 April 1916.
     Supplementary Notes: Enlisted: Galway. Born: Bohermore, Galway.
     Remembered: Basra Memorial – Iraq (40 & 64).

LEONARD, John   Private 95670   Connaught Rangers
     Death: (France) 1914–1918. Age 22.
     Supplementary Notes: Born: Galway.

LEONARD, Thomas   Private 15873   Tenth York & Lancaster Regiment
     Killed in Action: (France) 14 February 1917.
     Supplementary Notes: Born: Belclare.
     Buried: Philosophe British Cemetery – Mazingarbe – Pas de Calais – France (I. M. 27).

LESTER, John   Private 19863   Fourth South Wales Borderers
     Killed in Action: (Gallipoli) 7 January 1916.
     Supplementary Notes: Because of the date and location of Private John Lester's death, it was necessary to explain that this is the official recorded information. Born: Tuam.
     Remembered: Helles Memorial – Turkey (80 to 84 or 219 & 220).

LEWIS, W.H.   Officer   British Expeditionary Force
     Killed in Action: 26 May 1917.
     Supplementary Notes: Enlisted: November 1914. A former classical teacher at the Grammar School. Born: Galway.

LISTER, Albert John   Bandsman 6832   First Suffolk Regiment
     Died of Wounds: (Home) 26 March 1915. Age 26.
     Supplementary Notes: Enlisted: Colchester. Born: Galway.
     Buried: Colchester Cemetery – Essex – United Kingdom (H. 9. 78).

LLOYD, Albert V.   Private 201469   Fourth Seaforth Highlanders
     Killed in Action: (France) 8 or 10 April 1917.
     Supplementary Notes: Enlisted: Bradford. Born: Galway.

Buried: Nine Elms Military Cemetery – Thelus – Pas de Calais – France (Seaforth Grave Mem. 4).

LLOYD, John   Private 36909   Fifth King's Own (Yorkshire Light Infantry)
Killed in Action: (France) 25 August 1918. Age 28.
Supplementary Notes: Enlisted: Bradford. Formerly of the Royal Army Service Corps T/30491. Born: Galway.
Buried: Douchy-les-Ayette British Cemetery – Pas de Calais – France (IV. A. 4).

LOFTUS, Patrick   Private 16673   Eighth Royal Irish Fusiliers
Killed in Action: (France) 27 April 1916. Age 27.
Supplementary Notes: Enlisted: Tipperary. Born: Galway.
Remembered: Loos Memorial – Pas de Calais – France (124).

LOGAN, Michael   Private 25024   Fifteenth battalion Lancashire Fusiliers
Killed in Action: (Somme, France) 1 July 1916.
Supplementary Notes: Enlisted: Salford, Lancashire. Born: Galway. Same military number as Michael O'Connor, p. 193.
Remembered: Thiepval Memorial – Somme – France (3 C & 3 D).

LOHAN, Mark   Private 11451   Second Royal Dublin Fusiliers
Died of Wounds: (Mons, Belgium) 23 November 1914. Age 19.
Supplementary Notes: Enlisted: Dublin. Eldest son of Thomas & Kate Lohan (*nee* Duffey) of Tornacor, Ballinamore Bridge, Ballinasloe. There were five other children in the family.
Buried: Bailleul Military Cemetery – France (3A).

LONGMORE, Robert Wilfred   Private 104688 First Mounted Rifles Canadian Infantry
Death: (France) 29 September 1918. Age 22.
Supplementary Notes: Son of the Rev. Francis & Bessie Anna Longmore of The Rectory, Carman, Manitoba. Born: Galway.
Buried: Raillencourt Communal Cemetery Extension – Nord – France (I. F. 4).

LOUGHLIN, John   Private 73257   Royal Defence Corps
Death: (Irish Sea) 10 October 1918. Age 46.
Supplementary Notes: Enlisted: St Helens, Lancashire. Formerly of the Royal Dublin Fusiliers 13342. Drowned following the sinking of the SS *Leinster* by a German submarine. Son of Anne Loughlin of Ganaveen, Lawrencetown, Ballinasloe. The sinking of the SS *Leinster* was recorded in *Galway and the Great War*, pp. 98, 99, 100, 101.

Remembered: Hollybrook Memorial – Southampton – Hampshire – United Kingdom.

LOVE, John William   Private G/10912   Eleventh Middlesex Regiment
Killed in Action: (France) 4 March 1916.
Supplementary Notes: Born: Tuam.

LUCAS, Albert J.   Sergeant 6684   Second Irish Guards
Killed in Action: (France) 20 November 1916. Age 23.
Supplementary Notes: Born: Ardara.
Buried: Bancourt British Cemetery – Pas de Calais – France (IV. H. 1).

LUDLOW, Robert   Sergeant 9284   First Royal Dublin Fusiliers
Killed in Action: (Gallipoli) 30 April 1915. Age 28.
Supplementary Notes: Son of Robert & Susanna Ludlow of 6 Magdalen Terrace or Bohermore, Galway.
Buried: V Beach Cemetery – Turkey (Special Memorial B. 28).

LYDEN, James   Private 4821   First Irish Guards
Killed in Action: (France) 15 September 1916. Age 23.
Supplementary Notes: Son of James & Mary Lyden of Old Court, Roundstone, Connemara.
Buried: Guards' Cemetery – Lesboeufs – Somme – France (XII. N. 10).

LYDEN, Michael   Private 13515   Third Royal Scots Fusiliers
Death: (Galway) 7 January 1917. Age 34.
Supplementary Notes: Son of Michael & Honor Lyden of Letterfrack, Connemara; husband of M.A. Gordon Morrison Lyden of Western Crescent, Kilbirnie, Ayrshire.
Buried: Millburn United Free Churchyard – Dunbartonshire – United Kingdom (4. A. 17–1/2).

LYDON, James   Private 4821   First Irish Guards
Killed in Action: (France) 15 September 1916.
Supplementary Notes: Born: Roundstone, Connemara.

LYDON, John   Private 9251   First Connaught Rangers
Killed in Action: (France) 23 November 1914. Age 30.

Supplementary Notes: Enlisted: Galway. Son of Mary Lydon of Boliska, Spiddal, Connemara, and the late Patrick Lydon.

Remembered: Le Touret Memorial – Pas de Calais – France (43).

LYDON, Joseph Patrick   Private 1267   Forty-second Australian Infantry
    Killed in Action: (Belgium) 10 June 1917. Age 24.
    Supplementary Notes: Son of Michael & Delia Lydon of Eglinton Street, Galway.
    Buried: Bethleem Farm East Cemetery – Mesen, West-Vlaanderen – Belgium (A. 12).

LYDON, Mark   Private 7452   Fifth Connaught Rangers
    Death: (France) 31 December 1918. Age 39.
    Supplementary Notes: Son of Anthony Lydon of Myrus, Carna, Connemara.
    Buried: Duisans British Cemetery – Etrun – Pas de Calais – France (VIII. B. 62).

LYDON, McDara   Rifleman 5725   Seventh Royal Irish Rifles
    Killed in Action: (France) 16 August 1917. Age 20.
    Supplementary Notes: Son of Joseph & Kate Lydon of Carna, Connemara.
    Remembered: Tyne Cot Memorial Zonnebeke – West-Vlaanderen – Belgium (138 to 140 & 162 to 162A & 163A).

LYDON, Patrick   Private 5417   Second Royal Irish Regiment
    Killed in Action: (France) 8 September 1914.
    Supplementary Notes: Born: Glanmore, Spiddal, Connemara.
    Buried: Orly-Sur-Morin Communal Cemetery – France.

LYDON, Peter   Private 38986   Nineteenth Durham Light Infantry
    Killed in Action: (France) 23 April 1918.
    Supplementary Notes: Born: Billinskill.
    Remembered: Pozieres Memorial – Somme – France (68 to 72).

LYDON, Thomas   Private 4/9182   Second Durham Light Infantry
    Death: (Galway) 2 December 1915.
    Supplementary Notes: Enlisted: Newcastle. Born: Galway.
    Buried: Hebburn Cemetery – United Kingdom (I. 'U'. 879).

LYNCH, Patrick   Corporal 539   Fifth Connaught Rangers
    Killed in Action: (Gallipoli) 12 August 1915.
    Supplementary Notes: Enlisted: Galway. Served in the South African War. Husband of Helen Lynch (*nee* Hiland) of Water Lane, Bohermore, Galway. They had six children,

one of whom, Johnny, served as a fighter pilot in the RAF during the Second World War. He was killed in action while flying escort with a bombing mission.
Remembered: Helles Memorial – Turkey (181 to 183).

LYNCH, Patrick   Private 205005   Second & Sixth Lancashire Fusiliers
Killed in Action: (France) 4 September 1917.
Supplementary Notes: Enlisted: Liverpool. Born: Galway.
Buried: Gwalia Cemetery – West-Vlaanderen – Belgium (I. H. 18).

LYNCH, John   Deck Hand 933879   HM Tug *Frank*   Mercantile Marines
Death: 14 October 1919. Age 49.
Supplementary Notes: (Served as Martin Lynch.) Son of Patrick Lynch of Tuam; husband of Eliza Grace Lynch of 94 Gambam Street, Stoke Newington, London.
Buried: Abney Park Cemetery – London – United Kingdom (screen wall).

LYONS, Albert Alexander   Shoeing Smith 710   South Irish Horse
Died of Pneumonia: (France) 13 March 1915. Age 19.
Supplementary Notes: Enlisted: Oughterard. Awarded Mons Star. Son of Thomas & Eleanor Lyons of Tullaboy, Maam Cross, Connemara.
Buried: St Sever Cemetery – Rouen – Seine-Maritime – France (A. 5. 6).

LYONS, Joseph   Private 11481   ·   Irish Guards
Death: (Irish Sea) 10 October 1918. Age 25.
Supplementary Notes: Drowned following the sinking of the SS *Leinster* by a German submarine. Son of William Lyons of Craigue Caltra, Ballinasloe. The sinking of the SS *Leinster* is recorded in *Galway and the Great War,* pp. 98, 99, 100, 101.
Remembered: Hollybrook Memorial – Southampton – Hampshire – United Kingdom.

LYONS, Patrick   Private 137   Fifth Connaught Rangers
Death: (Gallipoli) 23 August 1915. Age 63.
Supplementary Notes: Enlisted: Galway. Born: St Jarlath's parish, Tuam. If his age is recorded correctly, he was the oldest known Galway soldier to die during the Great War. Tom Canavan was also aged 63, when he was lost following the sinking of the trawler *Pretty Polly*, and he was a civilian, not an enlisted man.
Remembered: Helles Memorial – Gallipoli – Turkey (185 to 190).

MACKEN, John   Private 5558   First Irish Guards
Killed in Action: (France) 18 May 1915.
Supplementary Notes: Enlisted: Greenock, Renfrew. Born: Ballinasloe.
Remembered: Le Touret Memorial – Pas de Calais – France (4).

MACKEN, Walter   Private G/18092   Fourth Royal Fusiliers
Killed in Action: (France) 27 March 1916. Age 27.
Supplementary Notes: Son of Mary Macken of Eyre Street, and the late Walter Macken; husband of Agnes Macken of 18 St Joseph's Avenue, Galway; father of the renowned author, Walter Macken. Three other brothers, John, Michael and Tom, also served in the war, and survived. He wrote many letters from the front, which have formed a valuable collection of Great War letters. Two of his letters were included in *Galway and the Great War*, pp. 245, 246, 247, 248.
Remembered: Ypres (Menin Gate) Memorial – Ieper – West-Vlaanderen – Belgium (6 & 8).

MACKEN, Walter   Private 2987   Connaught Rangers
Died of Wounds: (France) 8 December 1918. Age 26.
Supplementary Notes: Born: Galway.

MADDEN, James   Private 9243   Second Royal Irish Fusiliers
Died of Pneumonia: (Egypt) 8 December 1918. Age 30.
Supplementary Notes: Son of Mrs H. Madden of Munster Lane, Galway.
Remembered: Cairo War Memorial Cemetery – Egypt (M. 209).

MADDEN, John   Private 32503   First East Surrey Regiment
Killed in Action: (France) 10 October 1917. Age 32.
Supplementary Notes: Son of Thomas & Winifred Madden of Milltown, Tuam.
Remembered: Tyne Cot Memorial Zonnebeke – West-Vlaanderen – Belgium (79 to 80 & 163A).

MADDEN, Michael   Private 16928   Eleventh Manchester Regiment
Death: (Somme, France) 26 September 1916. Age 25.
Supplementary Notes: Son of James & Annie Madden of Derry, Mountbellew.
Remembered: Thiepval Memorial – Somme – France (13 A & 14 C).

MADDEN, Michael   Private 9425   First Leinster Regiment
Killed in Action: (Balkans) 21 May 1917. Age 28.
Supplementary Notes: Born: Clonford.
Buried: Struma Military Cemetery – Greece (VII. D. 14).

MADDEN, Patrick   Private 3586   Second Connaught Rangers
Killed in Action: (France) 22 October 1914. Age 29.
Supplementary Notes: Enlisted: Ballinasloe. Awarded Mons Star. Son of Elizabeth Madden (Keighrey) of Brackernagh, Ballinasloe.
Remembered: Ypres (Menin Gate) Memorial – Ieper – West-Vlaanderen – Belgium (42).

MADDEN, Patrick   Private 9108   First Royal Irish Regiment
Died of Wounds: (France) 17 February 1915.
Supplementary Notes: Born: Tuam.

MADDEN, William   Private G/4768   Eighteenth Middlesex Regiment
Died of Wounds: (France) 27 October 1916.
Supplementary Notes: Born: Tuam.
Buried: Carnoy Military Cemetery – Somme – France (V. 24).

MAHER, Michael John   Rifleman 8830   Seventh Royal Irish Rifles
Died of Wounds: (Ypres, Belgium) 8 August 1917. Age 24.
Supplementary Notes: Enlisted: Holborn. Born: Ballymacward.
Remembered: Ypres (Menin Gate) Memorial – Ieper – West-Vlaanderen – Belgium (40).

MAHER, Thomas   Sapper 168719   Royal Engineers
Death: (Home) 13 February 1917. Age 38.
Supplementary Notes: Born: Williamstown.
Buried: Liverpool (Ford) Roman Catholic Cemetery (R. 700).

MAHON, Dennis   Private 20518   Twenty-second Manchester Regiment
Killed in Action: (Guillemont, France) 3 September 1916. Age 31.
Supplementary Notes: Son of Dennis & Bridget Mahon; husband of Ellen Mahon of 2 School Street, London Road, Chorlton-on-Medlock. Born: Tuam.
Buried: Etaples Military Cemetery – Pas de Calais – France (X. B. 7).

MAHON, Michael Private 8625 First Connaught Rangers
Killed in Action: (France) 2 November 1914.
Supplementary Notes: Enlisted: Tuam. Nephew of Catherine Joyce of Louragh, Dunmore. Born: Dunmore.
Remembered: Le Touret Memorial – Pas de Calais – France (43).

MAHONY, John Private 8824 First Leinster Regiment
Killed in Action: (France) 12 May 1915.
Supplementary Notes: Born: Galway.
Remembered: Ypres (Menin Gate) Memorial – Ieper – West-Vlaanderen – Belgium (44).

MALONE, James Private 22616 Twentieth Lancashire Fusiliers
Died of Wounds: (France) 3 June 1916.
Supplementary Notes: Born: Moylough.
Buried: Le Touret Military Cemetery – Richebourg-L'Avoue – Pas de Calais – France (III. G. 8).

MALONEY, Arthur Private 100277 Royal Field Artillery
Death: (France) 1914–1918. Age 25.
Supplementary Notes: Born: Galway.

MALONEY, Patrick Private 10947 Second Connaught Rangers
Killed in Action: (France) 1 November 1914. Age 18.
Supplementary Notes: Enlisted: Galway. Awarded 1914 Star. Born: Oughterard.
Buried: Perth Cemetery (China Wall) – Australia (IV. C. 17).

MALONEY, Patrick Private 47349 Sixteenth T.W. Worcestershire Regiment
Death: (Home) 1 or 31 October 1917.
Supplementary Notes: Enlisted: Galway. Born: Galway.
Buried: Milford Haven Cemetery (C. 71).

MALONEY, W. Able Seaman SS *Taxandrier* Mercantile Marines
Presumed Drowned: 13 February 1917. Age 49.
Supplementary Notes: Born: Galway.
Remembered: Tower Hill Memorial – London – United Kingdom.

MANNION, John   Sergeant 1445   Fifth Connaught Rangers
Killed in Action: (Gallipoli) 21 August 1915.
Supplementary Notes: Enlisted: Cork. Born: Woodlawn.
Remembered: Helles Memorial – Gallipoli – Turkey (181 to 182).

MANNION, Martin   Private 129961   Thirty-fourth Machine Gun Corps
Killed in Action: (France) 12 September 1918. Age 24 or 25.
Supplementary Notes: Son of Michael & Margaret Mannion of Castleblakeney.
Buried: Reninghelst New Military Cemetery – Poperinge – West-Vlaanderen – Belgium (V. A. 6).

MANNION, Michael   Private 17100   Eighth Royal Dublin Fusiliers
Killed in Action: (France) 13 February 1916. Age 28.
Supplementary Notes: Son of John & Margaret Mannion of Derrymore, Clonberne.
Remembered: Loos Memorial – Pas de Calais – France (127 to 129).

MANNION, Patrick   Private 4174   First Connaught Rangers
Killed in Action: (France) 26 April 1915. Age 21.
Supplementary Notes: Enlisted: Galway. Son of Kate Mannion of Dunmore.
Remembered: Ypres (Menin Gate) Memorial – Ieper – West-Vlaanderen – Belgium (42).

MANNION, William   Private 236551   Labour Corps
Killed in Action: (France) 13 March 1918.
Supplementary Notes: Formerly of the Highland Light Infantry. Born: Athenry. There is a Royal Scot, W. Mannion 376080; recorded (United Kingdom) by the Commonwealth War Graves Commission as killed on 13 March 1918; and buried in Estaires Communal Cemetery Extension (V. C. 5). There is a possibility that this is the same soldier.

MARTIN, Geoffrey Clogstoun   Lieutenant   Ninth Royal Dublin Fusiliers
Killed in Action: (France) 2 August 1916. Age 24.
Supplementary Notes: Son of Captain Robert Walcott & Mrs Martin of 25 Longford Terrace, Monkstown, Blackrock. Born: Dunmore.
Buried: Vermelles British Cemetery – Pas de Calais – France (III. L. 8).

MARTYN, Christopher   Private 11831   Fifth Royal Irish Regiment
Killed in Action: (Ypres, Belgium) 9 October 1917 or 1918. Age 17.

Supplementary Notes: Born: Oranmore.

Buried: Doingt Communal Cemetery Extension – Somme – France (I. F. 16).

MARTYN, John   Private 10765   First Connaught Rangers
Killed in Action: (Mesopotamia) 21 January 1916. Age 21.

Supplementary Notes: Enlisted: Galway. Son of Thomas & Kate Martyn of Fairhill Road, Claddagh, Galway. He had escaped from a German prisoner of war camp in 1915.

Remembered: Basra Memorial – Iraq (40 & 64).

MATTHEWS, David   Lieutenant   Sixth Connaught Rangers
Killed in Action: (France) 29 May 1916. Age 27.

Supplementary Notes: Son of William & Catherine Matthews of Hardwood, Aughrim, Ballinasloe.

Buried: Noeux-Les-Mines Communal Cemetery – Pas de Calais – France (I. L. 6).

McCABE, John J.   Sergeant 19782   Eleventh Highland Light Infantry
Killed in Action: (Loos, France) 25 September 1915.

Supplementary Notes: Enlisted: September 1914. Son of James (Clerk of Petty Sessions, Eyrecourt) & Minnie A. McCabe of Eyrecourt (Athenry).

Remembered: Loos Memorial – Pas de Calais – France (108 to 112).

McCARTHY, Patrick   Gunner 6461   Seventeenth (Siege) Royal Garrison Artillery
Died of Wounds: (Egypt) 16 December 1915.

Supplementary Notes: Enlisted: Oranmore. Born: Ballinasloe.

Remembered: Helles Memorial – Gallipoli – Turkey (addenda panel).

McCASHIN, Henry   Rifleman 15351   Fourteenth Royal Irish Rifles
Killed in Action: (Somme, France) 1 July 1916.

Supplementary Notes: Enlisted: Belfast. Born: Galway.

Remembered: Thiepval Memorial – Somme – France (15 A & 15 B).

McCORMACK, Bernard   Private 8313   First Connaught Rangers
Killed in Action: (France) 5 November 1914.

Supplementary Notes: Enlisted: Ballinasloe. Born: Clonfert, Eyrecourt.

McCORMACK, Brian Private First Connaught Rangers
Killed in Action: (France). Age 25.
Supplementary Notes: Born: Galway.

McCORMACK, George Lieutenant British Expeditionary Force
Death: (Bovington Camp Hospital). Age 25.
Supplementary Notes: Son of the late William McCormack of Galway.
Remembered: Great War monument – St Nicholas' Collegiate Church – Galway.

McCORMACK, Thomas Private 13542 Ninth Royal Inniskilling Fusiliers
Killed in Action: (Somme, France) 1 July 1916. Age 40.
Supplementary Notes: Son of the late Thomas & Margaret McCormack of Ballinasloe; husband of Mary Elizabeth McCormack of 2 Anglesea Avenue, Blackrock, Co. Dublin.
Remembered: Thiepval Memorial – Somme – France (4 D & 5 B).

McDERMOTT, Daniel Private 34270 17th Manchester Regiment
Killed in Action: (France) 30 July 1916. Age 30 or 33.
Supplementary Notes: Born: Galway.
Remembered: Thiepval Memorial – Somme – France (13 A & 14 C).

McDERMOTT, John Francis Private 18294 20th Manchester Regiment
Killed in Action: (Somme, France) 1 July 1916. Age 18.
Supplementary Notes: Enlisted: Manchester. Born: Galway.
Buried: Dantzig Alley British Cemetery – Mametz – Somme – France (IV. I. 7).

McDERMOTT, Joseph Rifleman 2/7027 Second Royal Irish Rifles
Death: (France) 9 August 1915.
Supplementary Notes: Born: Galway.
Remembered: Ypres (Menin Gate) Memorial – Ieper – West-Vlaanderen – Belgium (60).

McDERMOTT, Joseph Private 49811 Connaught Rangers
Killed in Action: (France) 17 February 1916. Age 21.
Supplementary Notes: Born: Galway.

McDERMOTT, Patrick Private 10360 Sixth Royal Munster Fusiliers
Killed in Action: (Mecedonia or France) 4 October 1916 or 9 September 1917. Age 24.
Supplementary Notes: Born: Whitepark.

McDERMOTT, Patrick   Private 27/443   Thirteenth Northumberland
Fusiliers & Royal Field Artillery
>   **Killed in Action:** (Somme, France) 1 July 1916.
>   **Supplementary Notes:** Son of Patrick & Kate McDermott (*nee* Martyn) of Munster
>   Avenue, Galway.
>   **Remembered:** Thiepval Memorial – Somme – France (10 B. 11 B. & 12 B).

McDONAGH, James   Private 4115   First Connaught Rangers
>   **Killed in Action:** (France) 8 December 1918.
>   **Supplementary Notes:** Born: Galway.

McDONAGH, James   Private 7115   Second Irish Guards
>   **Died of Wounds:** (France) 18 September 1916. Age 23.
>   **Supplementary Notes:** Enlisted: Ballinasloe. Born: Ballygill.
>   **Buried:** St Sever Cemetery – Rouen – France (B. 22. 64).

McDONAGH, James   Lance Corporal 9579   Second Royal Irish Rifles
>   **Killed in Action:** (France) 11 August 1917.
>   **Supplementary Notes:** Son of Bridget McDonagh of New Road, Galway, and the late
>   James McDonagh; husband of Mary McDonagh of Presentation Road, Galway.
>   **Remembered:** Ypres (Menin Gate) Memorial – Ieper – West-Vlaanderen – Belgium
>   (40).

McDONAGH, John   Private 3610   Second Irish Guards
>   **Killed in Action:** (France). Age 22.
>   **Supplementary Notes:** Born: Galway.

McDONAGH, John   Private 5911   First Connaught Rangers
>   **Death:** 10 November 1918. Age 24.
>   **Supplementary Notes:** Son of John & Barbara McDonagh of Murvey, Roundstone,
>   Connemara.
>   **Buried:** Deir El Belah War Cemetery – Israel (B. 196).

McDONAGH, Joseph   Fisherman   Trawler *Pretty Polly*   Mercantile Marines
>   **Presumed Drowned:** 31 May 1918. Age 25.
>   **Supplementary Notes:** Son of Mary McDonagh of Ard East, Carna, and the late Col-
>   man McDonagh. Born: Ard East, Carna, Connemara. The sinking of the *Pretty Polly*
>   was recorded in *Galway and the Great War*, p. 98.

Remembered: Tower Hill Memorial – London – United Kingdom.

McDONAGH, Martin   Second Hand   Trawler *Neptune* Mercantile Marines
Died of Exposure: (Galway Bay) 17 December 1917. Age 58.
Supplementary Notes: Died as a result of enemy action. Son of the late Thomas &
Mary McDonagh; husband of Mary McDonagh (*nee* Gill) of Middle Street, Galway.
The sinking of the *Neptune* was recorded in *Galway and the Great War*, p. 98.
Remembered: Tower Hill Memorial – London – United Kingdom.

McDONAGH, Michael   Private 7034   Connaught Rangers
Death: (France). Age30
Supplementary Notes: Born: Galway.

McDONAGH, Michael   Private 4696   Sixth Connaught Rangers
Killed in Action: (France) 7 June 1917. Age 30
Supplementary Notes: Enlisted: Galway. Husband of J. McDonagh of Middle Street,
Galway.
Buried: La Laiterie Military Cemetery – Heuvelland – West-Vlaanderen – Belgium
(XII. A. 32).

McDONAGH, P.   Seaman 5050A   SS *Oristano*   Royal Navy Reserves
Death: 20 March 1917.
Supplementary Notes: Son of Mrs K. McDonagh of Ropewalk, Claddagh, Galway.
Buried: New York City, Brooklyn (The Evergreens) Cemetery – United States of
America (3. Ocean View Sector).

McDONAGH, Patrick   Fisherman   Trawler *Pretty Polly* Mercantile Marines
Presumed Drowned: 31 May 1918. Age 16.
Supplementary Notes: Son of John & Kate McDonagh of Ard West, Carna. Born:
Ard East, Carna, Connemara. The sinking of the *Pretty Polly* was recorded in *Galway
and the Great War*, p. 98.
Remembered: Tower Hill Memorial – London – United Kingdom.

McDONAGH, Patrick   Seaman 3130A   SS *Sonnie*   Royal Navy Reserves
Killed in Action: 11 August 1917. Age 24.
Supplementary Notes: Killed during action with an enemy submarine off the English
coast. Son of William & Kate McDonagh of Quay Street, Galway; husband of Sarah
McDonagh (*nee* Farrell) of Warmsley Street, Liverpool.

Remembered: Portsmouth Naval Memorial – Hampshire – United Kingdom (27).

McDONAGH, Patrick   Private 2224   Fifth Connaught Rangers
   Died of Wounds: (Alexandria) 21 April 1916. Age 20.
   Supplementary Notes: Born: Galway.

McDONAGH, Patrick   Private 5614   Fifth Connaught Rangers
   Died of Wounds: (Salonika) 10 December 1915.
   Supplementary Notes: Enlisted: Galway. Born: Galway.
   Buried: Salonika (Lembet Road) Military Cemetery – Greece (10).

McDONAGH, Patrick   Private 35614   Connaught Rangers
   Killed in Action: (France) 19 July 1915. Age 25.
   Supplementary Notes: Born: Galway.

McDONAGH, Thomas   Private 2798   Connaught Rangers
   Died of Wounds: (France) 24 October 1917. Age 21.
   Supplementary Notes: Born: Galway.

McDONALD, Patrick   Private 1181   Fifth Connaught Rangers
   Killed in Action: (Gallipoli) 28 August 1915.
   Supplementary Notes: Enlisted: Omagh. Born: Woodford.
   Remembered: Helles Memorial – Turkey (181 to 183).

McDONALD, William   Private 594   Fifth Connaught Rangers
   Died of Wounds: (Gallipoli) 23 August 1915.
   Supplementary Notes: Enlisted: Llanelly. Born: Clifden.
   Remembered: Helles Memorial – Turkey (181 to 183).

McDONAUGH, John   Lance Corporal 5933   First Connaught Rangers
   Death: (Mesopotamia) 20 April 1916.
   Supplementary Notes: Enlisted: Manchester. Born: Glenamaddy.

McDONNAGH, John   Private 5911   First Connaught Rangers
   Death: (Egypt) 10 November 1918.
   Supplementary Notes: Enlisted: Drumbarton. Born: Morriss.

McDONNELL, Bobbie　　　　Sergeant　　　　　　　Royal Dublin Fusiliers
Death: (Dardanelles) 11 May 1915.
Supplementary Notes: Son of Robert McDonnell (station master) of Galway.

McDONNELL, John　　　　Sergeant 23137　　Ninth Royal Inniskilling Fusiliers
Killed in Action: (France) 16 August 1917.
Supplementary Notes: Born: Inishmore.
Remembered: Tyne Cot Memorial Zonnebeke – West-Vlaanderen – Belgium (70 to 72).

McDONNELL, John　　　　Sapper 201091　　　　　　Royal Engineers
Death: 6 December 1916. Age 59.
Supplementary Notes: Enlisted: Ballinasloe. Inland Water Transport. Husband of Mary Anne McDonnell of Jubilee Street, Ballinasloe.
Buried: Minster (Thanet) Cemetery – Kent – United Kingdom (R.C. 249).

McDONNELL, Mark　　　　Private 43180　　Eighth Royal Inniskilling Fusiliers
Killed in Action: (France) 16 August 1917. Age 20.
Supplementary Notes: Born: Clifden.
Remembered: Tyne Cot Memorial Zonnebeke – West-Vlaanderen – Belgium (70 to 72).

McDONNELL, Martin　　　　Lieutenant　　　　　　　　Irish Guards
Died of Wounds: (Somme, France) 24 January 1917. Age 20.
Supplementary Notes: Enlisted: 1915. Born: Moycullen. Attached to the Royal Irish Rifles. Awarded Military Medal. Wounded on 23 January 1917. Eldest son of the late Farrell McDonnell of Glencoe House, Dunmore.

McDONNELL, Michael　　　Lance Corporal 8968　　First Royal Munster Fusiliers
Killed in Action: (France) 21 March 1918.
Supplementary Notes: Enlisted: Cork. Born: Galway.

McDONOUGH, Michael　　　Private 5/596　　　　Fifth Connaught Rangers
Died of Wounds: (Gallipoli) 14 September 1915.
Supplementary Notes: Enlisted: Leigh. Born: Tuam.
Buried: Leigh Cemetery (44 F. R.C. 56).

McDONOUGH, Patrick   Deck Hand 2773T5   Trawler *Charles Astie*
Royal Navy
>   **Death:** 26 June 1917. Age 47.
>   **Supplementary Notes:** Killed by a mine explosion in Lough Swilly. Son of Dominic
>   & Maggie McDonough of Cross Street, Galway; husband of Anne McDonough of
>   Whitehall.
>   **Remembered:** Portsmouth Naval Memorial – Hampshire – United Kingdom (28).

McDONOUGH, Patrick   Private 10975   First Irish Guards
>   **Died of Wounds:** (France) 4 July 1917. Age 19.
>   **Supplementary Notes:** Son of Patrick & Annie McDonough of Lettercallow, Letter-
>   more, Connemara.
>   **Buried:** Canada Farm Cemetery – Ieper – West-Vlaanderen – Belgium (I. A. I).

McGAWLEY, Patrick   Private 4478   Fourth Leinster Regiment
>   **Killed in Action:** (France) 4 September 1918. Age 20.
>   **Supplementary Notes:** Enlisted: Limerick. Son of Bridget McGawley of 10 Great
>   Snip Street, Dublin. Born: Ballinasloe.
>   **Remembered:** Ploegsteert Memorial – Comines-Warneton – Hainaut – Belgium
>   (10).

McGRATH, James   Lance Corporal 79173   Second Northumberland Fusiliers.
>   **Killed in Action or Died of Wounds:** (France) 4 November 1918. Age 24.
>   **Supplementary Notes:** Son of John & Anne McGrath of Meelick West, Carnane,
>   Tuam.
>   **Buried:** Fontaine-Au-Bois Communal Cemetery – Nord – France (C. 7).

McGRATH, Mathias   Private 22556   Seventh Royal Inniskilling Fusiliers
>   **Killed in Action:** (France) 16 August 1917. Age 28.
>   **Supplementary Notes:** Born: Moyrus.
>   **Remembered:** Tyne Cot Memorial Zonnebeke – West-Vlaanderen – Belgium (70 to 72).

McGRATH, Patrick   Stoker 251   Royal Navy Reserve
>   **Killed in Action:** (France) 18 May 1917. Age 30.
>   **Supplementary Notes:** Born: Galway.

McGRATH, Thomas   Private 24/247   24th Northumberland Fusiliers
>   **Killed in Action:** (Somme, France) 1 July 1916.

Supplementary Notes: Enlisted: Newcastle-on-Tyne. Born: Ballinasloe.
Remembered: Thiepval Memorial – Somme – France (10 B. 11 B. & 12 B).

McGRATH, Thomas   Lance Corporal 40624   Ninth Service York & Lancaster Regiment
Killed in Action: (France) 30 September 1917.
Supplementary Notes: Enlisted: Liverpool. Formerly of the Royal Field Artillery
162240. Awarded Military Medal. Born: Galway.
Buried: Hooge Crater Cemetery – West-Vlaanderen – Belgium (IX. G. 10).

McGUIRE, George   Acting Sergeant 9334   First Royal Irish Fusiliers
Killed in Action: (France) 21 March 1918.
Supplementary Notes: Enlisted: Cork. Awarded Military Medal. Born: Ballinasloe.
Remembered: Pozieres Memorial – Somme – France (76 & 77).

McHUGH, Martin   Private 5902   First Irish Guards
Killed in Action: (France) 6 April 1918. Age 32 or 36.
Supplementary Notes: Awarded Mons Star. Born: Tuam.
Buried: Gezaincourt Communal Cemetery Extension – Somme – France (II. J. 22).

McHUGH, Thomas   Deck Hand SD1562   Royal Naval Reserves
Died of Peritonitis: (Taranto) 27 November 1917.
Supplementary Notes: Enlisted: 10 June 1915. Born in 1874, the son of Patrick &
Ann McHugh of Bohermore; husband of Delia McHugh of 33 Upper Bohermore,
Galway. Served on HMS *Thetis*, HT *Daisy II*, *Manzanita*, *Admirable*, *Helgoland* and
HMS *Queen*.
Buried: Taranto Town Cemetery Extension – Italy (s. IV, r. F, p. 9).

McINTOSH, John   Private 5289   First Irish Guards
Killed in Action: (Loos, France) 27 September 1915. Age 24.
Supplementary Notes: Born: Clonbur.

McKEIGUE, Michael or John   Gunner 5390   121st Royal Field Artillery
Killed in Action: (France) 4 November 1918. Age 25.
Supplementary Notes: Enlisted: Earlstown, Lancashire. Son of Patrick & Bridget
McKeigue of Esher, Castleblakeney, Ballinasloe.
Remembered: Vis-En-Artois Memorial – Pas de Calais – France (3).

McKEIGUE, Michael   Lance Corporal 5930   First Connaught Rangers
Death: (Egypt) 16 October 1918. Age 32.
Supplementary Notes: Enlisted: Manchester. Born: Loughrea.
Buried: Haifa War Cemetery – Israel (A. 56).

McKEOWN, John   Private 19813   Eleventh Service Highland Light Infantry
Died of Wounds: (France) 1 October 1915.
Supplementary Notes: Enlisted: Glasgow. Born: Galway.
Buried: Longuenesse (St Omer) Souvenir Cemetery – Pas de Calais – France (II. A. 40).

McKEOWN, Peter   Private 9098   First Irish Guards
Killed in Action: (France) 15 September 1916. Age 24.
Supplementary Notes: Son of Thomas & Bridget McKeown of Rossaveel, Costello, Connemara (Spiddal).
Remembered: Thiepval Memorial – Somme – France (7 D).

McKERNAN, Michael   Lieutenant   Irish Guards
Died of Wounds: (France) May 1918. Age 22.
Supplementary Notes: Enlisted: Galway 1915. Awarded Military Medal. Born: Moycullen.

McKEW, Patrick   Private 27891   Connaught Rangers
Killed in Action: (France) 28 January 1918. Age 32.
Supplementary Notes: Born: Galway.

McKIERNAN, Michael Vincent   Second Lieutenant   Sixth Connaught Rangers
Died of Wounds: 11 May 1918. Age 22.
Supplementary Notes: Awarded Military Medal & Bar. Wounded on 21 March 1918. Son of James & Anna Maria McKiernan of Clooney, Quin, Co. Clare. Born: Moycullen.
Buried: St Sever Cemetery – Rouen – Seine-Maritime – France (Officers, B. 7. 3).

McLOUGHLIN, James   Private 9427   Second Irish Guards
Killed in Action: (France) 13 April 1918. Age 35.
Supplementary Notes: Enlisted: Galway. Son of Mr & Mrs John McLoughlin of Doonbeg, Cummer.
Remembered: Ploegsteert Memorial – Comines-Warneton – Hainaut – Belgium (1).

McLOUGHLIN, John   Private 599   First Royal Munster Fusiliers
Killed in Action: (France) 6 September 1916. Age 26.
Supplementary Notes: Enlisted: Warrington, Lancashire. Son of Thomas & Mary McLoughlin of Linagree Caltra, Ballinasloe.
Remembered: Thiepval Memorial – Somme – France (16 C).

McLOUGHLIN, Thomas   S/8317   Sixth Gordan Highlanders
Killed in Action: (France) 23 April 1917.
Supplementary Notes: Born: Cloon, Kelvey. His name is recorded as McLaughlin in *Ireland's Memorial Records 1914–1918*.
Buried: Struma Military Cemetery (VIII. E. 3).
Remembered: Helles Memorial – Turkey (178 to 180).

McLOUGHLIN, William   Private 1473   First Irish Guards
Killed in Action: (France) 20 September 1916.
Supplementary Notes: Enlisted: Dublin. Born: Clontuskert.
Buried: St Desir Cemetery – France.

McMANUS, Patrick   Private 6660   First Royal Munster Fusiliers
Killed in Action: (France) 4 July 1916.
Supplementary Notes: Born: Spiddal, Connemara.
Buried: Dud Corner Cemetery – Loos – Pas de Calais – France (II. F. 17).

McNAMARA, Michael   Private 7014   Seventh Leinster Regiment
Died of Wounds: (France) 10 August 1917.
Supplementary Notes: Born: Whitegate.
Buried: Brandhoek New Military Cemetery No. 3 – Ieper – West-Vlaanderen – Belgium (VI. B. 5).

McNAMEE, Patrick   Private 21020   Seventh & Eighth Royal Irish Fusiliers
Killed in Action: (France) 1 January 1917.
Supplementary Notes: Enlisted: Galway. Formerly of the Connaught Rangers 4217. Born: Galway.

McSWEENEY, Owen   Private 6444   Third King's Liverpool Regiment
Death: (Home) 27 September 1914.
Supplementary Notes: Born: Clonbern.
Buried: Liverpool (Everton) Cemetery (XV. R.C. 124).

McTIGHE, Patrick   Private 27946 (27964)   Household Cavalry
   Killed in Action: (Mesopotamia) 24 October 1918.
   Supplementary Notes: Born: Galway.
   Remembered: Basra Memorial – Iraq (1).

McTIGHE, William   Private 5876   Second South Lancashire Regiment
   Killed in Action: (France) 24 October 1914.
   Supplementary Notes: Enlisted: St Helens, Lancashire. Born: Galway.
   Remembered: Le Touret Memorial – Pas de Calais – France (23).

MEADE, Daniel   Private 21703   Eighth Royal Irish Fusiliers
   Death: (Galway) 4 July 1916.
   Supplementary Notes: Born: Loughrea.

MELIA, Matt   Private   Eighth Royal Munster Fusiliers
   Killed in Action: (France) 4 September 1916.
   Supplementary Notes: Wounded at Gallipoli in 1915. Stepson of Martin Melia of
   Mainguard Street, Galway. Two of his brothers also served, Pat with the First Connaught
   Rangers and Joseph with the Royal Munster Fusiliers & Royal Irish Regiment, and
   both survived.

MELIA, Matthew   Private 68711   First Connaught Rangers
   Killed in Action: (France) 18 August 1918. Age 37.
   Supplementary Notes: Born: Galway.

MELIADY, William   Private 9144   First Connaught Rangers
   Killed in Action: (France) 19 March 1915.
   Supplementary Notes: Enlisted: Dublin. Born: Loughrea.
   Remembered: Le Touret Memorial – Pas de Calais – France (43).

MELODY, Michael   Private 13911   Connaught Rangers
   Died of Wounds: (France) 19 February 1915. Age 41.
   Supplementary Notes: Born: Galway.

MELVIN, John   Private 10150   First Connaught Rangers
   Killed in Action: (France) 26 April 1915. Age 21.
   Supplementary Notes: Enlisted: Galway. Son of Mary Melvin of Suckeen, Wood
   Quay, Galway.

Remembered: Ypres (Menin Gate) Memorial – Ieper – West-Vlaanderen – Belgium (42).

MILLER, Cyril Roland Eyre   Lieutenant   Fourth Cameronians (Scottish Rifles)
Died of Wounds: (France) 23 November 1914. Age 32.
Supplementary Notes: Son of Captain J.B. (former Eighth Hussars & Forfar Light Horse) & Alice Maude Miller (*nee* Newton) of Upton Manor, Andover. Born: Eyrecourt Castle.
Buried: Boulogne Eastern Cemetery – Pas de Calais – France (I. B. 7).

MILLER, William   Private 10296   Second Leinster Regiment
Died of Wounds: (France) 3 August 1915. Age 27.
Supplementary Notes: Born: Loughrea.
Buried: New Irish Farm Cemetery – West-Vlaanderen – Belgium (XXVII. B. 1).

MISKELL, Patrick   Private 874   Second Royal Irish Regiment
Death: (France) 27 September 1918. Age 30.
Supplementary Notes: Son of John & Catherine Miskell (*nee* Gacquin) of Ballyforan, Ballinasloe.
Buried: Sucrerie British Cemetery – Graincourt-Les-Havrincourt – Pas de Calais – France (A. 53)

MITCHELL, Christopher   Private 25355   Tenth Royal Dublin Fusiliers
Death: (Dublin) 27 March 1916.
Supplementary Notes: Son of Mrs E. Mitchell of 76 Aughrim Street, Dublin. Born: Ballinasloe.
Buried: Grangegorman Military Cemetery – Dublin – Ireland (RC. 468).

MOLLOY, Martin William   Private 6649   Second Irish Guards
Killed in Action: (France) 13 September 1916. Age 29.
Supplementary Notes: Formerly of the RIC. Son of James & Mary Molloy of Carramore Knock, Rosscahill.
Buried: Guards' Cemetery – Lesboeufs – Somme – France (IV. Z. I).

MOLLOY, Michael   Private 7277   Second Connaught Rangers
Died of Wounds: (France) 4 September 1914.
Supplementary Notes: Enlisted: Ballinasloe. Awarded Mons Star. Born: Kilclooney,

Ballinasloe. He was with D Company when they were outflanked by the German advance at Mons and was wounded just outside the village of Grand Fayt during a counterattack.

Buried: Avesnes-sur-Helpe Communal Cemetery – Nord – France (A. 16).

MOLLOY, Patrick   Seaman 3243A Trawler *Malta*   Royal Navy Reserves
Death: (North Sea) 1 September 1915. Age 23.
Supplementary Notes: Killed by a mine explosion. Son of Mark & Nora Molloy of Long Walk, Galway. Served with the naval division at Antwerp.
Buried: Shotley (St Mary) Churchyard – Suffolk – United Kingdom (R.N. 55).

MOLLOY, Robert   Private 1545   First Irish Guards
Killed in Action: (France) 1 September 1914. Age 29.
Supplementary Notes: Enlisted: Birkenhead. Formerly of the RIC Reserve 64992. Born: Lawrencetown.
Remembered: La Ferte-Sous-Jouarre Memorial – Seine-et-Marne – France.

MOLLOY, Thomas Lewis   Sergeant (cook) 8877   Second Leinster Regiment
Killed in Action: (France) 20 August 1915. Age 27.
Supplementary Notes: Enlisted: Athlone. Son of Thomas & Mary Molloy of Market Hill, Ballinasloe.
Buried: Ramparts Cemetery – Lille Gate – Ieper – West-Vlaanderen – Belgium (H. 5).

MOLONEY, Arthur   Private 100277   Royal Field Artillery
Death: (France) 16 December 1916.
Supplementary Notes: Born: Suckeen, Woodquay, Galway.

MOLONEY, Thomas Anthony   Private 8/757   Otago regiment NZEF
Killed in Action: (Gallipoli) 1 or 23 May 1915. Age 21.
Supplementary Notes: Son of John & Kate Moloney of Upper Abbeygate Street, Galway.
Buried: The Nek Cemetery ANZAC – Turkey (A. 16).

MONAGHAN, James   Private 4237   Second Connaught Rangers
Killed in Action: (France) 2 November 1914. Age 23 or 25.
Supplementary Notes: Enlisted: Galway. Born: Oranmore.
Remembered: Ypres (Menin Gate) Memorial – Ieper – West-Vlaanderen – Belgium (42).

MONAGHAN, John   Private 4312   Fifth Connaught Rangers
Killed in Action: (Salonika) 7 December 1915. Age 22.
Supplementary Notes: Enlisted: Galway. Born: Oranmore.
Remembered: Doiran Memorial – Greece.

MONAGHAN, Joseph   Private 3605   Second Leinster Regiment
Killed in Action: 6 January 1915. Age 19 or 22.
Supplementary Notes: Son of John & Bridget Monaghan of Shannon Road, Portumna.
Buried: Cite Bonjean Military Cemetery – Armentieres – Nord – France (IX. B. 18).

MONAGHAN, Joseph   Private 7273   Sixth Connaught Rangers
Killed in Action: (Guillemont, France) 3 September 1916. Age 29.
Supplementary Notes: Enlisted: Tuam. Son of Anne Monaghan of Cloonthue Road, Tuam.
Remembered: Thiepval Memorial – Somme – France (15 A).

MONAGHAN, Patrick   Private 10700   Eighth Royal Munster Fusiliers
Killed in Action: (Guillemont, France) 3 September 1916. Age 27.
Supplementary Notes: Born: Tuam.
Remembered: Thiepval Memorial – Somme – France (16 C).

MONAGHAN, Thomas   Private 565   Fifth Connaught Rangers
Killed in Action: (Gallipoli) 28 August 1915.
Supplementary Notes: Enlisted: Galway. Born: Galway.

MONAHAN, J.   Sergeant 14730   Fourth Reserve Cavalry Regiment
Death: 4 April 1916. Age 41.
Supplementary Notes: Son of Laurence Monahan; husband of Lilian Monahan of 11 Plevna Crescent, St Ann's Road, Stamford Hill, London. Born: Galway.
Buried: Leytonstone (St Patrick's) Roman Catholic Cemetery – Essex – United Kingdom (XI.A. 5. 43).

MOORE, Alexander   Corporal 13853   Seventh Royal Dublin Fusiliers
Killed in Action: (Balkans) 23 September 1916. Age 26.
Supplementary Notes: Son of James Moore of Vicar Street, Tuam.
Remembered: Doiran Memorial – Greece.

MOORE, Patrick John   Private 4299   Second & Sixth Connaught Rangers
Killed in Action: (Guillemont, France) 3 September 1916. Age 35.
Supplementary Notes: Enlisted: Ballinasloe. Born: Portumna. Fought at Neuve Chapelle. He was wounded at Ypres. After three months in a British hospital, he was sent back to the front.
Remembered: Thiepval Memorial – Somme – France (15 A).

MOORE, Ulick   Lieutenant   Third Connaught Rangers
Killed in Action: (France) 22 March 1918. Age 22 or 35.
Supplementary Notes: Enlisted: Kinsale 20 November 1915. Second son of Cononel Maurice & Evelyn Moore of Carantrila Park. Wounded at Ginchy in September 1916.
Buried: St Emilie Valley Cemetery – Villers-Faucon – Somme – France (IV. D. 1).

MORAN, Michael James   Private 16748   Coldstream Guards
Death: (Home) 8 November 1915.
Supplementary Notes: Enlisted: Manchester. Born: Galway.
Buried: St Pancras Cemetery – London – United Kingdom (Special Memorial Row 1).

MORAN, Patrick   Private 6665   Second Irish Guards
Died of Wounds: 22 October 1915.
Supplementary Notes: Husband of Margaret Moran of Rehan, Tynagh, Loughrea.
Buried: Bethune Town Cemetery – Pas de Calais – France (IV. F. 59).

MORGAN, Thomas   Sergeant 4813   Sixth Royal Lancaster Regiment
Killed in Action: (Mesopotamia) 9 February 1917. Age 45.
Supplementary Notes: Enlisted: Barrow-in-Furness. Born: Galway.
Remembered: Basra Memorial – Iraq (7).

MORRIS, Charles Sabastian   Lieutenant Commander   Royal Navy
Killed in Action: (Jutland) 31 May 1916.
Supplementary Notes: Son of James Morris of Ballinboy House. His brother, James, also served in the navy. In 1941, he became commander and director of the Irish Naval Service. Another brother, George, served with the Indian cavalry.
Remembered: Portsmouth Naval Memorial – Hampshire – United Kingdom (11).

MORRIS, George Henry   Lieutenant Colonel   First Irish Guards
Killed in Action: (Mons, Belgium) 1 September 1914. Age 42.

Supplementary Notes: 'Mentioned in Despatches'. Son of Baron & Anna Morris (Killanin) of Spiddal (daughter of Hon. G.H. Hughes, Baron of the Court of Exchequer, Ireland); husband of Dora Morris of 4 Lancaster Gate Terrace, London. Descended from the famous tribal family of Galway. His only son, Michael Morris (Lord Killanin), was two months old when his father was killed. Lord Killanin, MBE, later served as a major with the armoured brigade during the Second World War.

Buried: Guards' Grave, Villers Cotterets Forest – Aisne – France (II. 1).

MORRIS, Lawrence   Private 9466   First Leinster Regiment
Killed in Action: (France) 4 May 1915.
Supplementary Notes: Born: Portumna.
Remembered: Ypres (Menin Gate) Memorial – Ieper – West-Vlaanderen – Belgium (44).

MORRISON, Alexander   Sergeant 10400   First Royal Dublin Fusiliers
Killed in Action: (France) 29 March 1918.
Supplementary Notes: Born: Gort.
Remembered: Pozieres Memorial – Somme – France (78 / 80).

MORRISON, William   Private 14141   Second Royal Munster Fusiliers
Killed in Action: (France) 24 September 1916.
Supplementary Notes: Born: Loughrea.
Remembered: Thiepval Memorial – Somme – France (16 C).

MOYLAN, John   Private 43160   Seventh / Eighth Royal Irish Fusiliers
Killed in Action: (France) 7 June 1917. Age 33.
Supplementary Notes: Son of John & Honor Moylan of Liss, Headford.
Remembered: Ypres (Menin Gate) Memorial – Ieper – West-Vlaanderen – Belgium (42).

MULCURRAN, Anthony   Private 3947   First Yorkshire Regiment
Death: (India) 28 December 1915.
Supplementary Notes: Born: Clifden.

MULDOON, Patrick   Sergeant 9902   Second Royal Dublin Fusiliers
Killed in Action: (France) 9 May 1915.
Supplementary Notes: Born: Portumna.
Remembered: Ypres (Menin Gate) Memorial – Ieper – West-Vlaanderen – Belgium (44 & 46).

MULLEN, John   Private 202690   Second Lancashire Fusiliers
Killed in Action: (France) 9 October 1917.
Supplementary Notes: Enlisted: Swinton, Lancashire. Born: Galway.
Remembered: Tyne Cot Memorial Zonnebeke – West-Vlaanderen – Belgium (54 to 60 & 163A).

MULLEN, Thomas   Private 24735   Ninth Cameronians (Scottish Rifles)
Killed in Action: (France) 3 May 1917.
Supplementary Notes: Enlisted: Glasgow. Born: Galway.
Remembered: Arras Memorial – Pas de Calais – France (6).

MULLIN, Thomas   Lance Corporal 12967   Ninth Royal Dublin Fusiliers
Killed in Action: (France) 6 September 1916. Age 37.
Supplementary Notes: Born: Ballymoe.
Remembered: Thiepval Memorial – Somme – France (16 C).

MULLINS, Patrick   Private 1722   Sixth Connaught Rangers
Killed in Action: (France) 5 August 1917.
Supplementary Notes: Enlisted: Liverpool. Born: Galway.
Remembered: Ypres (Menin Gate) Memorial – Ieper – West-Vlaanderen – Belgium (42).

MULLINS, Patrick   Corporal 250370   First & Sixth Manchester Regiments
Killed in Action: (France) 21 August 1918.
Supplementary Notes: Born: Dunmore.
Remembered: Vis-En-Artois Memorial – Pas de Calais – France (9).

MULVIHILL, William   Private 11916   First Irish Guards
Died of Wounds: (France) 3 December 1917.
Supplementary Notes: Born: Creete.
Buried: Rocquigny-Equancourt Road British Cemetery – Manancourt – Somme – France (VII. E. 26).

MURPHY, Michael   Private 12708   Fifth Royal Irish Fusiliers
Died of Wounds: (Egypt) 23 August 1915.
Supplementary Notes: Enlisted: Warrington. Born: Galway.
Remembered: Helles Memorial – Turkey (178 to 180).

MURPHY, Michael   Private 30089   First Royal Dublin Fusiliers
Died of Wounds: (POW Camp, Germany) 1 May 1918.
Supplementary Notes: Enlisted: Stirling. Born: Galway.
Buried: Cologne Southern Cemetery – Germany (XIII. F. 30).

MURPHY, Patrick   Private 2494   First Royal Inniskilling Fusiliers
Killed in Action: (Gallipoli) 19 June 1915.
Supplementary Notes: Enlisted: Ballinasloe. Born: Kilclooney, Ballinasloe.
Buried: Twelve Tree Copse Cemetery – Krithia – Turkey (XI. D. 4).

MURPHY, Patrick   Private 1/4410   First Irish Guards
Killed in Action: (France) 6 November 1914. Age 21 or 23.
Supplementary Notes: Awarded Mons Star. Born: Loughrea.
Remembered: Ypres (Menin Gate) Memorial – Ieper – West-Vlaanderen – Belgium
(11).

MURRAY, J.   Leading Seaman SS/2716   HMS *Erin*   Royal Navy
Death: 10 June 1916. Age 26.
Supplementary Notes: Son of John & Julia Murray of Flower Hill, Killimore, Ballinasloe.
Buried: Rosskeen Parish Churchyard Extensions (or Burial Ground) – Ross and Cromarty – United Kingdom (C. 386).

MURRAY, John   Private PW 5166   First Middlesex Regiment
Killed in Action: (France) 29 September 1918.
Supplementary Notes: Enlisted: Leicester. Born: Galway.
Buried: Domino British Cemetery – Epehy – Somme – France (II. B. 10).

MURRAY, John   Private 9923.   First Connaught Rangers
Death: (Mesopotamia) 21 January 1916. Age 24 or 30.
Supplementary Notes: Enlisted: Ballinasloe. Awarded Mons Star. Son of Margaret Murray of Liscune, Woodlawn.
Remembered: Basra Memorial – Iraq (40 & 64).

MURRAY, Martin   Corporal 9412   Second Leinster Regiment
Died of Wounds: (France) 13 March 1917. Age 22.
Supplementary Notes: Enlisted: Galway. Son of John & Mary Murray of St Augustine

Street, Galway; husband of Kathleen Murray of 3 Lower Terrace, Lower Mayfield, Cork.

Buried: Barlin Communal Cemetery Extension – Pas de Calais – France (I. G. 19).

MURTAGH, Michael   Private 10139   Second Leinster Regiment
Died of Wounds: (France) 10 April 1915.
Supplementary Notes: Born: Portumna.

MURTAGH, Robert   Lance Corporal 8118   First Connaught Rangers
Killed in Action: (Mesopotamia) 21 January 1916. Age 26.
Supplementary Notes: Son of Captain Michael Murtagh (Northumberland Fusiliers) of Rockbarton, Galway.
Remembered: Basra Memorial – Iraq (40 & 64).

NASH, Joseph   Private 43148   Fifth Connaught Rangers
Killed in Action: (France) 20 November 1917.
Supplementary Notes: Awarded Military Medal. Born: Galway.
Buried: Croisilles Railway Cemetery – Pas de Calais – France (II. C. 6).

NAUGHTON, Joseph   Private 4627   Sixth Connaught Rangers
Killed in Action: (France) 14 May 1916. Age 20.
Supplementary Notes: Enlisted: Galway. Born: Galway.
Buried: Dud Corner Cemetery – Loos – Pas de Calais – France (II. H. 11).

NAUGHTON, Michael Joseph   Private, 6/3410   First Canterbury Regiment NZEF
Killed in Action: 25 September 1916. Age 34.
Supplementary Notes: Son of Patrick Naughton of Rusheeny, Oughterard.
Remembered: Caterpillar Valley (New Zealand) Memorial – Somme – France.

NEE, Colman   Boatswain   Tanker *Progress*   Mercantile Marines
Death: 21 December 1916. Age 40.
Supplementary Notes: Killed when his ship was torpedoed off Hull. Son of Martin & Mary Nee; husband of Delia Nee of Lower Fairhill Road, Claddagh, Galway. He served on the SS *Granuaile*, a Congested Districts Board vessel, which carried supplies to offshore islands. He also served with the *Gunnamor* in the Claddagh.
Buried: Cruden Parish Churchyard and Extension – Aberdeenshire – United Kingdom (874).

NEE, Michael   Private 194   Sixth Royal Munster Fusiliers
   Death: (Gallipoli) 9 August 1915. Age 40.
   Supplementary Notes: Son of Michael & Honor Nee of Ballylara, Ardrahan (Kinvara).
   Remembered: Helles Memorial – Turkey (185 to 190).

NEE, Patrick   Private 18231   Seventh Royal Irish Regiment
   Killed in Action: (France) 21 March 1918. Age 21 or 23.
   Supplementary Notes: Son of the late Thomas & Bridget Nee (*nee* Shaughnessy) of
   Killola, Rosscahill (New Village).
   Remembered: Pozieres Memorial – Somme – France (30 & 31).

NEE, William   Private 5275   First Lancashire Fusiliers
   Killed in Action: (Somme, France) 1 July 1916. Age 32.
   Supplementary Notes: Born: Williamstown.
   Buiried: Auchonvillers Military Cemetery – Somme – France (II. E. 19).

NEEDHAM, James   Private   Fifth Connaught Rangers
   Killed in Action: (France) 11 October 1918. Age 20.
   Supplementary Notes: Born: Galway.

NEEDHAM, Martin   Private 5991   First Connaught Rangers
   Killed in Action or Died of Wounds: (Mesopotamia) 11 July 1917. Age 26.
   Supplementary Notes: Enlisted: Galway. Born: Clifden.
   Remembered: Basra Memorial – Iraq (40 & 64).

NEWELL, Charles Edward   Lieutenant   Eighth Royal Inniskilling Fusiliers
   Died of Wounds: (France) 25 May 1916. Age 19.
   Supplementary Notes: Wounds received at Loos. Son of A.C. Newell (former RM) &
   K.M. Newell of Romanesca, Sandycove, Kingstown. Born: Ballinasloe.
   Buried: Bethune Town Cemetery – Pas de Calais – France (III. K. 16).

NILAND, John   Private 3756   Second Connaught Rangers
   Killed in Action: (France) 10 November 1914. Age 21.
   Supplementary Notes: Enlisted: Galway. Son of John & Ellen Niland of Lakefield,
   Gort (Kilchreest, Loughrea).
   Remembered: Ypres (Menin Gate) Memorial – Ieper – West-Vlaanderen – Belgium
   (42).

NOLAN, Raymond Philip   Lieutenant   Third Black Watch
     Death: November 1914. Age 31.
     Supplementary Notes: Eldest son of Philip Nolan. Succeeded his uncle, Lieutenant Colonel J.P. Nolan, MP, in the Ballinderry Estate (1912). Educated at Beaumont, Stonyhurst and New College, Oxford.

NOON, John   Private 50   Second Manchester Regiment
     Killed in Action: (France) 26 August 1914. Age 30.
     Supplementary Notes: Enlisted: Ashton-Under-Lyne, Lancashire. Son of Patrick & Mary of Cloonthue, Tuam.
     Remembered: La Ferte-Sous-Jouarre Memorial – Seine-et-Marne – France.

NOONE, Martin   Driver 53837   Royal Horse Artillery
     Killed in Action: (France) 25 April 1915.
     Supplementary Notes: Enlisted: Galway. Born: Galway.
     Remembered: Le Touret Memorial – Pas de Calais – France (1).

NORMAN, George   Private 4987   First Connaught Rangers
     Killed in Action: (France) 17 February 1916. Age 29.
     Supplementary Notes: Born: Galway.

NORMAN, George   Able Seaman (deck hand) 3217/SD   Royal Navy Reserves
     Death: (Richmond Hospital, Dublin) 2 June 1915. Age 36.
     Supplementary Notes: Died having fallen from the Galway to Dublin train, near Kilcock. He was returning to his ship in Portsmouth having visited his wife and children in Galway. His name is also recorded as Ormonde. Born: Fairhill, Claddagh, Galway (Raven Terrace). Brother of James Norman, below.
     Buried: Fort Hill Cemetery – Galway – Ireland (near east boundary).

NORMAN, James   Able Seaman   Royal Navy Reserves
     Death: (Coast of Scotland) 11 July 1916.
     Supplementary Notes: Killed when his ship struck a mine. Born: Fairhill, Claddagh, Galway. Brother of George Norman, above.

NORMAN, William A.   Captain   Fifteenth Hussars
     Died of Wounds: (London) 29 May 1916. Age 31.
     Supplementary Notes: Son of the tenth earl of Westmeath, of Pallas, Tynage.

NUGENT, Thomas   Private 8598   Second Connaught Rangers
Killed in Action: (France) 6 November 1914. Age 29 or 33.
Supplementary Notes: Enlisted: Ballinasloe. Awarded Mons Star. Son of John & Mary Nugent of Kilmalan, Aughrim, Ballinasloe.
Remembered: Ypres (Menin Gate) Memorial – Ieper – West-Vlaanderen – Belgium (42).

O'BRIEN, Dennis   Private 11108   Ninth Royal Irish Fusiliers
Killed in Action or Died of Wounds: (France) 16 August 1917.
Supplementary Notes: Enlisted: Cavan. Born: Galway.
Remembered: Tyne Cot Memorial Zonnebeke – West-Vlaanderen – Belgium (140 to 141).

O'BRIEN, J.   Sapper 365924   Royal Engineers
Death: (Home) 27 December 1919. Age 50.
Supplementary Notes: Husband of Elizabeth O'Brien of St Vincent's Avenue, Woodquay, Galway.
Buried: Tipperary (St Michael's) new cemetery – Co. Tipperary – Ireland (E. H. 109).

O'BRIEN, John   Private 18242   Second Leinster Regiment
Died of Wounds: (France) 28 April 1918.
Supplementary Notes: Born: Tuam.
Buried: Ebblinghem Military Cemetery – Nord – France (I. D. 20).

O'BRIEN, John   Private 43889   Machine Gun Corps (Infantry)
Killed in Action: (France) 20 November 1916.
Supplementary Notes: Formerly of the First Royal Munster Fusiliers. Born: Loughrea.
Remembered: Thiepval Memorial – Somme – France (5 C & 12 C).

O'BRIEN, Martin   Private 12474   First Northumberland Fusiliers
Killed in Action: (France) 7 May 1915.
Supplementary Notes: Born: Ross.
Remembered: Ypres (Menin Gate) Memorial – Ieper – West-Vlaanderen – Belgium (8 & 12).

O'BRIEN, Michael   Private 7106   Second Royal Munster Fusiliers
Killed in Action: 27 August 1914. Age 30.

Supplementary Notes: Son of John & Bridget O'Brien of 9 Corporation Cottages, Sand Mall, Limerick; husband of Mary Margaret O'Brien. Born: Galway.
Buried: Etreux British Cemetery – Aisne – France (1. 14).

O'BRIEN, Michael   Leading Deck Hand 11868/DA   Royal Naval Reserves
Death: 1 January 1917.
Supplementary Notes: He was killed in an accident on board his ship. Born: Inishmore, Aran Islands. Husband of Barbara O'Brien (*nee* Conneely) of Inisheer; father of Edmond, Mary and Michael O'Brien. He was involved in the Gaelic League before enlisting. His son Michael, only an infant when his father was killed, was later killed at Monte Cassino during the Second World War.
Buried: Cardiff (Cathays) Cemetery – United Kingdom (C. 990).

O'BRIEN, Patrick   Private (boy) 10990   Third Connaught Rangers
Death: (Tuam, Co. Galway) 19 March 1915. Age 15.
Supplementary Notes: Enlisted: Galway. Born: St Jarlath's, Tuam. The youngest known Galway soldier to die during the Great War.
Buried: Kinsale (Old Abbey) Graveyard – Cork – Ireland (special memorial).

O'BRIEN, Patrick   Private 15451   Tenth Royal Welsh Fusiliers
Killed in Action: (France) 3 March 1916.
Supplementary Notes: Born: Tuam.
Remembered: Ypres (Menin Gate) Memorial – Ieper – West-Vlaanderen – Belgium (22).

O'BRIEN, William   Private 8139   First East Lancashire Regiment
Killed in Action: (France) 3 November 1914.
Supplementary Notes: Enlisted: Ennis, Co. Clare. Born: Galway.
Remembered: Ploegsteert Memorial – West-Vlaanderen – Belgium (5 & 6).

O'CONNOR, Christopher   Private 4543   Second & Fourth Leinster Regiment
Killed in Action: (France) 30 November 1917.
Supplementary Notes: Enlisted: Ballinasloe. Formerly of the South Irish Horse 2567. Son of Mrs K. O'Connor of Brackermagh, Ballinasloe (Kilclooney).
Buried: Hargicourt British Cemetery – Aisne – France (I. H. 5).

O'CONNOR, Joe   Lieutenant   British Expeditionary Force
Death: 1914–1918.

Supplementary Notes: From Ballinasloe.

Remembered: Roll of Honour – Killed in Action – 1914–1918 – Ballinasloe – Ireland.

O'CONNOR, Joseph   Corporal 112157   First King's Liverpool Regiment

Killed in Action: (Loos, France) 25 September 1915. Age 35

Supplementary Notes: Enlisted: Swansea. Attached to the Royal Engineers. Formerly of the 187th Special Company RE Manchester Regiment 3/28110. Youngest son of Andrew O'Connor of Hazlewood, Tuam. He also served in the Boer War.

O'CONNOR, Michael   Private 5024   Eighth Royal Dublin Fusiliers

Killed in Action: (France) 18 May 1917. Age 32.

Supplementary Notes: Born: Galway.

O'CONNOR, Michael   Private 25024 Eighth & Ninth Royal Dublin Fusiliers

Died of Wounds: (France) 29 November 1917. Age 22.

Supplementary Notes: Enlisted: Galway. Son of Patrick & Margaret O'Connor; husband of Josephine O'Connor of St Helen Street, Galway.

Buried: Bucquoy Road Cemetery – Ficheux – Pas de Calais – France (11. J. 12).

O'CONNOR, Michael   Private   British Expeditionary Force

Death: (France or Flanders) 1914–1918. Age 21.

Supplementary Notes: Family believe he was in the Connaught Rangers. His brother, Patrick, also served in the Connaught Rangers. Born: Suckeen, Woodquay, Galway.

O'CONNOR, P.   Private 5696   Sixth Connaught Rangers

Death: 20 November 1917. Age 28.

Supplementary Notes: Son of John & Mary O'Connor of Cottage, Barnaderg.

Buried: Croisilles Railway Cemetery – Pas de Calais – France (I. C. 13).

O'CONNOR, Patrick   Leading Stoker 172086   HMS *Black Prince Royal Navy*

Killed in Action: (Jutland) 31 May 1916. Age 43.

Supplementary Notes: Born: Galway.

Remembered: Plymouth Naval Memorial – Devon – United Kindom (15).

O'CONNOR, Patrick   Private 9979   Second Leinster Regiment

Killed in Action: (France) 9 July 1915.

Supplementary Notes: Enlisted: Longford. Born: St John's Parish, Galway.

Buried: Potijze Burial Ground Cemetery – West-Vlaanderen – Belgium (Y. 24).

O'DONALD, Peter   Gunner 11378   Royal Field Artillery
Died of Wounds: (France) 20 July 1916.
Supplementary Notes: Born: Tuam.
Buried: Corbie Communal Cemetery Extension – Somme – France (1. F. G17).

O'DONNELL, Colman   Seaman 5054A   HMS *Laurentic* Royal Navy Reserves
Death: 25 January 1917. Age 25.
Supplementary Notes: Ship was struck by a mine and sank off Lough Swilly on the northern coast of Donegal. Son of Mr P. O'Donnell of Long Walk, Galway.
Buried: Upper Fahan Church of Ireland Churchyard – Co. Donegal – Ireland.

O'DONNELL, Martin   Private 14118   Fourteenth Durham Light Infantry
Died of Wounds: (France) 26 February 1916.
Supplementary Notes: Born: Roundstone, Connemara.
Remembered: Ypres (Menin Gate) Memorial – Ieper – West-Vlaanderen – Belgium (36 & 38).

O'DONNELL, Martin   Seaman 2749A HMS *Cressy* Royal Navy Reserves
Killed in Action: (North Sea) 22 September 1914. Age 46.
Supplementary Notes: Killed during action with an enemy submarine. Son of Martin & Anne O'Donnell of the Aran Islands; husband of Mary O'Donnell of Kilronan, Aran Islands.
Remembered: Portsmouth Naval Memorial – Hampshire – United Kingdom (6).

O'DONNELL, Michael   Private 4628   Sixth Connaught Rangers
Killed in Action: (France) 20 November 1917. Age 21 or 23.
Supplementary Notes: Enlisted: Galway. Son of Thomas & Mary O'Donnell (*nee* Conneely) of Tiernee, Lettermore, Connemara. He was home on leave shortly before being killed.
Buried: Croisilles Railway Cemetery – Pas de Calais – France (I. D. 21).

O'DONNELL, Patrick Joseph   Private 26901   Tenth Royal Dublin Fusiliers
Died of Wounds: (France) 13 February 1917.
Supplementary Notes: Born: Gort.
Remembered: Portsmouth Naval Memorial – Hampshire – United Kingdom (6).

O'DONNELL, Thomas Private 315 29th Australian Infantry Australian Imperial Force
Death: 4 December 1916. Age 23.
Supplementary Notes: Son of Patrick & Catherine O'Donnell of 212 High Street, Shepparton, Victoria. Born: Galway.
Remembered: Villers-Bretonneux Memorial – Somme – France.

O'DONOGHUE, James Gunner 13515 Royal Field Artillery
Killed in Action: (France) 26 October 1917.
Supplementary Notes: Enlisted: Manchester. Born: Galway.

O'DOWD, John Private 4718 Sixth Connaught Rangers
Died of Wounds: 26 April 1918. Age 29.
Supplementary Notes: Enlisted: Galway. Son of Michael & Mary O'Dowd of Maum, Errislannan, Clifden.
Buried: Le Cateau Military Cemetery – Nord – France (I. B. 75).

O'FARRELL, Maurice Driver T/26133 Army Service Corps
Killed in Action: (France) 27 April 1915. Age 28.
Supplementary Notes: Attached to the Sixty-second Royal Field Artillery. Son of Dr H. O'Farrell of Portumna (Salthill).
Remembered: Ypres (Menin Gate) Memorial – Ieper – West-Vlaanderen – Belgium (8 & 9).

O'FLAHERTY, Arthur Private 6261 First Irish Guards
Killed in Action: (Belgium) 26 March 1915. Age 20.
Supplementary Notes: Enlisted: Galway. Son of Michael & Anne O'Flaherty of 37 St Bridget's Terrace, Galway. The Commonwealth War Graves Commission record the date of death as 28 March 1916. However, the family have a letter of condolence written by Fr Browne (Irish Guards chaplain) dated 27 March 1915. The letter states that he was killed on 26 March 1915. It was included in *Galway and the Great War*, p. 175.
Buried: Potijze Burial Ground Cemetery – Ieper – West-Vlaanderen – Belgium (E. 14).

O'FLAHERTY, Fr Coleman Chaplain Twenty-Eighth Infantry US army
Killed on Duty: (France) 1917.
Supplementary Notes: Awarded Distinguished Service Cross. Son of Patrick & Catherine O'Flaherty (*nee* Clancy) of Upper Dominick Street, Galway. Having been ordained he went to America and eventually ended up as a chaplain in the US army. He

was killed while attending to wounded soldiers on the battlefield. One of his brothers, Patrick, was killed during the Irish War of Independence fighting against crown forces.

O'GORMAN, John Francis   Fireman   SS *Aylevarroo*   Mercantile Marines
Presumed Drowned: 7 October 1917. Age 20.
Supplementary Notes: Son of Mary O'Gorman of Whitehall, Galway, and the late Thomas O'Gorman.
Remembered: Tower Hill Memorial – London – United Kingdom.

O'GRADY, Robert   Private 2340   South Irish Horse
Death: (Home) 12 December 1917.
Supplementary Notes: Born: Galway.
Buried: Birmingham (Lodge Hill) Cemetery (screen wall B10. 6. 475C).

O'HAIRE, Thomas   Fireman   SS *Era*   Mercantile Marines
Death: 1 May 1918. Age 23.
Supplementary Notes: Drowned as a result of an attack by an enemy submarine. Son of Thomas & Margaret O'Haire of Kilnadeema, Loughrea.
Remembered: Tower Hill Memorial – London – United Kingdom.

O'HARA, Michael   Private 6576   First Connaught Rangers
Death: (Mesopotamia) 2 May 1916.
Supplementary Notes: Enlisted: Manchester. Born: Galway.
Buried: Amara War Cemetery – Amara – Iraq (XX. C. 2).

O'HARE, Patrick   Private 1591   Second Royal Warwickshire Regiment
Killed in Action: (France) 19 December 1914. Age 24
Supplementary Notes: Born: Clifden.

OLIVER, John   Seaman 2269A   HMS *Laurentic*   Royal Navy Reserves
Death: 25 January 1917. Age 27.
Supplementary Notes: Ship was struck by a mine and sank off Lough Swilly on the northern coast of Donegal. Son of Patrick & Mary Oliver of Rope Walk, Claddagh, Galway.
Remembered: Portsmouth Naval Memorial – Hampshire – United Kingdom (27).

OLIVER, John   Private 63911   Royal Field Artillery
Killed in Action: November 1916. Age 21.
Supplementary Notes: Born: Galway.

O'MALLEY, Coman Geoffrey   Lance Corporal 30165   First Royal Dublin Fusiliers
Killed in Action: (Dadizeele) 14 October 1918. Age 19.
Supplementary Notes: Son of Dr D.T. & Mrs O'Malley of Glenamaddy. One of six brothers who served in the war.
Buried: Ledeghem Military Cemetery – Ledegem – West-Vlaanderen – Belgium (B. 4).

O'MALLEY, M.   Private 18021   Eighth Royal Munster Fusiliers
Death: (France) 4 September 1916. Age 39.
Supplementary Notes: Son of Catherine O'Malley (*nee* Egan) and the late Patrick O'Malley; husband of Bridget O'Malley of Mainguard Street, Galway.
Buried: Dive Copse British Cemetery – Sailly-Le-Sec – Somme – France (I. B. 22).

O'MALLEY, Martin   Rifleman 4858   Eighteenth London Irish Rifles
Killed in Action: (France) 15 September 1916.
Supplementary Notes: Enlisted: London. Formerly of the Twenty-sixth London Regiment 253. Born: Galway.
Remembered: Thiepval Memorial – Somme – France (13 C).

O'MALLEY, Matthew   Private 18024   Eighth Royal Munster Fusiliers
Died of Wounds: (France) 4 September 1916.
Supplementary Notes: Born: St Nicholas' Parish, Galway.

O'MALLEY, Patrick   Lance Sergeant 9174   First Irish Guards
Died of Wounds: (Cambrai, France) 5 December 1917. Age 21 or 22.
Supplementary Notes: Son of Martin & Bridget O'Malley of River Street, Ballinasloe.
Remembered: Cambrai Memorial – Lou Verval – Nord – France (2 & 3).

O'MALLEY, Thomas   Private 21121   First Royal Dublin Fusiliers
Killed in Action: (France) 3 April 1918.
Supplementary Notes: Born: Bohermore, Galway.
Remembered: Pozieres Memorial – Somme – France (79 & 80).

O'MALLEY, Vincent   Private 5/3913   Fifth Connaught Rangers
Killed in Action: (Gallipoli) 21 August 1915. Age 21.
Supplementary Notes: Enlisted: Galway. Born: Ross (Maam, Connemara). The family was only informed of his death after the US ambassador to Turkey made inquiries on behalf of the family.

Remembered: Helles Memorial – Turkey (181 to 183).

O'MALLEY, William (Willie)   Second Lieutenant   Royal Field Artillery
Killed in Action: (France) 9 April 1917.
Supplementary Notes: Son of William O'Malley, MP for Connemara. Before enlisting he wrote: 'When I see the young men of my own station pushing to join the Colours to defeat the War Lords, or perhaps defend their country, I feel that to hide behind their courage and their guns would be an overwhelming shame.'
Buried: Bedford House Cemetery – West-Vlaanderen – Belgium (Enclosure No. 4. I. H. 13).

O'NEILL, Christy   Private 8343   First Connaught Rangers
Died of Wounds: (France) 28 September 1914.
Supplementary Notes: Enlisted: Tuam. Born: Tuam.
Buried: Mazargues War Cemetery – Marseilles – France (III. A. 39).

O'NEILL, Lawrence Justin F.   Sergeant 279872   Canadian Railway Troops
Died of Pneumonia: (England) 30 April 1917. Age 54.
Supplementary Notes: Son of Lany & Mary O'Neill; husband of Mary Ann O'Neill of 465, 12th Street, N.W., Calgary, Alberta. Born: Ballinasloe.
Buried: Liverpool (Kirkdale) Cemetery – Lancashire – United Kingdom (II. R.C. 224).

O'RORKE, Michael   Private 24232   Thirteenth King's Liverpool Regiment
Died of Wounds: (France) 17 August 1918. Age 23.
Supplementary Notes: Awarded Military Medal. Born: Galway.
Buried: Rosieres Communal Cemetery Extension – Somme – France (I. E. 2).

O'SHAUGHNESSY, Patrick   Private 36882   Third Otago Regiment NZEF
Killed in Action: (Belgium) 16 August 1917.
Supplementary Notes: Son of Mr J. O'Shaughnessy of Ballylin East, Craughwell.
Buried: Motor Car Corner Cemetery – Comines-Warneton – Hainaut – Belgium (B. 23).

O'SULLIVAN, William Henry   Lance Corporal 29889   Second Royal Dublin Fusiliers.
Killed in Action: (France) 20 November 1917. Age 22.
Supplementary Notes: Enlisted: Glasgow, Scotland. Son Michael & Hannah O'Sullivan of Snave House, Bantry. Born: Ballinasloe.
Remembered: Arras Memorial – Pas de Calais – France (9).

O'TOOLE, Joseph   Private 11643   Second Irish Guards
Killed in Action: (France) 13 September 1917. Age 19.
Supplementary Notes: Son of Mr & Mrs Festus O'Toole of Streamstown, Clifden.
Remembered: Tyne Cot Memorial Zonnebeke – West-Vlaanderen – Belgium (10 to 11).

OWENS, Michael   Private 3028   Second Connaught Rangers
Killed in Action: (France) 21 or 30 October 1914. Age 30.
Supplementary Notes: Enlisted: Oranmore. Born: Oranmore.
Remembered: Ypres (Menin Gate) Memorial – Ieper – West-Vlaanderen – Belgium (42).

ORMONDE, F.   Lance Corporal 1035   Fifth Connaught Rangers
Death: 7 December 1915. Age 40.
Supplementary Notes: Son of Mr & Mrs Richard Ormonde of Galway; husband of Mary Josephine Ormonde of Barrack Street, Mullingar.
Remembered: Doiran Memorial – Greece.

PAISLEY, John   Corporal   British Expeditionary Force
Died of Wounds: (London) June 1918.
Supplementary Notes: Born: Ballinasloe.
Buried: Creagh new cemetery – Ballinasloe – Ireland.

PATTON, Timothy   Private   First Connaught Rangers
Killed in Action: (France) 18 September 1916.
Supplementary Notes: Born: Galway.

PATTON, Timothy   Private 7125   Second Royal Irish Rifles
Killed in Action: (France) 26 October 1914.
Supplementary Notes: Born: Dunmore.
Remembered: Le Touret Memorial – Pas de Calais – France (42 & 43).

PAYNE, George Frederick   Private 8130   Second Border Regiment
Killed in Action: (France) 28 November 1914. Age 28.
Supplementary Notes: Enlisted: Woodbridge, Suffolk. Born: Galway.
Remembered: Ploegsteert Memorial – West-Vlaanderen – Belgium (6).

PEARSON, Henry   Private 726049   109th Canadian Infantry
Death: (France or Flanders) 1914–1918.

Supplementary Notes: Enlisted: Canada. Born: Galway.

PERSSE, Cecil de Burge   Second Lieutenant   Seventh Dragoon Guards
Died of Wounds: (Netley Hospital, France) 19 July 1915. Age 40.
Supplementary Notes: Wounded at Featubert on 18 May 1915. Son of the late Henry
S. Persse of Glenarde, Galway.
Remembered: Great War monument – St Nicholas' Collegiate Church – Galway –
Ireland.

PERSSE, Dudly Eyre   Lieutenant   Second Royal Dublin Fusiliers
Died of Wounds: (France) 1 February 1915. Age 22.
Supplementary Notes: Son of Alfred Persse of Ross Park. His grandfather was Dudly
Persse (Persse's Distillery) of Roxborough House.
Buried: Bailleul Communal Cemetery – Nord – France (F. 6).

PERSSE, Randolph   Lieutenant   Second King's Royal Rifles
Killed in Action: (France) 1 January 1915.
Supplementary Notes: Only son of Algernon Persse of Cregclare, Ardrahan.
Remembered: Le Touret Memorial – Pas de Calais – France (44).

PETERS, Arthur Kersaw   Sapper 59299   Royal Engineers
Death: 18 February 1916. Age 33.
Supplementary Notes: He was former building trades instructor in the Galway tech-
nical school. A letter from him was included in *Galway and the Great War*, p. 227, 228.
Buried: Boulogne Eastern Cemetery – Pas de Calais – France (VIII. D. 56).

PHILLIPS, Charles   Quarter Master Sergeant   Connaught Rangers
Killed in Action: (France) 15 August 1916. Age 35.
Supplementary Notes: Born: Galway.

PHILLIPS, Henry J.   Private D/7934   Second Inniskilling Dragoon Guards
Death: (Milbank Hospital, London) 28 February 1917. Age 30.
Supplementary Notes: Enlisted: Dublin. Son of Henry J. Phillips of 10 Arbour Terrace,
Arbour Hill, Dublin. Born: Galway.
Buried: Brompton Cemetery – London – United Kingdom (H. 174141).

PHILLIPS, Joseph   Company Sergeant Major 6669   Sixth Connaught Rangers
Killed in Action: (France) 21 March 1918. Age 36.

Supplementary Notes: Enlisted: Renmore barracks 1899. Served in the Boer War and India. He married in India in 1907 and had five children: Myra, Phyllis, Bernie, Leo, Alby. Born: Rahoon.

Buried: St Emilie Valley Cemetery – Villers-Faucon – Somme – France (I. F. 1).

PICKETT, James   Private 16849   Eighth Royal Dublin Fusiliers
Death: 29 April 1916. Age 30.
Supplementary Notes: Son of James & Catherine Pickett of Duras, Kinvara.
Remembered: Loos Memorial – Pas de Calais – France (127 to 129).

PITTMAN, William   Private 3453   Seventh Leinster Regiment
Death: 1 September 1916. Age 17.
Supplementary Notes: Son of William & Mary Ellen Pittman of Parochial Hall, Wood Quay, Galway.
Remembered: Thiepval Memorial – Somme – France (16 C).

POLAND, Patrick   Private 10876   Sixth Connaught Rangers
Killed in Action: (France) 21 March 1918. Age 21.
Supplementary Notes: Enlisted: Galway. Son of John & Margaret Poland of Kylemore, Lawrencetown, Ballinasloe.
Remembered: Pozieres Memorial – Somme – France (77).

POLLINGTON, Charles J.   Able Seaman 116563   HMS *Indus*   Royal Navy
Death: 30 May 1918. Age 52.
Supplementary Notes: Son of Henry & Louisa Pollington; husband of Margaret Pollington of 64 Fairhill, Galway.
Buried: Ford Park Cemetery (Plymouth Old Cemetery & Pennycomequick) – Devon – United Kingdom (L. 10. 17).

POWER, Patrick   Private 9892   First Connaught Rangers
Killed in Action: (France) 1 June 1915.
Supplementary Notes: Youngest son of Sergeant Major Power (Army Service Corps) of Castle barracks and St Augustine Street, Galway.

POWER, Thomas   Private 2464   Sixth South Lancashire Regiment
Killed in Action: (Mesopotamia) 5 April 1915.
Supplementary Notes: Born: Williamstown.

POWER, Thomas   Private 6359   Second Royal Irish Regiment
Died of Wounds: (France) 27 May 1915. Age 22

Supplementary Notes: Born: Bohermore, Galway.

Buried: Hazebrouck Communal Cemetery – Nord – France (II. B. 28).

PURCELL, John Joseph   Lance Sergeant 10588   Sixth Connaught Rangers
   Killed in Action: (France) 20 November 1917.
   Supplementary Notes: Enlisted: Paisley, Renfrew. Born: Castlegar, Galway.

PURCELL, Michael   Gunner 91165   Sixty-third Royal Field Artillery
   Death: (Mesopotamia) 5 September 1916. Age 36.
   Supplementary Notes: Son of John & Bridget Clancy Purcell. Born: Kinvara.
   Buried: Baghdad (North Gate) War Cemetery – Iraq (XXI. F. 27).

QUEENAN, Patrick   Private 8801   First Connaught Rangers
   Killed in Action: (France) 23 November 1914.
   Supplementary Notes: Enlisted: Warrington. Born: Woodlawn.
   Remembered: Le Touret Memorial – Pas de Calais – France (43)

QUIGLEY, Alfred   Private 9328   First Connaught Rangers
   Killed in Action: (France) 8 November 1914.
   Supplementary Notes: Enlisted: Boyle, Co. Roscommon. Born: Galway.
   Buried: Rue-du-Bacquerot No. 1 Military Cemetery – Laventie – Pas de Calais – France
   (I. A. 14).

QUINN, John   Private 122   Fifth Connaught Rangers
   Killed in Action: (Gallipoli) 21 August 1915.
   Supplementary Notes: Enlisted: Galway. Son of Patrick & Bridget Quinn of Middle
   Street, Galway.
   Remembered: Helles Memorial – Turkey (181 to 183).

QUINN, John   Private 3917   First Connaught Rangers
   Killed in Action: (France) 19 February 1916. Age 38
   Supplementary Notes: Born: Galway.

QUINN, John Jama Patrick   Lieutenant Colonel   117th Mahratta
   Death: 25 September 1915. Age 47.
   Supplementary Notes: Son of Michael Quinn; husband of Florence Quinn (*nee*
   Esmond–White) of Cloonmore, Tuam. Brother of William Quinn, p. 204.
   Remembered: Kirkee 1914–1918 Memorial – India (G).

QUINN, Patrick   Private 2518   First York & Lancaster Regiment
Killed in Action: (France) 13 August 1915. Age 25
Supplementary Notes: Enlisted: Wath-on-Dearne. Son of Thomas Quinn of Ballina-mona, Ballyglunin.
Buried: Talana Farm Cemetery – Ieper – West-Vlaanderen – Belgium (IV. A. 15).

QUINN, Patrick   Private 24/506   Twenty-forth Northumberland Fusiliers
Died of Wounds: 9 July 1916. Age 28 or 35.
Supplementary Notes: Son of Martin & Bridget Quinn of Aran, Kilcolgan, Oranmore (Ballinderran).
Buried: St Sever Cemetery – Rouen – Seine-Maritime – France (A. 24. 27).

QUINN, Thomas   Private 14   Fifth Connaught Rangers
Died of Wounds: (Gallipoli) 30 August 1915. Age 34 or 35.
Supplementary Notes: Enlisted: Galway. Son of John & Mary Quinn; husband of Mary Ellen Quinn of New Road, Galway (Rahoon).
Remembered: Helles Memorial – Turkey (181 to 183).

QUINN, William   32513   First Connaught Rangers
Death: 31 December 1919.
Supplementary Notes: Son of Mr & Mrs Michael Quinn of Cloonmore, Tuam. Brother of John Jama Quinn, above.
Remembered: Kirkee 1914–1918 Memorial – India (10).

QUOYLE, Thomas Nicholas   Private 3828   Fifth Connaught Rangers
Killed in Action: (Gallipoli) 21 August 1915. Age 24.
Supplementary Notes: Enlisted: Ballinasloe. Former teacher. His father was a teacher in the Claddagh national school, while his brother, John, taught at the Galway workhouse, before he joined the Connaught Rangers. Born: Galway.
Remembered: Helles Memorial – Turkey (181 to 183).

RABBIT, James   Private 6988   First Connaught Rangers
Killed in Action: (Mesopotamia) 21 January 1916. Age 38.
Supplementary Notes: Enlisted: Warrington. Born: Mountbellew.
Remembered: Basra Memorial – Iraq (40 & 64).

RAE, Thomas   Private 41228   Sixteenth Royal Scots
Killed in Action: (France) 22 October 1917. Age 38.

Supplementary Notes: Born: Ballingall.

Remembered: Tyne Cot Memorial Zonnebeke – West-Vlaanderen – Belgium (10 to 14 & 162).

RAFFERTY, Michael   Greaser   SS *Arabic*   Mercantile Marines

Death: 19 August 1915. Age 58.

Supplementary Notes: Drowned as a result of an attack by an enemy submarine. Husband of Maria Rafferty (*nee* Dougherty) of 28 Burns Street, Bootle, Lancs. Born: Galway.

Remembered: Tower Hill Memorial – London – United Kingdom.

RAFFERTY, Michael   Private 29584   Second & Sixth Royal Warwickshire regiments

Died of Wounds: (Belgium) 12 April 1918.

Supplementary Notes: Enlisted: St Helens, Lancashire. Formerly of the South Lancashire regiment 40517. Born: Ballinasloe.

Remembered: Ploegsteert Memorial – Comines-Warneton – Hainaut – Belgium (2 & 3).

RAFTERY, John   Private   British Expeditionary Force

Death: 1914–1918.

Supplementary Notes: From Ballinasloe.

Remembered: Roll of Honour – Killed in Action – 1914–1918 – Ballinasloe – Ireland.

RAFTERY, Peter   Private 25976   Tenth Royal Dublin Fusiliers

Killed in Action: (Somme, France) 13 November 1916.

Supplementary Notes: Enlisted: Boyle, Co. Roscommon. Born: Claddagh, Galway.

Remembered: Thiepval Memorial – Somme – France (16 C).

REA, Dennis   Acting Sergeant 41599   Royal Field Artillery

Death: (Salonika) 26 November 1916.

Supplementary Notes: Born: Loughrea.

Buried: Karasouli Military Cemetery – Greece (D. 883).

REGAN, Robert   Lance Corporal 43099   Eighth Royal Inniskilling Fusiliers

Killed in Action: (France) 28 May 1917. Age 17.

Supplementary Notes: Enlisted: Ballinasloe. Formerly of the Connaught Rangers 5231. Son of Thomas & Ellen Regan of Haymarket Street, Ballinasloe (Killclooney).

Buried: Loker Churchyard – Heuvelland – West-Vlaanderen – Belgium (I. C. 13).

REGAN, Thomas   Private 1502   Fifth Royal Irish Lancers
Killed in Action: (France) 2 May 1915. Age 25.
Supplementary Notes: Born: Kilclooney, Ballinasloe.
Remembered: Ypres (Menin Gate) Memorial – Ieper – West-Vlaanderen – Belgium (5).

REILLY, Alfred   Rifleman 8393   Second Royal Irish Rifles
Killed in Action: (France) 27 October 1914.
Supplementary Notes: Born: Eyrecourt.
Remembered: Le Touret Memorial – Pas de Calais – France (42 & 43).

REILLY, James   Private 3775   Second Connaught Rangers
Killed in Action: (France) 7 November 1914. Age 33.
Supplementary Notes: Enlisted: Galway. Awarded Mons Star. Born: Rahoon (Tuam).
Remembered: Ypres (Menin Gate) Memorial – Ieper – West-Vlaanderen – Belgium (42).

REILLY, James   Private 41131   Connaught Rangers
Killed in Action: (France) 18 August 1916. Age 36.
Supplementary Notes: Born: Galway.

REILLY, Michael   Private 16191   Second Connaught Rangers
Killed in Action: (France) 29 September 1914. Age 30.
Supplementary Notes: Awarded 1914 Star. Born: Galway.

REILLY, Patrick   Private 31129   Second Connaught Rangers
Killed in Action: (France) 1 November 1914. Age 27.
Supplementary Notes: Awarded 1914 Star. Born: Galway.

REILLY, Thomas   Corporal 4204   Sixth Connaught Rangers
Killed in Action: (France) 7 March 1917. Age 22.
Supplementary Notes: Enlisted: Ballinasloe. Son of Thomas Reilly of Haymarket Street, Ballinasloe (Kilclooney).
Buried: Kemmel Chateau Military Cemetery – Heuvelland – West-Vlaanderen – Belgium (M. 72).

RIDGE, Patrick   Deck Hand 22485DA   HMS *Vivid*   Royal Navy Reserves
Death: 28 October 1918. Age 20.
Supplementary Notes: Son of Colman & Mary Ridge of Carna, Connemara.

Buried: Ford Park Cemetery (Plymouth Old Cemetery & Pennycomequick) – Devon – United Kingdom (L. 21. 4).

RIELLY, Patrick   Sapper 144978   Royal Engineers
Killed in Action: (France) 27 January 1916.
Supplementary Notes: Formerly of the Highland Light Infantry. Born: Kilkerran.
Buried: Noeux-Les-Mines Communal Cemetery – Pas de Calais – France (I. G. 7).

RILEY, James   Private 26534   Tenth Sherwood Foresters
Killed in Action: (France) 23 April 1917.
Supplementary Notes: Enlisted: Nottingham. Born: Ballinasloe.
Remembered: Arras Memorial – Pas de Calais – France (7).

RILEY, John   Private 5052   First Connaught Rangers
Death: (Mesopotamia) 2 October 1916.
Supplementary Notes: Enlisted: Melton Mowbray. Born: Ballymoe.
Buried: Basra War Cemetery – Iraq (V. R. 13).

RILEY, William   Acting Corporal 8721   Second Royal Inniskilling Fusiliers
Killed in Action: (France) 16 May 1915.
Supplementary Notes: Born: Ballinahinch, Connemara.
Remembered: Le Touret Memorial – Pas de Calais – France (16 & 17).

ROACH, Michael   Private 11173   Eighth Northumberland Fusiliers
Died of Wounds: (France) 20 August 1917. Age 26 or 27.
Supplementary Notes: Son of Thomas & Celia Roach of Fahey, Clifden.
Buried: Brandhoek New Military Cemetery No. 3 – Ieper – West-Vlaanderen – Belgium (H. G. 19).

ROBERTS, William James   Private 2271   Fourth City of London, Royal Fusiliers
Killed in Action: (France) 26 April 1915.
Supplementary Notes: Enlisted: Shaftesbury. Born: Galway.

ROCHE, Mark   Private 16397   Tenth Yorkshire Light Infantry
Died of Wounds: (France) 4 July 1916.
Supplementary Notes: Born: Tuam.
Buried: Heilly Station Cemetery – Mericourt-L'Abbe – Somme – France (I. A. 20).

ROCHE, Thomas   Private   First Connaught Rangers
Killed in Action: (France) 1917. Age 32.

Supplementary Notes: Born: Galway.

ROGERSON, Patrick   Private 3218   Seventh Leinster Regiment
Death: (Ypres, Belgium) 2 August 1917.
Supplementary Notes: Son of Pat & Bridget Rogerson of Newbridge, Ballinasloe.
Remembered: Ypres (Menin Gate) Memorial – Ieper – West-Vlaanderen – Belgium
(44).

ROLAND, David   Private 3903   Second Connaught Rangers
Killed in Action: (France) 21 October 1914.
Supplementary Notes: Enlisted: Galway. Born: Oughterard.
Remembered: Ypres (Menin Gate) Memorial – Ieper – West-Vlaanderen – Belgium (42).

ROLAND, Frederick   Lance Corporal 2/7725   Second Irish Guards
Killed in Action: (France) 14 January 1916. Age 29.
Supplementary Notes: Born: Ballyshea.

ROLAND, Michael   Private 5/4102   First Connaught Rangers (Depot)
Death: (Galway) 9 April 1915.
Supplementary Notes: Enlisted: Galway. Born: Tuam.
Buried: St Mary's – (new cemetery) – Bohermore – Galway – Ireland.

ROLAND, John   Private 2189   First Irish Guards
Killed in Action: (France) 6 November 1914. Age 28 or 30.
Supplementary Notes: Son of Mrs M. Roland of Camp Street, Oughterard.
Buried: Poperinge Old Military Cemetery – Poperinge – West-Vlaanderen – Belgium
(I. L. 29).

RUANE, James   Private 29842   Royal Inniskilling Fusiliers
Death: 16 August 1917. Age 20.
Supplementary Notes: From Ballinasloe.
Remembered: Tyne Cot Memorial Zonnebeke – West-Vlaanderen – Belgium (70 to
72) & Roll of Honour – Killed in Action – 1914–1918 – Ballinasloe – Ireland.

RUFFLEY, John   Private 7910   First Irish Guards
Killed in Action: (France) 15 September 1916.
Supplementary Notes: Born: Bohermore, Galway.
Buried: Guillemont Road Cemetery – Guillemont – Somme – France (I. B. 12).

RUFFLEY, John　　　　　　　　Private 11419　　　　　　　Royal Dublin Fusiliers
Died of Wounds: (France) Age 32.
Supplementary Notes: Born: Galway.

RUSHE, John　　　　　　　　Private 18015　　　　　　Ninth Sherwood Foresters
Killed in Action: (Gallipoli) 10 August 1915.
Supplementary Notes: Born: Glenamaddy.
Remembered: Helles Memorial – Turkey (150 to 152).

RYAN, James　　　　Private 292074　　　　First & Seventh Northumberland Fusiliers
Death: 17 April 1917. Age 34.
Supplementary Notes: Brother of Marcus J. Ryan of Castle Street, Dunmore. Born:
Galway.
Remembered: Arras Memorial – Pas de Calais – France (2–3).

RYAN, James　　　　　　　　Officer　　　　　　　　　Royal Engineers
Killed in Action: 6 May 1917. Age 33.
Supplementary Notes: Son of the late William Ryan of Galway.
Remembered: Great War monument – St Nicholas' Collegiate Church – Galway
– Ireland.

RYAN, James　　　　　　　Rifleman 11366　　　　Third King's Royal Rifle Corps
Died of Wounds: (France) 17 May 1915.
Supplementary Notes: Born: Galway.

RYAN, James Joseph　　　　Able Seaman Z/1488　　　　　Royal Navy Reserve
Death: (Belgium) 26 October 1917. Age 26.
Supplementary Notes: Hood Division. Son of Martin & Ellen Ryan of Cloonkeen,
Mountbellew.
Buried: Dozinghem Military Cemetery – Poperinge – West-Vlaanderen – Belgium
(X. C. 17).

RYAN, John　　　　　　　　Private 3216　　　　　　　First Irish Guards
Killed in Action: (France) 1 September 1914.
Supplementary Notes: Born: Tuam.
Remembered: La Ferte-Sous-Jouarre Memorial – Seine-et-Marne – France.

RYAN, John　　　　　　　　Private 4239　　　　　　First Connaught Rangers
Killed in Action: (Mesopotamia) 17 January 1917. Age 24.

Supplementary Notes: Enlisted: Ballinasloe. Born: Kilrickle (Loughrea).
Buried: Amara War Cemetery – Amara – Iraq (XXVII. F. 5).

RYAN, John   Gunner 53237   Royal Garrison Artillery
    Killed in Action: (France) 14 August 1915. Age 27.
    Supplementary Notes: Born: Galway.
    Buried: Talana Farm Cemetery – Ieper – West-Vlaanderen – Belgium (IV. A. 20).

RYAN, Fr Michael   Chaplain   Royal Army Chaplain's Department
    Death: 1 November 1916. Age 59.
    Supplementary Notes: Son of Patrick & Sabina Ryan of Loughrea.
    Remembered: Kirkee 1914–1918 Memorial – India (11).

RYAN, William George   Corporal 18093   Sixteenth Royal Army Medical Corps
    Killed in Action: (Hooge) 9 August 1915. Age 30.
    Supplementary Notes: Son of William & Phoebe Ryan of Newcastle, Galway.
    Buried: Ramparts Cemetery, Lille Gate – Ieper – West-Vlaanderen – Belgium (H. 7).

SATCHWELL, Ralph William   Second Lieutenant   76th (Siege) Royal Garrison Artillery
    Death: (France) 31 January 1917. Age 21.
    Supplementary Notes: Son of Hubert & Anna Satchwell of Mount Mary, Creggs.
    Buried: Ovillers Military Cemetery – Somme – France (I. A. 27).

SAVAGE, George   Private   Royal Dublin Fusiliers
    Death: 1914–1918.
    Supplementary Notes: From Ballinasloe.
    Remembered: Roll of Honour – Killed in Action – 1914–1918 – Ballinasloe and St John's Church Roll of Honour – Ballinasloe – Ireland.

SCAFFE, John   Private 21119   Connaught Rangers
    Died of Wounds: (France) 19 February 1915. Age 39.
    Supplementary Notes: Born: Galway.

SCHOFIELD, John   Leading Seaman 5781A   SS *Frimaire*   Royal Navy Reserve
    Killed in Action: 15 March 1917. Age 20.
    Supplementary Notes: Killed during action with an enemy submarine near Belle Isle. Son of Colman Schofield of Spanish Parade, Galway.
    Remembered: Portsmouth Naval Memorial – Hampshire – United Kingdom (27).

SCULLY, Thomas   Private 20753   Eighth Royal Inniskilling Fusiliers
Died of Wounds: (France) 29 April 1916.
Supplementary Notes: Born: Loughrea.
Remembered: Loos Memorial – Pas de Calais – France (60).

SHAUGHNESSY, George   Gunner 44176   Royal Field Artillery
Killed in Action: (Egypt) 10 September 1916.
Supplementary Notes: (Royal Horse Artillery). Enlisted: Glasgow. Born: Galway.
Buried: Struma Military Cemetery – Greece (V. H. 13).

SHAUGHNESSY, John   Private 242   Fifth Connaught Rangers
Killed in Action: (Gallipoli) 28 August 1915.
Supplementary Notes: Enlisted: Merthyr, Glam. Born: Galway.
Remembered: Helles Memorial – Turkey (181 to 183).

SHAUGHNESSY, Michael   Lance Corporal 10823   First Royal Irish Fusiliers
Killed in Action: (France) 12 October 1914. Age 27.
Supplementary Notes: Enlisted: Ballinasloe. Born: Ballinasloe.
Remembered: Thiepval Memorial – Somme – France (15 A).

SHAUGHNESSY, Patrick   Private 7303   Second Leinster Regiment
Killed in Action: (France) 20 October 1914. Age 32.
Supplementary Notes: Born: Tuam.

SHAUGHNESSY, Patrick   Private 1323   Second Leinster Regiment
Death: 20 October 1914. Age 29.

Supplementary Notes: Son of Patrick & Bridget Shaughnessy of Tierboy Road, Tuam.
Remembered: Ploegsteert Memorial – Comines-Warneton – Hainaut – Belgium (10).

SHAUGHNESSY, Thomas   Private 7740   First Connaught Rangers
Death: (India) 9 October 1918.
Supplementary Notes: Enlisted: Sligo. Born: Ballymoe.
Remembered: Kirkee 1914–1918 Memorial – India (E).

SHAUGHNESSY, William   Private 6722   Sixth Connaught Rangers
Killed in Action: (France) 4 June 1917. Age 38.
Supplementary Notes: Enlisted: Northwich. Son of the late Darby & Annie Shaughnessy of Ardskeabeg, Ballyglunin.

Buried: La Laiterie Military Cemetery – Heuvelland – West-Vlaanderen – Belgium (IX. B. 4).

SHAUGHNESSY, William   Private T/439889   Royal Army Service Corps
Died of Wounds: 18 January 1920. Age 40.
Supplementary Notes: Son of John Shaughnessy of Moyne, Ballyglunin; husband of Ellen Shaughnessy of New Road, Anderton, Northwich.
Buried: Barnton Cemetery – Cheshire – United Kingdom (N.C. 93).

SHERIDAN, A.   Gunner 33794   Thirteenth Royal Field Artillery
Killed in Accident: (Mesopotamia) 14 October 1920. Age 38.
Supplementary Notes: Son of Hugh & Nora Sheridan of Prospect Hill, Galway.
Buried: Basra War Cemetery – Iraq (IV. Q. 18).

SHIELDS, Thomas   Private 3/7512   First Connaught Rangers
Killed in Action: (Mesopotamia) 6 April 1917.
Supplementary Notes: Enlisted: Wallasey. Born: Drimkary.
Buried: Baghdad (North Gate) War Cemetery – Iraq (V. D. 1).

SLATER, Daniel   Private 3303   Second Royal Irish Fusiliers
Killed in Action: (France) 15 March 1915.
Supplementary Notes: Enlisted: Cavan. Born: Galway.
Remembered: Ypres (Menin Gate) Memorial – Ieper – West-Vlaanderen – Belgium (42)

SMALL, John   Private 6994   Second Connaught Rangers
Killed in Action: (France) 8 November 1914. Age 32.
Supplementary Notes: Enlisted: Ballinasloe. Son of Patrick Joseph & Ann Small of Main Street, Ballinasloe; husband of Nora Small (*nee* Clinton) of 5 Phoenix Square, Rochdale (Kilclooney).
Remembered: Ypres (Menin Gate) Memorial – Ieper – West-Vlaanderen – Belgium (42) & Roll of Honour – Killed in Action – 1914–1918 – Ballinasloe – Ireland.

SMALL, Martin   Private 659642   Labour Corps
Died of Wounds: (Ballinasloe, Co. Galway) 3 February 1919.
Supplementary Notes: Formerly of the Fourth Connaught Rangers 4865. Born: Ballinasloe.
Buried: Creagh new cemetery – Ballinasloe – Ireland (D. 78).

Remembered: Roll of Honour – Killed in Action – 1914–1918 – Ballinasloe – Ireland.

SMITH, Dick   Officer   Third Seaforth Highlanders
    Died of Wounds: (Beaumont Hammell, France) September 1917.
    Supplementary Notes: Wounded while escorting prisoners back to allied lines. Son of R.J. Smith, superintendent of the agriculture station, Athenry.

SMYTH, John Edward   Private 26160   Eighth Royal Inniskilling Fusiliers
    Died of Wounds: (France) 1 May 1916. Age 24.
    Supplementary Notes: Son of Thomas & Brigid Smyth of Galway Road, Loughrea.
    Buried: Noeux-Les-Mines Communal Cemetery – Pas de Calais – France (I. M. 10).

SMYTH, Patrick   Private 10655   First Irish Guards
    Killed in Action: (France) 1 December 1917. Age 28.
    Supplementary Notes: Son of Patrick & Bridget Smyth of Muckanagh, Ballygar. Born: Galway.
    Remembered: Cambrai Memorial – Lou Verval – Nord – France (2 & 3).

SMYTH, Thomas   Private 2/7076   First Irish Guards
    Died of Wounds: (Loughrea) 10 August 1918. Age 20.
    Supplementary Notes: Born: Loughrea.
    Buried: St Brendan's Church of Ireland Churchyard – Loughrea – Co. Galway – Ireland (south-east section).

SOMERVILLE, Richard Newman   Lieutenant   Ninety-fourth Field Coy. Royal Engineers
    Death: (France) October 1915. Age 28.
    Supplementary Notes: Son of Mr R.N. & Mrs J.D. Somerville of Atbara, Osborne Park, Belfast. Born: Galway.
    Buried: St Vaast Post Military Cemetery – Richebourg-L'Avoue – Pas de Calais – France (II. A. 10).

SOMERVILLE, William   Lance Corporal 3929   Second Royal Irish Rifles
    Killed in Action: (France) 17 May 1916.
    Supplementary Notes: Born: Kilclooney, Ballinasloe.
    Buried: Ecoivres Military Cemetery – Mont-St Eloi – Pas de Calais – France (I. M. 17).

SPAIN, Henry   Private 427901   Thirteenth Canadian Infantry.
    Death: (France) 1 December 1916. Age 32.

Supplementary Notes: (Quebec Regiment) Enlisted: Canada. Son of Mr & Mrs Spain of Palmerston, Portumna. Four other brothers served, Joseph, Connaught Rangers; Michael and Patrick, Leinster Regiment; Christopher, Royal Field Artillery. His father also had four nephews, two grandsons, and a son-in-law serving.
Buried: Villers Station Cemetery – Alers-Au-Bois – Pas de Calais – France (II. C. 8).

STACIE, R.   Captain   Fourteenth Canadian Infantry
Killed in Action: (Ypres, Belgium) 1915.
Supplementary Notes: Son of the late E. Stacie (former Town Clerk) of Ballinasloe.

STANLEY, S.   Gunner 226540   162nd Royal Field Artillery
Killed in Action: (Belgium) 1 May 1918. Age 20.
Supplementary Notes: Son of Samuel & Elizabeth Stanley of Woodford.
Buried: Nine Elms British Cemetery – Poperinge – West-Vlaanderen – Belgium (XI. C. 8).

STAUNTON, John   Private 11166   First Irish Guards
Death: 9 October 1917. Age 24.
Supplementary Notes: Son of Delia Staunton of Trenanerla, Killimore.
Remembered: Tyne Cot Memorial Zonnebeke – West-Vlaanderen – Belgium (10 to 11).

STAUNTON, John Francis   Rifleman H/49937   Second & Third New Zealand Rifle Brigade
Died of Wounds: (France) 12 April 1918. Age 36.
Supplementary Notes: Son of Thomas & Bridget Staunton of Galway.
Buried: Doullens Communal Cemetery Extension No. 1 – Somme – France (VI. C. 30).

STAUNTON, Joseph   Corporal 40446   First Royal Dublin Fusiliers
Death: 28 March 1918. Age 40.
Supplementary Notes: Formerly of the Connaught Rangers 6140. Husband of Mary Staunton of Harbour Cottages, Ballinasloe. Born: Galway.
Remembered: Pozieres Memorial – Somme – France (79 & 80).

STAUNTON, Thomas Joseph   Lance Corporal 18445   First Royal Munster Fusiliers
Killed in Action: (France) 2 September 1918. Age 22.
Supplementary Notes: Son of John & Ellen Staunton of Doone, Kilconnell.
Buried: St Martin Cal Vaire British Cemetery – St Martin-Sur-Cojeul – Pas de Calais – France (II. C. 2).

STEWART, George Henry   Sergeant 29332   Tenth Royal Inniskilling Fusiliers
Killed in Action: (France) 10 August 1917.
Supplementary Notes: Son of Mrs K. Stewart of 10 Courtown Terrace, Clonliffe Road, Dublin, and the late William Stewart. Born: St Nicholas' Parish, Galway.
Buried: New Irish Farm Cemetery – Ieper – West-Vlaanderen – Belgium (XV. A. 17).

STOKES, John   Private 6009   First Royal Munster Fusiliers
Killed in Action: (Gallipoli) 28 June 1915.
Supplementary Notes: Born: Gort.
Remembered: Helles Memorial – Turkey (185 to 190).

STOKES, Sammy   Quarter Master Sergeant 6941   Second Connaught Rangers
Killed in Action: (France) 20 September 1914.
Supplementary Notes: Born: Galway. His death is mentioned in a letter by William Glinn to *The Galway Express* (17 October 1914). It was included in *Galway and the Great War*, p. 153.
Buried: Vailly British Cemetery – Aisne – France (I. G. 1).

SULLIVAN, John   Private 3893   Second Connaught Rangers
Killed in Action: (France) 4 November 1914. Age 40.
Supplementary Notes: Enlisted: Galway. Born: Ballinafad, Clifden.
Remembered: Ypres (Menin Gate) Memorial – Ieper – West-Vlaanderen – Belgium (42).

SULLIVAN, John   Private 10583   First Connaught Rangers
Killed in Action: (France) 26 April 1915.
Supplementary Notes: Enlisted: Curragh, Co. Kildare. Born: Oranmore.

SWEENEY, Edward   Private 10372   First Connaught Rangers
Died of Wounds: (Mesopotamia) 17 April 1916.
Supplementary Notes: Enlisted: Renmore barracks, Galway. Born: Gort. Brother of Michael Sweeney, below. Five brothers of this family served.
Buried: Amara War Cemetery – Iraq (XXI. G. 15).

SWEENEY, James   Private 6078   Thirteenth Manchester Regiment
Killed in Action: (Salonika) 11 November 1916.

Supplementary Notes: Born: Galway.

Buried: Karasouli Military Cemetery – Greece (A. 124).

SWEENEY, James   Private 9960   Eighth East Yorkshire Regiment

Died of Wounds: (France or Flanders) 23 July 1916.

Supplementary Notes: Enlisted: Beverley. Born: Galway.

Buried: Abbeville Communal Cemetery – Somme – France (IV. G. 13).

SWEENEY, John   Gunner 47173   Royal Garrison Artillery

Killed in Action: (France) 24 March 1918.

Supplementary Notes: Born: Kilconley.

Remembered: Arras Memorial – Pas de Calais – France (1).

SWEENEY, Michael   Private 3539   Second Connaught Rangers

Killed in Action: (France) 28 November 1914.

Supplementary Notes: Enlisted: Renmore barracks, Galway. Awarded Distinguished Conduct Medal. Born: Gort. Brother of Edward Sweeney, above.

Remembered: Ypres (Menin Gate) Memorial – Ieper – West-Vlaanderen – Belgium (42).

SWEENEY, Patrick   Private 6937   Second Connaught Rangers

Died of Wounds: (France) 21 February 1919.

Supplementary Notes: Enlisted: Galway. Born: Lisannany, Tuam.

Remembered: Cologne Memorial (south wall in north shelter at entrance to burial plots).

TARMERY, Thomas   Private 17145   Sixth York & Lancaster Regiment

Killed in Action: (Gallipoli) 7 August 1915.

Supplementary Notes: Born: Williamstown.

Remembered: Helles Memorial – Turkey (171 to 173).

THOMPSON, Edward   Private 4214   First Leinster Regiment

Killed in Action or Died of Wounds: (France) 14 September 1915. Age 38.

Supplementary Notes: Born: Licklemass.

TIERNEY, Patrick   Private 7897   First Connaught Rangers

Killed in Action: (France) 8 November 1915. Age 34.

Supplementary Notes: Enlisted: Galway. Born: Suckeen, Woodquay, Galway.

TIERNEY, Thomas   Corporal 3125   Second Connaught Rangers
Killed in Action: (France) 29 October 1914.
Supplementary Notes: Enlisted: Galway. Born: Oranmore.
Remembered: Ypres (Menin Gate) Memorial – Ieper – West-Vlaanderen – Belgium
(42).

TIGHE, Andrew   Private 41451   First & Seventh Worcestershire Regiment
Killed in Action: (France) 17 August 1917. Age 21.
Supplementary Notes: Enlisted: Widnes, Lancaster. Son of Norah Tighe of Garbally,
Menlough, Ballinasloe.
Remembered: Tyne Cot Memorial Zonnebeke – West-Vlaanderen – Belgium (75 to 77).

TIMLIN, James   Private 10030   Second Royal Scots Fusiliers
Killed in Action: (France) 29 September 1918.
Supplementary Notes: Enlisted: Kilmarnock, Ayrshire. Born: Galway.

TREACY, John   Company Quarter Master Sergeant 7455   Fifth Connaught Rangers
Died of Wounds: (France) 20 October 1918. Age 37.
Supplementary Notes: Enlisted: Dublin. Son of Edward & Maria Treacy of Ballinderry,
Ballinasloe; husband of Annie Treacy of Rossmore, Woodford (Kilconnell).
Buried: Maurois Communal Cemetery – Nord – France (17).

TREACY, Jonn   Private H/73495   First South Irish Horse
Death: (Egypt) 20 September 1918. Age 24.
Supplementary Notes: Son of Michael & Mary Treacy of Ballyboggin, Athenry.
Buried: Haifa War Cemetery – Israel (A. 57).

TREACY, Michael   Second Lieutenant   First & Fourth Royal Munster Fusiliers
Death: 21 March 1918. Age 27.
Supplementary Notes: Son of the late Patrick & Mary Treacy of Kiltullagh, Glena-
maddy.
Remembered: Pozieres Memorial – Somme – France (78 & 79).

TREACY, Thomas   Private 14185   First Royal Munster Fusiliers
Died of Wounds: (France) 2 June 1918. Age 27.
Supplementary Notes: Born: Ahascreagh, Ballinasloe.

TRENCH, The Hon. Frederic Sydney   Lieutenant   First King's Royal Rifle Corps
Died of Wounds: (France) 16 November 1916. Age 21.
Supplementary Notes: Gazetted to the First King's Royal Rifle Corps on 2 November 1914. He was wounded at Beaumont Hamel on the previous day. Eldest son of Frederic Oliver (Third Baron Ashtown) & Violet Grace Trench (Baroness Ashtown) of Woodlawn House, Woodlawn. Educated at Eton and Magdalen College, Oxford.
Buried: Mailly Wood Cemetery – Somme – France (I. D. 28).

TRESTON, William   Gunner 90794   Sixty-third Royal Field Artillery
Death: (Mesopotamia) 29 April 1916. Age 27.
Supplementary Notes: Son of Elizabeth Treston of Kilmacduagh, Gort. Stepson of James Keran.
Buried: Kut War Cemetery – Iraq (B. 12).

TROTTER, Claude Handley   Lieutenant   Forty-fourth Royal Air Force
Killed in Air Crash: 13 October 1918. Age 23.
Supplementary Notes: Formerly of the Canadian Infantry (Alberta regiment). Son of the Rev. Canon John Crawford & Fanny R. Trotter of The Rectory, Ardrahan.
Buried: Chigwell Row (All Saints) Churchyard – Essex – United Kingdom.

TUITE, Albert   Private 11496   Second Royal Dublin Fusiliers
Death: (France) 27 August 1914. Age 25.
Supplementary Notes: Brother of Michael Tuite of Dangan Dereen, Ballyglunin.
Buried: Honnechy British Cemetery – Nord – France (1. C. 28).

TULLEY, James   Gunner 99969   189th Heavy Royal Garrison Artillery
Died of Pneumonia: 1 December 1918. Age 34.
Supplementary Notes: Son of Thomas & Mary Tulley of Timiduane, Clonburn, Ballinasloe.
Buried: Alexandria (Hadra) War Memorial Cemetery – Egypt (C. 14).

TULLY, Patrick   Private 5775   Connaught Rangers
Killed in Action: (France) 12 July 1916. Age 31.
Supplementary Notes: Born: Galway.

TULLY, Patrick Martin   Private 10862   First Connaught Rangers
Killed in Action: (France) 10 April 1915.
Supplementary Notes: Enlisted: Galway. Born: St Patrick's Parish, Galway.

Remembered: Le Touret Memorial – Pas de Calais – France (43).

TURLEY, John　　　　　　　Private 36544　　　Sixth South Lancashire Regiment
Death: 17 June 1918. Age 24.
Supplementary Notes: Lost his life by drowning. Son of Pat & Mary Turley of Ballina-more Bridge, Ballinasloe.
Remembered: Basra Memorial – Iraq (23).

TURNER, James　　　　　　Lance Corporal 6111　　First Royal Munster Fusiliers
Killed in Action: (France) 9 September 1916.
Supplementary Notes: Enlisted: Earlestown, Lancashire. Born: Galway.
Remembered: Thiepval Memorial – Somme – France (16C).

VAREKER, R.H.M.　　　　　　Lieutenant　　　　　　Grenadier Guards
Killed in Action: (France) Age 22.
Supplementary Notes: Enlisted: September 1914. Son of Captain George Vareker (Royal Dublin Fusiliers) of Co. Galway; grandson of Lord Gort of Lough Cutra Castle, Gort.

VAUGHAN, John　　　　　　Rifleman 7232　　　　Second Royal Irish Rifles
Killed in Action: (France) 20 or 29 September 1914.
Supplementary Notes: Enlisted: Galway. Born: Galway.
Buried: Vailly British Cemetery – Aisne – France (II. D. 18).

WAITES, Charles James　　　Second Lieutenant　　Sixth Connaught Rangers
Killed in Action: (France) 10 October 1918. Age 31.
Supplementary Notes: Son of William & Mary J. Waites of Kilcolgan.
Buried: Montay-Neuvilly Road Cemetery – Montay – Nord – France (. I. F. I).

WALLACE, Patrick J.　　　　Private 8455　　　　　First Irish Guards
Killed in Action: (France) 11 September 1916.
Supplementary Notes: Born: Ballinderry.
Remembered: Thiepval Memorial – Somme – France (7D).

WALSH, Coleman　　　　　Private 7718 (119917)　Sixth Connaught Rangers
Killed in Action: (France) 8 March 1917.
Supplementary Notes: Enlisted: Ennis. Son of Barbara Walsh of Rosmuck, Connemara.
Remembered: Ypres (Menin Gate) Memorial – Ieper – West-Vlaanderen – Belgium (42).

WALSH, James   Private 6888   First Canadian Infantry
Death: (France or Flanders) 22 December 1914. Age 37.
Supplementary Notes: Born: Galway.
Remembered: Le Touret Memorial – Pas de Calais – France (27 & 28).

WALSH, John   Private 4309   Fifth Connaught Rangers
Killed in Action: (Salonika) 7 December 1915. Age 18.
Supplementary Notes: Enlisted: Galway. Son of Michael & Kate Walsh of Wood Quay, Galway.
Remembered: Doiran Memorial – Greece.

WALSH, John   Private 47634   Fourth Worcestershire Regiment
Killed in Action: 9 October 1917. Age 22.
Supplementary Notes: Son of Thomas Walsh of William Street West, Galway.
Remembered: Tyne Cot Memorial Zonnebeke – West-Vlaanderen – Belgium (75 to 77).

WALSH, John   Corporal 4506   Second Leinster Regiment
Killed in Action: (Ypres, Belgium) 31 July 1917. Age 21.
Supplementary Notes: Enlisted: Galway. Formerly of the Royal Field Artillery 100275. Son of Philip Walsh of Foster Street, Galway. He was a member of St Patrick's band in Galway. He wrote a letter to his mother just six days before he was killed at the third Battle of Ypres (Passchendaele). The letter was included in *Galway and the Great War,* p. 184, 185.
Remembered: Ypres (Menin Gate) Memorial – Ieper – West-Vlaanderen – Belgium (44).

WALSH, John   Private 5406   Second Leinster Regiment
Killed in Action: (France) 28 March 1917. Age 22.
Supplementary Notes: Born: Galway.

WALSH, John   Leading Seaman 8200A   SS *Uniy*   Royal Navy Reserves.
Killed in Action: 2 May 1918. Age 22.
Supplementary Notes: Killed during action with an enemy submarine in the Straits of Dover. Son of Martin & Mary Walsh of Long Walk, Galway.
Remembered: Portsmouth Naval Memorial – Hampshire – United Kingdom (21).

WALSH, Joseph Augustine   Leading Telegraphist J/41572 HMS *Victory I* Royal Navy.
Died of Wounds: 29 February 1920. Age 21.

Supplementary Notes: (Shore-base) Son of Michael & Anne Barnett Walsh of Ganaveen, Laurencetown, Ballinasloe.

Buried: Haslar Royal Naval Cemetery – Hampshire – United Kingdom (B. 12. 9).

WALSH, Martin   Seaman J/29903   HMS *Formidable*   Royal Navy
Killed in Action: (English Channel) 1 January 1915 or 9 May 1917. Age 18 or 28.
Supplementary Notes: Killed during action with an enemy submarine. Son of Philip & Alice Walsh of St Helen Street, Galway.
Remembered: Portsmouth Naval Memorial – Hampshire – United Kingdom (6).

WALSH, Michael   Private 6056   Second Irish Guards
Killed in Action: (France) 15 September 1916.
Supplementary Notes: Born: Kilconnolly.
Remembered: Thiepval Memorial – Somme – France (7D).

WALSH, Michael   Guardsman 12445   First Grenadier Guards
Killed in Action: (France) 14 or 19 September 1914 or 1916.
Supplementary Notes: Born: Tuam.
Remembered: Thiepval Memorial – Somme – France (8D).

WALSH, Michael   Private 18290   Second Leinster Regiment
Killed in Action: (France) 23 May 1918.
Supplementary Notes: Born: Dooris.
Buried: Cinq Rues British Cemetery – Hazebrouck – Nord – France (D 28).

WALSH, Michael   Private   British Expeditionary Force
Killed in Action: (Belgium) October 1914.
Supplementary Notes: Family believe he served with the Connaught Rangers. Another brother, Patrick Walsh, survived the war. Born: Oughterard. Brother of Peter Walsh, p. 223.

WALSH, Patrick   Private 4728   Sixth Connaught Rangers
Death: (France) 21 December 1917. Age 29.
Supplementary Notes: Enlisted: Galway. Son of Thomas & Mary Walsh of McDonnell's Lane, Athenry.
Buried: Ronssoy Communal Cemetery – Somme – France (D. 5).

WALSH, Patrick   Private 5834   First Connaught Rangers
Death: (Mesopotamia) 15 October 1916. Age 42.

Supplementary Notes: Enlisted: Pontefrack. Son of John & Kate Walsh of Headford.
Buried: Amara War Cemetery – Iraq (VII. A. 11).

WALSH, Patrick   Boy   Trawler *Neptune*   Mercantile Marines
Death: (Galway bay) 17 December 1917. Age 15.
Supplementary Notes: Drowned as a result of enemy action. Son of Ann Walsh of
20 Quay Street, Galway, and the late William Walsh. The sinking of the *Neptune* was
recorded in *Galway and the Great War*, p. 96, 96.
Remembered: Tower Hill Memorial – London – United Kingdom.

WALSH, Patrick   Private 4728   Sixth Connaught Rangers
Killed in Action: (France) 21 December 1917. Age 29.
Supplementary Notes: Born: Athenry.
Buried: Ronssoy Communal Cemetery – Somme – France (D5).

WALSH, Patrick   Private 5834   First Connaught Rangers
Killed in Action: (Mesopotamia) 15 October 1916.
Supplementary Notes: Born: Galway.

WALSH, Peter   Private   British Expeditionary Force
Killed in Action: (France) October / November 1918.
Supplementary Notes: Family believe he served with the Connaught Rangers. Another
brother, Patrick Walsh, survived the war. Born: Oughterard. Brother of Michael Walsh,
p. 221. There is a Connaught Ranger, P. Walsh 4491; recorded (United Kingdom) by the
Commonwealth War Graves Commission as killed on 10 October 1918; and buried in
Highland Cemetery – Le Cateau – Nord – France (VIII. A. 9). There is a possibility
that this is the same soldier.

WALSH, Thomas   Private 9239   First Connaught Rangers
Death: 5 November 1914. Age 27.
Supplementary Notes: Son of William & Bridget Walsh of Tullinadaly Road, Tuam.
Remembered: Le Touret Memorial – Pas de Calais – France (43).

WALSH, Timothy   Private 9871   First Connaught Rangers
Killed in Action: (Mesopotamia) 21 January 1916. Age 24 or 32.
Supplementary Notes: Enlisted: Glasgow. Son of Michael & Mary Anne Walsh of
Bridge, Oughterard.
Remembered: Basra Memorial – Iraq (40 & 64).

WARD, Bernard   Private 3108   First Connaught Rangers
    Died of Wounds: (Mesopotamia) 27 January 1916. Age 27.
    Supplementary Notes: Enlisted: Oranmore. Born: Kilclooney, Ballinasloe.
    Buried: Basra War Cemetery – Iraq (VI. F. 3).

WARD, Charles   Private 2457   Second Royal Irish Regiment
    Died of Wounds: (Ballinasloe, Co. Galway) 21 November 1917. Age 33.
    Supplementary Notes: Enlisted: Galway. Formerly of the Connaught Rangers 588.
Son of Jane Ward of Harbour Street, Ballinasloe (Kilclooney).
    Buried: Grangegorman Military Cemetery – Dublin – Ireland (RC. 540).

WARD, James   Private 4180   First Connaught Rangers
    Killed in Action: (Mesopotamia) 11 March 1916.
    Supplementary Notes: Enlisted: Galway. Born: Tuam.

WARD, James Thomas   Private 4815   Second Leinster Regiment
    Killed in Action: (France) 20 October 1914. Age 26.
    Supplementary Notes: Son of Martin & Mary Ward of Timiduane, Clonburn, Ballinasloe.
    Remembered: Ploegsteert Memorial – Comines-Warneton – Hainaut – Belgium (10).

WARD, John   Private 7754   First Connaught Rangers
    Killed in Action: (France) 20 October 1914.
    Supplementary Notes: Born: Kilclooney, Ballinasloe.
    Remembered: Ploegsteert Memorial – Comines-Warneton – Hainaut – Belgium.

WARD, Laurence   Gunner 26545   Royal Field Artillery
    Killed in Action: (France) 13 February 1916.
    Supplementary Notes: Born: White Park.
    Buried: Erquinghem Churchyard Extension – Nord – France (I. G. 19).

WARD, Laurence   Private 4191   Sixth Connaught Rangers
    Killed in Action: (France) 20 November 1917.
    Supplementary Notes: Enlisted: Ballinasloe. Born: Tuam.
    Buried: Croisilles Railway Cemetery – Pas de Calais – France (I.C. 9).
    Remembered: Roll of Honour – Killed in Action – 1914–1918 – Ballinasloe – Ireland.

WARD, Martin   Private 3819   Second Connaught Rangers
Died of Wounds: (Tuam, Co. Galway) 10 November 1914.
Supplementary Notes: Enlisted: Galway. Born: Tuam (Loughrea).
Buried: Tidworth Military Cemetery – Wiltshire – United Kingdom (A. 26).
Remembered: Roll of Honour – Killed in Action – 1914–1918 – Ballinasloe – Ireland.

WARD, Mich   Fireman   SS *Lusitania* Mercantile Marines
Death: 7 May 1915. Age 28.
Supplementary Notes: Drowned as a result of an attack by an enemy submarine. Born: Galway.
Remembered: Tower Hill Memorial – London – United Kingdom.

WARD, Michael   Private 9221   First Royal Irish Regiment
Death: (Mesopotamia) 29 October 1915.
Supplementary Notes: Born: Tuam.
Buried: Alexandria (Hadra) War Memorial Cemetery – Egypt (C. 28).

WARD, Patrick   Private 10112   First Connaught Rangers
Died of Wounds: (Mesopotamia) 17 January 1917. Age 22.
Supplementary Notes: Enlisted: Galway. Awarded Mons Star. Son of Dennis & M.A. Ward of Barrack Street, Tuam.
Remembered: Basra Memorial – Iraq (40 & 64).

WARD, Patrick   Private 8100   Second Connaught Rangers
Killed in Action: (France) 26 August 1914. Age 38.
Supplementary Notes: Enlisted: Galway. Awarded 1914 Star. Brother of James Ward of Kinvarra. Born: Kinvarra.
Remembered: La Ferte-Sous-Jouarre Memorial – Seine-et-Marne – France.

WARD, Thomas   Private 6911   Second Royal Munster Fusiliers
Killed in Action: (France) 4 October 1918. Age 26.
Supplementary Notes: Son of Martin Ward of Cloonbern, Moylough, Ballinasloe.
Buried: Templeux-le-Guerard British Cemetery – Somme – France (I. H. 39).

WARD, Thomas   Private 5939   Second Royal Munster Fusiliers
Killed in Action: (France) 9 May 1915. Age 26.
Supplementary Notes: Born: Gort.

Remembered: Le Touret Memorial – Pas de Calais – France (43 & 44).

WARD, William   Private 16495   First Royal Irish Fusiliers
 Died of Wounds: (France) 6 September 1918.
 Supplementary Notes: Enlisted: Galway. Formerly of the Royal Irish Regiment. Born: Galway.
 Buried: Arneke British Cemetery – Nord – France (III. D. 27).

WARD, William   Private 39467   Royal Irish Regiment
 Killed in Action: (France) 13 November 1917. Age 29.
 Supplementary Notes: Born: Gort.

WELSH, James   Private 47011   Fourth King's Liverpool Regiment
 Killed in Action: (France) 20 March 1918.
 Supplementary Notes: Born: Glenamaddy.
 Buried: Potijze Burial Ground Cemetery – West-Vlaanderen – Belgium (I. E. 24).

WELSH, John   Private 8323   First King's Liverpool Regiment
 Killed in Action: (France) 10 March 1915. Age 35.
 Supplementary Notes: Enlisted: Warrington. Born: Galway.
 Remembered: Le Touret Memorial – Pas de Calais – France (6 to 8).

WESTCOTT, Ernest   Sergeant 9320   First Yorkshire Regiment
 Death: (India) 23 July 1918.
 Supplementary Notes: Born: Castlegar, Galway.

WHITE, Edward   Private 20829   First Royal Irish Regiment
 Death: (Egypt) 16 October 1918.
 Supplementary Notes: Born: Tuam.
 Remembered: War Memorial Cemetery – Cairo – Egypt (M. 183).

WHITE, Laurence   Private 5231   First Connaught Rangers
 Died of Wounds: (Mesopotamia) 24 April 1916.
 Supplementary Notes: Enlisted: Northwich. Born: Mullochmore.
 Remembered: Basra Memorial – Iraq (40 & 64).

WHITE, William M.M.   Lance Sergeant 9806   Second Leinster Regiment
 Killed in Action: (France) 4 September 1918. Age 26.

Supplementary Notes: Awarded Military Medal. Son of John & Bedelia White of Dooras, Woodford, Loughrea (Portumna).
Buried: Wulverghem-Lindenhoek Road Military Cemetery – Heuvelland – West-Vlaanderen – Belgium (V. C. 3).

WHYTE, Valentine   Private 9897   First Irish Guards
Killed in Action: (France) 13 April 1918. Age 24.
Supplementary Notes: Born: Woodford.
Remembered: Ploegsteert Memorial – Comines-Warneton – Hainaut – Belgium (1).

WILKINSON, William Martin   Private 42693   Eleventh Suffolk Regiment
Killed in Action: (France) 8 August 1918.
Supplementary Notes: Enlisted: Tottenham, Middlesex. Formerly of the Labour Corps 161450. Born: Galway.
Remembered: Ploegsteert Memorial – Comines-Warneton – Hainaut – Belgium (3).
WILLIAMS, John   Private 5464   First Irish Guards
Killed in Action: (France) 6 October 1915.
Supplementary Notes: Born: Woodford.

WILLSON, Frederick James   Lieutenant   Indian Army Reserve
Died of Wounds: (Mesopotamia) 10 January 1917. Age 27.
Supplementary Notes: Attached to the Third Company, First King George's Own Sappers & Miners. Eldest son of James & Alice Willson of Mill House, Ballinasloe. His father had served in the Indian educational service. Brother of William Alick Willson, below.
Buried: Amara War Cemetery – Iraq.
Remembered: St John's Church Roll of Honour – Ballinasloe – Ireland.

WILLSON, William Alick   Lieutenant   Twelfth Royal Irish Rifles
Died of Wounds: 1 April 1916. Age 24.
Supplementary Notes: Attached to the Twenty-second (Entrenching) Royal Irish Rifles. 'Mentioned in Despatches'. Youngest son of James & Alice Willson and brother of Frederick James Willson, above.
Buried: Moreuil Communal Cemetery Allied Extension – Somme – France. (Y. 5.).
Remembered: St John's Church Roll of Honour – Ballinasloe – Ireland.

WILSON, F.J.   Lieutenant   British Expeditionary Force
Death: 1914–1918.

Supplementary Notes: From Ballinasloe.
Remembered: Roll of Honour – Killed in Action – 1914–1918 – Ballinasloe & St John's Church Roll of Honour – Ballinasloe – Ireland.

WILSON, J.M.   Lieutenant   Royal Flying Corps
 Killed in Air Crash: (Dromore, Co. Tyrone) 13 November 1918. Age 36.
 Supplementary Notes: (Royal Air Force) Killed in mid-air collision. Newspaper report states that he was a Galwayman.

WILSON, Matthew   Private 7010   Second Connaught Rangers
 Killed in Action: (Belgium) 25 February 1915. Age 36.
 Supplementary Notes: Enlisted: Galway. Awarded Mons Star. Born: Ahascragh.

WOODS, John   Private 5815   Eighth Royal Munster Fusiliers
 Killed in Action: (France) 4 September 1916.
 Supplementary Notes: Born: Inisheer, Aran Islands.
 Remembered: Thiepval Memorial – Somme – France (16C).

WRIGHT, Allen   Private 40421   Second Royal Scots Fusiliers
 Killed in Action: (France) 7 April 1917.
 Supplementary Notes: Born: Nuns' Island, Galway.
 Remembered: Arras Memorial – Pas de Calais – France (5).

WRIGHT, John   Private 3030248   Fifty-fourth Canadian Infantry
 Killed in Action: (France) 2 September 1918. Age 39.
 Supplementary Notes: (Central Ontario division). Son of Thomas & Katherine Wright (*nee* Deshel) of Ballyconneely, Connemara.
 Buried: Dury Mill British Cemetery – Pas de Calais – France (II. A. 33).

WYNNE, John   Lance Sergeant 5/368   Fifth Connaught Rangers
 Died of Wounds: (Gallipoli) 20 August 1915.
 Supplementary Notes: Enlisted: Dublin. Born: Ballyglunin.
 Buried: Seventh Field Ambulance Cemetery – Gallipoli – Turkey (Sp. Mem. C. 24).

YARNELL, Victor   Private 25907   Seventh Royal Irish Regiment
 Killed in Action: (France) 27 March 1918. Age 24.
 Supplementary Notes: Formerly of the South Irish Horse 933. Born: Ballinasloe.
 Remembered: Pozieres Memorial – Somme – France (30 &31) & St John's Church Roll of Honour – Ballinasloe – Ireland.

YOUNG, Alexander (VC)   Lieutenant   South African Forces

Killed in Action: (Delville Wood, Somme, France) 19 October 1916. Age 43.

Supplementary Notes: Enlisted: Second Dragoon Guards 1890, Renmore barracks. He was born in Ballynamanagh (Oranmore), Clarinbridge. Brother of Galway businessman, politician and recruiting committee member, Joseph Young. Educated in the Model School, Galway. An excellent horseman, and was noted as one of the finest rough riders in the British army. He later joined the Scotch Greys, and became a riding instructor at Canterbury. On 13 August 1901, Young earned the Victoria Cross in action against several companies of Boers under the command of Commandant Erasmus. The Boers were setting explosives, intending to blow up a railway line to prevent the train carrying troops reaching their comrades. Young ordered his men to attack and galloped ahead of his troops, reaching the enemy first. He shot several of them and captured their commander. His bravery was commended by Field Marshal Roberts, and he was presented with his VC by King Edward VII.

Remembered: Thiepval Memorial – Somme – France (4C).

GALWAY MEN'S S & B ASSOCIATION NEW YORK AMERICAN ARMY BANNER LIST

A list of American soldiers, who were of Galway origin, and who lost their lives in the Great War. They were recorded on a banner that was later presented to the Renmore barracks museum by the Galway Men's S & B Association New York.

Ballanger, Thomas

Bowler, William

Brennan, Dan

Canning, John

Charles, James

Collins, Thomas

Connolly, Patrick

Conroy, Michael

Devaney, Martin

Devaney, Robert

Donlon, Martin

Fahey, John

Fahey, Mathew

Fallon, Bernard

Farrell, Patrick

Ford, Thomas

Gill, John

Goode, James

Hanrahan, Francis

Hanrahan, John

Hennessy, John

Hoban, Steve

Holden, Frank

Holden, John

Kelly, Malachy

Kelly, Micheal

Kenny, Thomas

Kiely, Michael

Mackin, James

Mahoney, Timothy

Manning, Michael

Mitchill, Michael

THEIR NAME LIVETH FOR EVERMORE

NOTES

WAR IN EUROPE

1. Cassells, L., *The Archduke and the Assassin: Sarajevo, June 28th 1914* (Stein & Day, New York, 1985).

   Ferguson, N., 'Public Finance and National Security: The Domestic Origins of the First World War Revisited', *Past & Present*, Vol. 142 (1994), pp. 141–68.

   'British and German Cases', *Journal of Modern History*, Vol. 46 (1974), pp. 191–216.

   Hamilton, R.F., *The Origins of the Great War* (Cambridge University Press, Cambridge, 2003).

   Joll, J., *The Origins of the First World War* (Longmans Publishing Group, Harlow, 2000).

   Kaiser, D.E., 'Germany and the Origins of the First World War', *Journal of Modern History*, Vol. 55 (1983), pp. 442–74.

   Steiner, Z.S., *Britain and the Origins of the First World War* (Macmillan, London, 1977).

   Williamson, S.R., *Austria-Hungary and the Origins of the First World War* (Macmillan, Basingstoke, 1991).

2. Lieven, D.C.B., *Russia and the Origins of the First World War* (Macmillan, London, 1983).

   Mombauer, A., *Helmuth von Moltke and the Origins of the First World War* (Cambridge University Press, Cambridge, 2001).

   Seligmann, M.S., 'A Barometer of National Confidence: A British Assessment of the Role of Insecurity in the formulation of German Military Policy Before the First World War', *English Historical Studies*, Vol. 117 (2002), pp. 333–55.

3. Bartlett, T. and Jeffery, K. (eds), *A Military History of Ireland* (Cambridge University Press, Cambridge, 1996).

   Blake, J., 'Field-Marshal Sir John French', *Journal of the Galway Archaeological & Historical Society*, Vol. 8, No. 4 (1913–1914), p. 247.

   Fitzpatrick, D., *The Two Irelands, 1912–1939* (Oxford University Press, Oxford, 1998).

   Fitzpatrick, D., *Ireland and the First World War* (Trinity History Workshop, Dublin, 1986).

Glover, M., *Warfare from Waterloo to Mons* (Book Club Associates, London, 1980), pp. 243–5.

Henry, W., *Supreme Sacrifice: The Story of Eamonn Ceannt 1881–1916* (Mercier Press, Cork, 2005), p. 35.

BATTLELINES DEFINED

4. Bowman, T., *The Irish Regiments in the Great War: Discipline and Morale* (Manchester University Press, Manchester, 2003), pp. 49, 50.

    Glover, M., *Warfare from Waterloo to Mons*, pp. 248, 249.

    Harris, H.E.D., *The Irish Regiments in the First World War* (Mercier Press, Cork, 1968), pp. 35, 36.

    Hogg, I.V., *Dictionary of World War I* (Brockhampton Press, London, 1997), pp. 156, 157.

    Johnson, T., *Orange, Green and Khaki, The Story of the Irish Regiments in the Great War, 1914–18* (Gill and Macmillan Ltd, Dublin, 1992), pp. 2, 20, 21.

    Jourdain, H.F.N., *The Connaught Rangers 2nd Battalion, Formerly 94th Foot*, Volume II (Schull Books, Fraser, E. Cork, 1999), p.412.

5. Harris, H.E.D., *The Irish Regiments in the First World War*, pp. 35, 36.

    Hogg, I.V., *Dictionary of World War I*, p. 4.

    Johnson, T., *Orange, Green and Khaki*, pp. 29–35.

    Marshall, S., *The American Heritage History of World War I* (American Heritage Publishing Company Inc. USA, 1964), pp. 73, 78, 239.

    Sheffield, G., *Forgotten Victory. The First World War: Myths and Realities* (Headline Book Publishing, London, 2001), p. 90.

ANSWER THE CALL

6   *Galway Advertiser*, 'The Connaught Rangers go to War', *19 November 1998*.

    Henry, W., *Galway and the Great War* (Mercier Press, Cork, 2006).

    Sheerin, N., *On Your Doorstep* (Sheerin, Galway, 1977), pp. 20, 21.

    Galway Advertiser, 'The Forgotten Heroes of the Great War', 13 October 2005.

    The Galway Express, 'Duration of the War', 9 January 1915; 'Local War Items', 17 October 1914; 9 January 1915; 23 January 1915; 13 February 1915.

7. Henry, W., *Galway and the Great War*.

    The Connacht Tribune, 'Aggressive Politics – Striking Pronouncement by Bishop of Clonfert', 15 June 1915; 'Come With Me', 3 August 1917; 'Co. Galway Farms Mapped Out in Berlin', 8 April 1916; 'Great Recruiting Demonstration at Clifden',

15 January 1916; 'Irish Bishops and the War', 11 March 1916; 'The Recruiting Committee', 3 July 1915.

The Galway Express, 'Call of the Drum', 24 April 1915; 'Conceived by Satan – Matured in Hell', 15 May 1915; 'Irish Guards Visit', 1 May 1915.

The Tuam Herald, 'Recruiting at Williamstown', 4 September 1915'; 'The Irish Brigade – Recruiting Meeting in Tuam', 15 May 1915.

8   Henry, W., *Galway and the Great War.*

9   Henry, W., *Galway and the Great War.*

The Connacht Tribune, 'Galway Munition Factory', 7 August 1916; 'Galway Woollen Industry', 20 February 1915; 'Munitions Factory', 25 March 1917; 'Order for Galway Woollen Factory', 19 September 1914; 'Prisoners of War Entertainment', 19 January 1918; 'Soldiers and Sailors Comforts', 6 April 1918; 'War Funds – Over £12,000 Subscribed by Co. Galway', 20 June 1919; 'Women and the War', 2 October 1915.

The Galway Express, '15 Per Cent – Thriving Condition of Galway Woollen Mills', 2 March 1918; 'Connaught Rangers Comfort Fund', 12 September 1914; 'Galway Prisoners of War Fund – Appeal for a Co. Galway War Plate', 4 September 1915; 'The Connaught Rangers – An Appeal', 15 August 1914; 'Comforts in the Trenches', 28 November 1914; 'Red Cross Flag Day', 28 November 1914.

The Tuam Herald, 'Galway Notes', 27 March 1915; 'The County of Galway Naval and Military War Fund', 4 September 1915.

CHRISTMAS 1914

10. Hogg, I.V., *Dictionary of World War I*, p. 237.

Holt, Major & Mrs, *Battlefield Guide to the Ypres Salient* (Leo Cooper, London, 2000), pp. 19, 20.

Johnson, T., *Orange, Green and Khaki*, pp. 52–4.

Keegan, J., *The First World War: an Illustrated History* (Pimlico, London, 2002), p. 116.

Marshall, S., *The American Heritage History of World War I*, pp. 76, 77.

The Galway Express, 'Connaught Rangers Heavy Losses at Ypres – A Perfect Hell on Earth', *5 June 1915.*

11. Armes, Captain R. J, 'Christmas Day 1914' [Letter].

'Christmas Day 1914 The Day World War I Fighting Stopped in France', *Ireland's Eye*, No. 240 (December 2000).

Internet: The Christmas Day Truce of 1914 http://www.worldwar1.com/heritage/xmast.htm

The Christmas Truce. http://www.firstworldwar.com/features/christmastruce.htm

12. Hogg, I.V., *Dictionary of World War I*, pp. 130, 163.

Johnson, T., *Orange, Green and Khaki*, pp. 72, 156–8.

Keegan, J., *The First World War: an Illustrated History*, pp. 172–84, 267.

Marshall, S., *The American Heritage History of World War I*, pp. 77, 135, 136.

'The Irish in the Great War' (Tony Finnerty Archives).

13. Hogg, I.V., *Dictionary of World War I*, pp. 45, 84, 86.

Johnson, T., *Orange, Green and Khaki*, p. 100.

World Book Encyclopaedia: 'Dardanelles' (Surrey 1986), pp. 28, 29.

FIGHT TO A FINISH

14. Hogg, I.V., *Dictionary of World War I*, pp. 110, 185, 193.

Keegan, J., *The First World War: an Illustrated History*, pp. 245–9.

Marshall, S., *The American Heritage History of World War I*, pp. 176, 177.

Spector, R.H., *At War at Sea: Sailors and Naval Combat in the Twentieth Century* (Viking Penguin, New York 2001), pp. 83–92.

15. Documentary: 'The Battle of the Somme; the Bloodiest Battle of World War One', A Lamancha/Castle Co-Production, 1993.

East Galway Democrat, 'Guillemont and Ginchy', 7 September 1918.

Hogg, I.V., *Dictionary of Battles* (Brockhampton Press, London, 1997), p. 152.

Hogg, I.V., *Dictionary of World War I*, p. 203.

Johnson, T., *Orange, Green and Khaki*, pp. 225, 226.

Keegan, J., *The First World War: an Illustrated History*, p. 271.

Larkin Family Archives.

Marshall, S., *The American Heritage History of World War I*, pp. 180, 181.

Stedman, M., *Gullemont Somme Battleground Europe* (Leo Cooper, South Yorkshire, 1998), p. 116.

The Connacht Tribune, 'Gullemont and Ginchy – Anniversary of the Charge of the Irish Braigades', 7 September 1918.

'The Irish in the Great War' (Tony Finnerty Archives).

16. Bowman, T., *The Irish Regiments in the Great War*, pp. 332, 442, 443.

Hogg, I.V., *Dictionary of World War I*, pp. 39, 100, 238.

Holt, Major & Mrs, *Battlefield Guide to the Ypres Salient*, p. 22.

Internet: 'Battle of Cambrai.' http://www.firstworldwar.com/battles/cambrai.htm

Johnson, T., *Orange, Green and Khaki*, pp. 309–15, 415, 424–27.

Keegan, J., *The First World War: an Illustrated History*, pp. 345–9, 405–7.

Marshall, S., *The American Heritage History of World War I*, pp. 214–20.

Sheffield, G., *Forgotten Victory. The First World War: Myths and Realities*, pp. 174–81.

BROTHERS IN ARMS

17. *The Connacht Tribune*, 'Flight Lieutenant Kelly', 3 March 1917; 'Military Awards', 12 January 1918; 'Sent Down 27 Enemy Aeroplanes', 18 January 1919.
18. *The Tuam Herald*, 'A Brave Galway Family – A Loughrea Batch of Heroes', 28 August 1915; 'Connaught Officers', 8 January 1916; 'Death of Major Robert Gregory M.C., R.F.C.', 9 February 1918; 'Our Irish Soldiers', 29 April 1916; 'From Wounds Received', 30 June 1917.
19. *The Tuam Herald*, 'A Brave Galway Family – A Loughrea Batch of Heroes', 28 August 1915; 'From Wounds Received', 30 June 1917.
    State Records of Birth – District of Loughrea.
    State Records of Marriage – District of Ballinasloe.
20. *The Tuam Herald*, 'A Brave Galway Family – A Loughrea Batch of Heroes', 28 August 1915; 'From Wounds Received', 30 June 1917.
    State Records of Birth – District of Loughrea.
    State Records of Marriage – District of Ballinasloe.

PEACE AND REMBRANCE

21. *East Galway Democrat*, 'Peace At Last', 16 November 1918.
    Henry, W., *Galway and the Great War*.
22. Henry, W., *Galway and the Great War*.
    The Connacht Tribune, 'Grammar School War Memorial', 14 June 1919.
23. Henry, W., *Galway and the Great War*.

ROLL OF HONOUR

Profiles: submitted by family members
Dominick Burke by Damian Burke and Anne O'Flaherty, 2006.
John Caulfield by Douglas Rafter, 2005.
James (Jim) Comber by Gerald Comber, 2002.
James Connolly by Noel & Madeleine King, 2005.
James Conolly by Seán Malone, 14 April 2003.

Thomas Corcoran by Mary Deely, 2005.
Coleman Farmer by Colm Walsh, 2005.
Larry Farmer by Colm Walsh, 2005.
John Finnerty by Tony Finnerty, 2005.
John Gilmore by Christy Craughwell, 2007.
John Keaney by Francis Keaney, 2006.
Joseph Keaney by Francis Keaney, 2006.
Thomas Keaney by Francis Keaney, 2006.
Robert Thomas Kennedy by John Kennedy, 22 January 2007.
John Joe Leonard by Val Raftery, 27 November 2004.
Martin William Molloy by Mary Jane Carter, 2001.
Thomas McHugh by Damian Burke and Anne O'Flaherty, 2006.
James Murphy by Paddy Cunningham, 2005.
Coleman Nee by Michael Connelly, 2004.
Michael O'Connor by Anne O'Flaherty, 2006.
Patrick O'Donnell by Bill & Alice Scanlan, 2006.
James Ollington by Michael Conneely, 2006.
Pat Purcell by Seán Purcell, 2006.
Michael Lavelle by Kathleen Villers-Tuthill, 2007.
John Madden by Finbarr O'Shea, 2007.

'Ballinasloe Local History' (Internet) http://www.ballinasloe.org/articles/people.php
'Clontuskert – Great War 1914–1918' (Douglas Rafter), unpublished article.
'Our Boys in service for God & Country', Galway Men's S & B Association New York American Army Banner, Renmore barracks museum, Galway.
Great War monument – St Nicholas' Collegiate Church – Galway – Ireland.
Ireland's Memorial Records 1914–1918, compiled by the Committee of the Irish National War Memorial, 1923.
Soldiers Died in the Great War, CD ROM by Naval and Military Press Ltd.
'Ballinasloe Local History' (Internet), list of Ballinasloe men who died in World War One (Damian Mac Con Uladh). http://www.ballinasloe.org/articles/people.php
Records of Colm McDonogh, his personal list of Ballinasloe soldiers killed
Roll of Honour – Killed in Action – 1914-1918 – Ballinasloe. Banner held in Ballinasloe.
'Soldiers Died in the Great War 1914 – 19 Part 69', The Connaught Rangers, The

Connaught Rangers. His Majesty's Stationery Office, 1921 (Piction Publishing [Chippenham] Ltd., 1988).

St John's Church Roll of Honour – Ballinasloe, monument in St John's Church, Ballinasloe.

REFERENCES

ARCHIVES AND MANUSCRIPTS:

American Army Service Records.

Army Service Records of World War I, Public Records Office, Kew, Surrey.

Ashe Family Archives.

Attestation Papers: Canada www.canadiangreatwarproject.com

Burgess Family Archives.

Campell Family Archives: 1] Archives of the Naval Saving Bank, Portsmouth: 2] Account Number 19688; Census of Ireland 1901 & 1911, 3] Commissioners of the Admiralty Document; Certificate for Wounds and Hurts, Naval Service

'Clontuskert – Great War 1914–1918' (Douglas Rafter), unpublished article.

Commonwealth War Graves Commission Archives, Maidenhead, Berks, UK

Documentary: The Battle of the Somme; the Bloodiest Battle of World War One, A Lamancha/Castle Co-Production, 1993.

Fahy Family Archives.

Furey Research Report, March (2005).

Flynn Family Archives: Pensions Appeal Tribunal Document; Ref.: 13/MF/ 2160.

Ireland's Memorial Records 1914–1918, compiled by the Committee of the Irish National War Memorial. 1923.

Irish Guards Archives.

Kennedy Family Archives.

Jordan Family Archives.

Larkin Family Archives.

Loughrea Church Records.

Macken Family Archives.

McElroy Family Archives.

Noonan and Ward Family Archives.

O'Connor Family Archives.

O'Donnell Family Archives.

O'Farrell Family Archives.

O'Flaherty Family Archives.

O'Malley Family Archives.

Records of Colm McDonogh, his personal list of Ballinasloe soldiers killed

Renmore Barracks Museum Archives.

Soldiers Died in the Great War, CD ROM by the Naval and Military Press Ltd.

State Records of Birth – District of Loughrea.

State Records of Marriage – District of Ballinasloe.

Tom Kenny Archives.

Tony Finnerty Archives.

BOOKS:

O'Dowd, P., *Down by the Claddagh* (Kennys Bookshop & Art Galleries Ltd., Galway 1993), p. 48.

Heringklee, S., Higgins, J. (eds), *Monuments of St. Nicholas' Collegiate Church, Galway, A Historical Genealogical Archaeological Record* (Rock Crow's Press, Galway, 1991).

'Soldiers Died in the Great War 1914–19 Part 69', *The Connaught Rangers*, The Connaught Rangers, His Majesty's Stationery Office, 1921 (Piction Publishing [Chippenham] Ltd., 1988).

Villiers-Tuthill, K., *Beyond the Twelve Bens* (Kathleen Villiers-Tuthill. Galway 1990), pp. 148, 149.

INTERNET:

'Ballinasloe Local History' http://www.ballinasloe.org/articles/people.php

'Ballinasloe Local History' (Internet), list of Ballinasloe men who died in World War One (Damian Mac Con Uladh). http://www.ballinasloe.org/articles/people.php

'Battle of Cambrai' http://www.firstworldwar.com/battles/cambrai.htm

'Spanish Flu' http://en.wikipedia.org/wiki/Spanish_flu

'The Christmas Day Truce of 1914' http://www.firstworldwar.com/features/christmastruce.htm

'The Christmas Truce' http://www.worldwar1.com/heritage/xmast.htm

'The Influenza Pandemic of 1918' http://virus.stanford.edu/uda/

INTERVIEWS:

John Jordan, 12 November 2000; Jonie Fallon, 13 November 2000; Elizabeth Hackett, 13 November 2000; Mary Walsh, 13 November 2000; Patsy O'Connor, 15 November 2000; Sheila Jordan, 28 June 2001; Annie Burke, 27 August 2001; Frances Kenneen, 19 September 2001; Johnny Flaherty, 23 September 2001; Billy Lally, 26 September 2001; Nora Cahill, 8 October 2001; Carmel Colgan, 25 June 2002; Paddy O'Neill, 13 November 2002; Anne Everiss, 19 November

2002; Brian Fahy, 5 March 2003; Michael Conneely, 28 November 2003; Mike Flynn, 28 November 2003; Anne Campbell, 29 November 2003; Billy Carr, 29 November 2003; Tommy Carr, 29 November 2003; Dickie Byrne, 29 November 2003; Noel Heaney, 8 August 2004; Michael Lynskey, 21 November 2004; Patrick Heaney, 23 November 2004; Val Raftery, 27 November 2004; Dennis Kearney, 5 February 2005; Frank Costello, 15 October 2005; Gerry Crane, 16 October 2005; Paddy Curran, 16 October 2005; Maureen Oliver, 16 October 2005; Christy Craughwell, 20 October 2005; James Casserly, 18 November 2005; Paddy O'Neill, 25 November 2005; Martin Flaherty, 26 January 2006; Mary Lambe, 11 February 2006. Ronny & Barbara Ward, 9 December 2006; Mickey & Marie Fitzgerald, 20 January 2007; John Kelly, 20 January 2007; Thomas Feeney, 24 January 2007; Mary McGrath, 26 January 2007; Paddy Monaghan, 26 January 2007; Johnny Murphy, 27 January 2007; Mary Duane, 3 February 2007; Micheal Howley, 3 February 2007; Vincent Griffin, 22 February 2007; Patsy & Rita O'Connor, 26 February 2007.

JOURNALS:

Blake, J., 'Field-Marshal Sir John French', *Journal of the Galway Archaeological and Historical Society*, Vol. 8, No. 4 (1913–14).

Ferguson, N., 'Public Finance and National Security: The Domestic Origins of the First World War Revisited', *Journal of the Galway Archaeological and Historical Society*, Vol. 142 (1994).

Kaiser, D.E., 'Germany and the Origins of the First World War', *Journal of the Galway Archaeological and Historical Society*, Vol. 55 (1983).

Seligmann, M.S., 'A Barometer of National Confidence: A British Assessment of the Role of Insecurity in the formulation of German Military Policy before the First World War', *Journal of the Galway Archaeological and Historical Society*, Vol. 117 (2002).

LETTERS:

Captain R.J. Armes, 1914; Corporal G. Gill, 8 December 1918; John Lawless, 8 February 1999; Pat Costello, 18 December 2002; P.J Summerly, 2002; Richard Conneely, 9 December 2002; Michael Joseph Gardiner, 26 November 2002; Mary Jane Carter, 2002; Michael Coughlan, 2002; Leo Larkin, 2002 & 1 February 2007; Francis Kearney, 2002; Se‡n Malone, 14 March 2003; John Lawless, 2003; Vivienne O'Connor, 2002; Michael Coughlan, 7 February 2005; Aidan O'Malley,

8 March 2005; Seán Ashe, 18 March 2005; Jack Ward, 28 December 2005; Tony Finnerty, 2 February 2006; Francis Keaney, 20 December 2006; John Kennedy, 22 January 2007.

MAGAZINES:

Aide Memoire, Ulster Military Historical Society.

'Remember John Condon, Age 14', *Aide Memoire*, No. 51 (November, 2001).

'Christmas Day 1914, The Day World War I Fighting Stopped in France', *Ireland's Eye*, Issue No. 240 (December, 2000).

MONUMENTS:

Great War monument – St Nicholas' Collegiate Church – Galway – Ireland.

Roll of Honour – Killed in Action – 1914–1918 – Ballinasloe. Banner held in Ballinasloe.

St John's Church Roll of Honour – Ballinasloe, monument in St John's Church, Ballinasloe.

NEWSPAPERS:

East Galway Democrat: 'Death of Corporal Paisley', 22 June 1918; 'Guillemont and Ginchy', 7 September 1918; 'Peace At Last', 16 November 1918; 'The Flu Spreading', 9 November 1918; 'Virus of Influenza Discovered', 3February 1919.

Galway Advertiser: The Connaught Rangers go to War', 19 November 1998.

The Connacht Tribune: '4 Questions to the Women of Ireland', 20 February 1915; '5 Reasons why Irishmen should join the Army', 20 March 1915; 'A Cameo Sketch of a Galway Hero', 24 October 1916; 'A Hero's Death', 21 April 1917; 'Amongst The Fallen – Lieut. Alexander Young, V.C., Killed', 28 October 1916; 'An Officer's Letter of Condolence', 7 October 1916; 'Clifden Meeting', 3 July 1915; 'Come With Me', 3 August 1917; 'Co. Galway Farms Mapped Out in Berlin – What Are You Going to Do about It – Irishmen Have Something to Defend – Your Farm Has Been 'Mapped' by the Germans – What Would the Germans Do', 8 April 1916;'Death of Lieut. D. Mathews, Connaught Rangers', 17 June 1916; 'Death of Lieut. Mattie Glynn', 9 November 1918; 'Death of Major Robert Gregory M.C., R.F.C.', 9 February 1918; 'Death of Naval Man', 12 June 1915; 'Distinguished Lieutenant's Death', 23 May 1918; 'Footwear for the Men at the

Front', 23 January 1915; 'Flight Lieutenant Kelly', 3 March 1917; 'From Rostrum to Trench – Galway Technical Instructor's Experiences', 9 October 1915; 'Galway Airmen Killed', 16 November 1918; 'Galway and Recruiting', 16 November 1918; 'Galway Men Drowned', 1 September 1917; 'Galway Man Killed at the Dardanelles', 29 May 1915; 'Galway Reserve Man Killed Near Dublin', 5 June 1915; 'Galway Shell Factory', 14 July 1917; 'Great Recruiting Demonstration at Clifden', 15 January 1916; 'Gullemont and Ginchy – Anniversary of the Charge of the Irish Braigades', 7 September 1918; 'Harbour Board – Excellent Work of Galway Munition Factory', 20 June 1917; 'His Experiences in the Fateful Landing at Gallapoli – Chaplain's Story – Graphic Pictures of the Flanders Battlefield', 26 June 1915; "How a Brave Galway Soldier Died', November/December 1916; 'Irish Bishops and the War', 11 March 1916; 'Killed in Action', 30 December 1916; 'Lieut. Fisher Killed', 15 July 1916; 'Notes & News', 14 July 1916; 'Portumna Soldier's Death', 8 June 1918; 'Recruiting Committee', 3 July 1915; 'Recruiting Council Appointment', 5 October 1918; 'Recruiting Meeting at Loughrea', 10 July 1915, 'Recruiting Rally', 9 October 1915; 'Renmore Tragedy', 10 April 1915; 'Sent Down 27 Enemy Aeroplanes', 18 January 1919; 'Soldiers and Sailors' Comforts', 6 April 1918; 'The Recruiting Campaign', 17 July 1915; 'Three Soldier Brothers – One Falls', 7 October 1916; 'Two Galway Seamen Lost', 10 June 1916.

The Galway Express: '2nd Lieut. Hubert Patrick Fisher', 15 July 1916; 'A Gallant Galway Soldier', 22 September 1917; 'A Tragic Mistake', 20 May 1916; 'Answering the Call – Claddagh's Magnificent Response', 24 April 1915; 'Call of the Drum', 24 April 1915; 'Captain Mahon', 18 September 1915; 'Captain Noel G. Holmes', 24 April 1915; 'Comforts for our Fighters – Concert and Operatic Performance in Galway', 12 December 1914; 'Conceived by Satan – Matured in Hell', 15 May 1915; 'Connaught Rangers Comfort Fund', 12 September 1914, 'Connaught Heavy Losses at Ypres – A Perfect Hell on Earth', 5 June 1915; 'Connaughts at Gallipoli', 24 March 1917; 'Dreadful Suicide at Renmore', 10 April 1915; 'Duration of the War', 9 January 1915; 'Fall from a Train', 5 June 1915; 'Frozen to Death', 3 February 1917; 'Galwaymen Fall', 15 July 1916; 'Galway Soldier Killed in German East Africa', 1 April 1916; 'Galway Woollen Industry', 20 February 1915; 'Hon. Colonel George Morris', 31 October 1914; 'Irish Guards Visit', 1 May 1915; 'Last Roll Call', 31 March 1917; 'Lieutenant R.A. Persse Killed', 9 January 1915; 'Lieutenant Robert de Stacpoole', 3 October 1914; 'Lieut.-Col. The Hon. George Morris', 17 October 1914; 'Mr. W.G. Todd, M.P., Off to the War', 17 April 1915; 'Mr. Woods. D.I., for the Front', 17 October 1914; 'Order for Galway Woollen Factory', 19 September 1914; 'Our Oldest Lieutenant: Past M.F.H., Galway', 17 October 1914; 'Roll of Fame', 28 August 1915; 11 September 1915; 'Second Lieutenant Roderick de Stacpoole, R.F.A.', 29 May 1915; 'The Late Lieutenant Cecil de Burgh Persse', 24 July 1915; 'The Late Lieut. R.P.D. Nolan', 21 November 1914; 'The Late Mr. Stephen King', 24 June 1916; 'Toll of Empire', 15 July 1916; 'Toll of War', 11 November 1916; 'Vote of Condolence with Mr. and Mrs. Berry', 20 May 1916.

The Times: 'Killed in Action', 4 January 1918; 'The Fallen Officers', 16 November 1914; 'The Official Lists', 16 November 1914.

The Tuam Herald: 'A Brave Galway Family – A Loughrea Batch of Heroes', 28 August 1915; 'A Brave Galway Man', 6 January 1917; 'Connaught Officers', 8 January 1916; 'County of Galway Red Cross Flag Week', 2 January 1915; 'Death of a Brave Galway Gentleman', 31 March 1917; 'Death of a Young Tuam Man at the Front', 5 June 1915; 'Death of Lieutenant-Colonel George Morris', 28 November 1914; 'Death of Lieutenant Gerald J. Cloran, RNR', 17 November 1917; 'Death of Lieutenant Lynch Staunton', 7 April 1914; 'Death of Lieutenant Martin McDonnell, R.I.R.', 10 February 1917; 'Death of Lieutenant Philip Nolan of Ballinderry', 28 December 1918; 'Death of Major Robert Gregory, M.C., R.F.C.', 9 February 1918; 'From Wounds Received', 30 June 1917; 'Galway War Fund Association', 5 August 1916, 'Heroic Death of Lieut. Ulick A. Moore, 3rd Connaught Rangers', 10 August 1918; 'How Lieutenant Daly Died', 9 September 1916; 'Last Roll Call', 31 March 1917; 'Lieutenant Martin McDonnell', 17 March 1917; 'Our Irish Soldiers', 29 April 1916; 'Second Lieutenant Gabriel P. Costello, R.E.', 28 August 1915; 'The County of Galway Naval and Military War Fund', 4 September 1915; 'The Connaught Rangers – (1793–1916) – At Guillemont and Ginchy', 14 October 1916; 'The Late Mr Stephen King', 24 June 1916; 'The Roll of Honour – Second Lieutenant Gabriel P. Costello, R.E.', 28 August 1915.

PROFILES:

Submitted by family members
Dominick Burke by Damian Burke and Anne O'Flaherty, 2006.
John Caulfield by Douglas Rafter, 2005.
James (Jim) Comber by Gerald Comber, 2002.
James Connolly by Noel & Madeleine King, 2005.
James Conolly by Seán Malone, 14 April 2003.
Thomas Corcoran by Mary Deely, 2005.

Coleman Farmer by Colm Walsh, 2005.

Larry Farmer by Colm Walsh, 2005.

John Finnerty by Tony Finnerty, 2005.

John Gilmore by Christy Craughwell, 2007.

John Keaney by Francis Keaney, 2006.

Joseph Keaney by Francis Keaney, 2006.

Thomas Keaney by Francis Keaney, 2006.

Robert Thomas Kennedy by John Kennedy, 22 January 2007.

John Joe Leonard by Val Raftery, 27 November 2004.

Martin William Molloy by Mary Jane Carter, 2001.

Thomas McHugh by Damian Burke and Anne O'Flaherty, 2006.

James Murphy by Paddy Cunningham, 2005.

Coleman Nee by Michael Connelly, 2004.

Michael O'Connor by Anne O'Flaherty, 2006.

Patrick O'Donnell by Bill & Alice Scanlan, 2006.

James Ollington by Michael Conneely, 2006.

Pat Purcell by Seán Purcell, 2006.

Michael Lavelle by Kathleen Villers-Tuthill, 2007.

John Madden by Finbarr O'Shea, 2007.

World Book Encyclopaedia: 1986, Surrey
'Dardanelles', Jutland, *Battle of*', '*World War I*'.

BIBLIOGRAPHY

Bartlett, T. and Jeffery, K. (eds), *A Military History of Ireland* (Cambridge University Press, Cambridge, 1996).

Bowman, T., *The Irish regiments in the Great War: Discipline and morale* (Manchester University Press, Manchester, 2003).

Cassells, L., *The Archduke and the Assassin: Sarajevo, June 28th 1914* (Stein & Day, New York, 1985).

Fitzpatrick, D., *Ireland and the First World War* (Trinity History Workshop, Dublin, 1986).

— *The Two Irelands (1912–1939)* (Oxford University Press, Oxford, 1998).

Glover, M., *Warfare from Waterloo to Mons* (Book Club Associates, London, 1980).

Hamilton, R.F., *The Origins of the Great War* (Cambridge University Press, Cambridge, 2003).

Harris, H.E.D., *The Irish Regiments in the First World War* (Mercier Press, Cork, 1968).

Henry, W., *Supreme Sacrifice. The Story of Eamonn Ceannt 1881–1916* (Mercier Press, Cork, 2005).

— Galway and the Great War (Mercier Press, Cork, 2005

— St Clerans, *The Tale of a Manor House* (Merv Griffin. USA, 1999).

— *The Galway Arms Golfing Society:, A History* (The Galway Arms Golfing Society, 2003).

Heringklee, S., Higgins, J. (eds), *Monuments of St. Nicholas' Collegiate Church, Galway, A Historical Genealogical Archaeological Record,* Rock Crow's Press, Galway (1991).

Hogg, I.V., *Dictionary of Battles* (Hutchinson Dictionaries) (Brockhampton Press, London, 1997).

— *Dictionary of World War I* (Hutchinson Dictionaries) (Brockhampton Press, London, 1997).

Holt, Major & Mrs, *Battlefield Guide to the Ypres Salient* (Leo Cooper, London, 2000).

Jeffery, K., *Ireland and the Great War* (Cambridge University Press, Cambridge, 2000).

Johnson, T., *Orange, Green and Khaki, The Story of the Irish Regiments in the Great War (1914–18)* (Gill and Macmillan Ltd, Dublin, 1992).

Joll, J., *The Origins of the First World War* (Longmans Publishing Group, Harlow, 2000).

Jourdain, H.F.N., *The Connaught Rangers 1st Battalion, Formerly 88th Foot,* Volume 1 (Schull Books, Fraser, E. Cork, 1999).

— *The Connaught Rangers 2nd Battalion, Formerly 94th Foot*, Volume 2 (Schull Books, Fraser, E. Cork, 1999).

Junger, Ernst, *Storm of Steel* (Penguin Books, London, 2004).

Keegan, J., *The First World War: an Illustrated History* (Pimlico, London, 2002).

Keiger, J.V.F., *France and the Origins of the First World War* (Macmillan, London, 1983).

Kipling, R., *The Irish Guards In The Great War; Volume II The Second Battalion and Appendices* (Macmillan, London, 1923).

Lieven, D.C.B., *Russia and the Origins of the First World War* (Macmillan, London, 1983).

Loades, D., *Kings & Queens, An Essential A-Z Guide* (Starfire, London, 2001).

MacDonald, L., *Somme* (Papermac, London, 1988).

MacLochlainn, A., and Regan, T., *Two Galway Schools, The Salthill Industrial School & The Claddagh Piscatory School* (Galway Labour History Group, Galway, 1993).

Marshall, S., *The American Heritage History of World War I* (American Heritage Publishing Company Inc., USA, 1964).

McGuinn, James J., *Sligo Men in the Great War 1914–1918* (Naughan Press, County Cavan, 1994).

Mombauer, A., *Helmuth von Moltke and the Origins of the First World War* (Cambridge University Press, Cambridge, 2001).

O'Dowd, P., *Down by the Claddagh* (Kennys Bookshop & Art Galleries Ltd,. Galway, 1993).

— *Galway in old Photographs* (Gill & Macmillan, Dublin, 2003).

— *Galway Lawn Tennis Club – a History* (Galway Lawn Tennis Club, Galway, 2005).

O'Flaherty, M., *The Claddagh Boy* (Carlton Press, New York, 1963).

O'Hara, B., *Regional Technical College Galway, the First 21 Years* (The Research & Consultancy Unit, Regional Technical College Galway, 1993).

Sheerin, N., *On Your Doorstep* (Norbert Sheerin, 1977).

Sheffield, G., *Forgotten Victory. The First World War: Myths and Realities* (Headline Book Publishing, 2001).

Spector, R.H., *At War at Sea. Sailors and Naval Combat in the Twentieth Century* (Viking Penguin (member of Penguin Putnam Inc.), 2001).

Stedman, M., *Gullemont Somme Battleground Europe* (Leo Cooper, South Yorkshire, 1998).

Steiner, Z.S., *Britain and the Origins of the First World War* (Macmillan, London, 1977).

Villiers-Tuthill, K., *Beyond the Twelve Bens* (Kathleen Villiers-Tuthill, 1990).

Williamson, S.R., *Austria-Hungary and the Origins of the First World War* (Macmillan, Basingstoke, 1991).

INDEX

A

Africa 20, 53, 141, 144
Ahern, Bertie 33
Aisne 19, 41, 108, 115, 117, 124, 131,
    146, 159, 186, 193, 215, 219
Amara 25, 116, 129, 137, 139, 140, 155,
    197, 210, 215, 222, 226
America 174, 196
Ardrahan 64, 120, 142, 190, 201, 218
Asia 20
Athenry 42, 52, 53, 99, 103, 112, 116,
    120, 134, 138, 154, 170, 171, 213,
    217, 221, 222
Austria 17

B

Balkans 20, 118, 168, 184
Ballinasloe 16, 21, 28, 29, 31, 37, 38, 44,
    48, 73, 76, 77, 78, 79, 80, 81, 82,
    84, 85, 86, 87, 88, 89, 91, 93, 95,
    96, 97, 98, 100, 102, 103, 104,
    106, 107, 110, 111, 114, 115, 116,
    117, 118, 125, 127, 128, 129, 130,
    131, 133, 135, 136, 137, 139, 140,
    141, 146, 147, 149, 150, 151, 152,
    153, 155, 161, 163, 166, 167, 168,
    171, 172, 173, 176, 177, 178, 180,
    182, 183, 185, 188, 190, 192, 193,
    194, 198, 199, 200, 202, 204, 205,
    206, 207, 208, 210, 211, 212, 213,
    214, 217, 218, 219, 221, 223, 224,
    226, 227
Basra 12, 25, 74, 75, 86, 90, 100, 104,
    106, 110, 119, 120, 125, 141, 150,
    162, 171, 181, 185, 188, 189, 190,
    204, 207, 212, 219, 222, 223, 224,
    225
Beattystown 36, 63

Belgium 17, 18, 21, 31, 42, 43, 63, 70,
    71, 73, 75, 76, 77, 78, 79, 81, 82,
    83, 84, 86, 88, 90, 91, 92, 94, 95,
    96, 98, 99, 101, 103, 104, 105,
    106, 107, 108, 111, 115, 116, 117,
    118, 120, 121, 122, 123, 124, 125,
    126, 128, 129, 131, 132, 133, 134,
    135, 136, 137, 138, 139, 141, 142,
    143, 144, 145, 146, 148, 149, 150,
    151, 152, 153, 154, 155, 156, 157,
    158, 159, 161, 163, 165, 166, 167,
    168, 169, 170, 172, 173, 174, 176,
    177, 178, 179, 180, 182, 183, 185,
    186, 187, 188, 190, 192, 193, 195,
    196, 198, 199, 200, 204, 205, 206,
    207, 208, 209, 210, 211, 212, 214,
    215, 216, 217, 219, 220, 221, 223,
    225, 226, 227
Betty, Admiral David 25
Black Watch 22, 55, 116, 191
Bohermore 36, 37, 38, 39, 44, 45, 46,
    47, 49, 50, 55, 56, 58, 59, 62, 63,
    64, 65, 67, 70, 109, 146, 156, 162,
    164, 165, 178, 198, 203, 208
British Expeditionary Force 18, 46, 47,
    72, 73, 77, 84, 88, 89, 90, 93, 99,
    104, 116, 147, 150, 162, 172, 193,
    194, 200, 205, 221, 222, 226
Bulgaria 18, 118

C

Cambrai 26, 27, 39, 44, 88, 96, 111, 121,
    126, 127, 149, 198, 213
Canada 43, 44, 70, 74, 80, 91, 101, 105,
    116, 147, 148, 177, 201, 214
Cardiff 79, 124, 193
Claddagh 21, 25, 27, 36, 37, 39, 41, 42,
    43, 44, 45, 48, 50, 56, 57, 58, 60,
    61, 62, 63, 70, 71, 85, 92, 94, 95,

109, 113, 114, 120, 121, 131, 135, 157, 158, 159, 171, 174, 189, 191, 197, 204, 205

Clifden 21, 39, 46, 54, 55, 71, 74, 78, 83, 84, 87, 90, 114, 122, 123, 125, 127, 130, 133, 134, 136, 138, 145, 153, 161, 175, 176, 186, 190, 196, 197, 200, 207, 215

Clonbrock 136

Coldstream Guards 81, 82, 137, 185

College Road 63, 108, 136, 150

Conde 18

Condon, Pte John 24

Connacht 14, 20, 31

Connaught Rangers 19, 20, 22, 23, 27, 28, 29, 30, 41, 44, 46, 47, 49, 50, 53, 54, 55, 56, 60, 61, 62, 63, 64, 65, 66, 67, 70, 71, 72, 73, 75, 76, 77, 78, 79, 80, 81, 82, 83, 84, 85, 86, 87, 88, 90, 91, 92, 94, 95, 96, 97, 98, 99, 100, 101, 102, 103, 104, 105, 106, 107, 108, 109, 110, 111, 112, 113, 114, 115, 116, 117, 118, 119, 120, 122, 123, 124, 125, 126, 127, 129, 130, 131, 132, 133, 134, 135, 136, 137, 138, 139, 140, 142, 143, 144, 145, 146, 149, 150, 151, 152, 153, 154, 155, 157, 158, 159, 160, 161, 162, 164, 165, 166, 167, 168, 169, 170, 171, 172, 173, 174, 175, 176, 179, 180, 181, 182, 183, 184, 185, 187, 188, 189, 190, 191, 192, 193, 194, 195, 196, 197, 198, 199, 200, 201, 202, 203, 204, 205, 206, 207, 208, 209, 210, 211, 212, 214, 215, 216, 217, 218, 219, 220, 221, 222, 223, 224, 225, 227

Cork 81, 85, 97, 115, 170, 176, 178, 189, 193

D

Dardanelles 71, 132, 176

Dublin 11, 22, 33, 45, 48, 52, 53, 58, 73, 74, 75, 76, 77, 78, 79, 86, 88, 90, 91, 97, 100, 106, 109, 118, 120, 121, 124, 127, 128, 130, 134, 138, 142, 143, 146, 147, 148, 149, 152, 153, 154, 163, 164, 170, 172, 176, 177, 180, 181, 182, 184, 186, 187, 188, 191, 194, 195, 198, 199, 201, 202, 205, 209, 210, 214, 215, 217, 218, 219, 223, 227

E

Egypt 20, 41, 50, 56, 71, 86, 95, 104, 107, 110, 113, 114, 123, 124, 130, 143, 153, 167, 171, 175, 179, 187, 211, 217, 218, 224, 225

England 45, 55, 57, 72, 117, 154, 161, 199

Europe 17, 18, 21, 24, 26, 32, 33

Eyre Square 59

F

Flanders 29, 33, 72, 80, 90, 101, 130, 132, 134, 147, 148, 149, 194, 200, 216, 220

Forster Street 13, 47, 65

France 13, 17, 18, 26, 29, 37, 40, 42, 43, 45, 47, 51, 53, 54, 56, 57, 59, 60, 62, 63, 65, 70, 71, 72, 73, 74, 75, 76, 77, 78, 79, 80, 81, 82, 83, 84, 85, 86, 87, 88, 89, 90, 91, 92, 93, 94, 95, 96, 97, 98, 99, 100, 101, 102, 103, 104, 105, 106, 107, 108, 109, 110, 111, 112, 113, 114, 115, 116, 117, 118, 119, 120, 121, 122, 123, 124, 125, 126, 127, 128, 129, 130, 131, 132, 133, 134, 135, 136, 137, 138, 139, 140, 141, 142, 143, 144, 145, 146, 147, 148, 149, 150, 151, 152, 153, 154, 155, 156, 157, 158, 159, 160, 161, 162, 163, 164,

165, 166, 167, 168, 169, 170, 171,
172, 173, 174, 175, 176, 177, 178,
179, 180, 181, 182, 183, 184, 185,
186, 187, 188, 189, 190, 191, 192,
193, 194, 195, 196, 197, 198, 199,
200, 201, 202, 203, 204, 205, 206,
207, 208, 209, 210, 211, 212, 213,
214, 215, 216, 217, 218, 219, 220,
221, 222, 223, 224, 225, 226, 227,
228

Franz Ferdinand 17
French, Sir John 18, 46
Furey Brothers 28, 29, 30, 31

G

Gallipoli 20, 24, 35, 38, 52, 60, 78, 79,
80, 86, 93, 95, 100, 106, 111, 113,
114, 116, 117, 118, 123, 124, 134,
137, 138, 139, 145, 148, 149, 152,
154, 155, 160, 162, 164, 165, 166,
170, 171, 175, 176, 181, 183, 184,
188, 190, 198, 203, 204, 209, 211,
215, 216, 227

Galway 11, 12, 13, 14, 15, 16, 20, 21, 22,
26, 27, 28, 32, 36, 37, 38, 39, 40,
41, 42, 43, 45, 46, 47, 48, 49, 50,
51, 54, 55, 56, 57, 58, 59, 62, 63,
65, 66, 70, 71, 72, 73, 74, 75, 76,
77, 78, 79, 80, 81, 82, 83, 84, 85,
86, 87, 89, 90, 91, 92, 93, 94, 95,
96, 97, 98, 99, 101, 102, 103, 104,
105, 106, 107, 108, 109, 110, 111,
112, 113, 114, 115, 116, 117, 118,
119, 120, 121, 122, 123, 124, 125,
126, 127, 128, 129, 131, 132, 133,
134, 135, 136, 137, 138, 139, 140,
141, 142, 143, 144, 145, 146, 147,
148, 149, 150, 151, 152, 153, 154,
155, 156, 157, 158, 159, 161, 162,
163, 164, 165, 166, 167, 169, 170,
171, 172, 173, 174, 175, 176, 177,
178, 179, 180, 181, 183, 184, 185,

186, 187, 188, 189, 190, 191, 192,
193, 194, 195, 196, 197, 198, 199,
200, 201, 202, 203, 204, 205, 206,
207, 208, 209, 210, 211, 212, 213,
214, 215, 216, 217, 218, 219, 220,
221, 222, 223, 224, 225, 226, 227,
228, 229

Germany 17, 18, 33, 109, 125, 188
Gibraltar 50
Ginchy 26, 33, 114, 185
Glynn, Frank 28
Grattan-Bellew, Major William 28, 132
Gregory, Lady Augusta 28
Gregory, Major Robert 28, 133
Grenadier Guards 19, 103, 126, 156,
219, 221
Guillemont 26, 33, 34, 74, 117, 122, 125,
126, 127, 129, 152, 168, 184, 185,
208

H

Hazell, Major T. Falcon 28
Hindenburg Line 26, 27

I

Inniskilling 36, 37, 47, 65, 72, 85, 146,
151, 172, 176, 177, 188, 190, 201,
205, 207, 208, 211, 213, 215
Ireland 14, 15, 16, 18, 21, 31, 32, 33, 47,
49, 52, 55, 57, 70, 71, 72, 73, 74,
75, 77, 81, 82, 84, 85, 86, 87, 88,
89, 93, 100, 101, 104, 105, 109,
111, 116, 117, 119, 120, 131, 141,
142, 144, 146, 147, 150, 153, 154,
159, 180, 182, 186, 191, 192, 193,
194, 195, 200, 201, 205, 208, 209,
210, 212, 213, 223, 224, 226, 227
Irish Guards 19, 22, 26, 39, 40, 45, 51,
58, 59, 64, 67, 76, 78, 80, 87, 88,
91, 93, 94, 97, 99, 101, 104, 105,
107, 110, 111, 112, 114, 115, 119,

120, 122, 124, 125, 126, 129, 131,
133, 134, 137, 138, 140, 142, 144,
145, 146, 149, 151, 154, 155, 158,
159, 160, 164, 166, 167, 173, 176,
177, 178, 179, 180, 182, 183, 185,
187, 188, 196, 198, 200, 208, 209,
213, 214, 219, 221, 226

J

Jelliceo, Sir Admrial John 25
Jerusalem 117
Jourdain, Lt Col H.F. 20, 50, 51
Jutland 25, 43, 74, 124, 158, 185, 194

K

Kelly, Flight Lieutenant E.C. 28
King's Liverpool Regiment 111, 112,
118, 136, 180, 194, 199, 225
Kinsale 29, 87, 185, 193
Kluck, Alexander von 19

L

Leinster 22, 65, 84, 86, 92, 93, 94, 95,
98, 99, 100, 102, 108, 109, 114,
117, 118, 120, 121, 122, 131, 137,
145, 149, 150, 155, 158, 163, 166,
168, 169, 177, 180, 182, 183, 184,
186, 188, 189, 192, 193, 194, 202,
208, 211, 214, 216, 220, 221, 223,
225
Leinster Regiment 22, 65, 84, 86, 92, 93,
94, 95, 98, 99, 100, 109, 114, 117,
118, 121, 122, 131, 137, 145, 149,
150, 155, 158, 168, 169, 177, 180,
182, 183, 184, 186, 188, 189, 192,
193, 194, 202, 208, 211, 214, 216,
220, 221, 223, 225
Lewin, Colonel 29
Lille 183, 210
Limerick 59, 177, 193

Liverpool 22, 70, 93, 97, 102, 109, 111,
112, 118, 120, 136, 144, 156, 166,
174, 178, 180, 187, 194, 199, 225
London 22, 34, 40, 42, 49, 82, 83, 85, 87,
88, 89, 106, 108, 109, 112, 121,
128, 132, 139, 145, 156, 159, 160,
166, 168, 169, 174, 184, 185, 186,
191, 197, 198, 200, 201, 205, 207,
222, 224
Long Walk 39, 48, 66, 94, 127, 183, 195,
220
Loos 24, 26, 45, 58, 76, 85, 93, 130, 135,
142, 143, 146, 160, 163, 170, 171,
178, 180, 189, 190, 194, 202, 211
Loughrea 21, 27, 28, 29, 30, 31, 55, 57,
61, 72, 78, 79, 80, 86, 89, 102,
107, 111, 114, 125, 127, 128, 135,
147, 150, 160, 179, 181, 182, 185,
186, 188, 190, 192, 197, 205, 210,
211, 213, 224, 226

M

Macken, Private Walter 56, 167
Malta 47, 63, 97, 141, 183
Manchester 22, 84, 116, 129, 138, 153,
160, 167, 168, 172, 175, 179, 185,
187, 191, 194, 196, 197, 215
Marne 19, 41, 108, 115, 135, 139, 183,
191, 209, 224
McAleese, Mary 33
Mediterranean 71
Menin Gate 23, 73, 76, 78, 79, 83, 88,
90, 91, 95, 99, 101, 104, 106, 111,
115, 116, 120, 122, 124, 125, 126,
128, 129, 132, 133, 137, 139, 142,
143, 144, 145, 148, 151, 154, 155,
161, 167, 168, 169, 170, 172, 173,
182, 183, 186, 187, 188, 190, 192,
193, 195, 196, 200, 206, 208, 212,
215, 216, 217, 219, 220
Mesopotamia 20, 25, 44, 56, 74, 86, 90,
91, 92, 95, 100, 104, 106, 109,

116, 119, 120, 123, 127, 129, 136,
137, 139, 140, 141, 150, 155, 162,
171, 175, 181, 185, 188, 189, 190,
197, 202, 203, 204, 207, 209, 212,
215, 218, 221, 222, 223, 224, 225,
226
Middle Street 59, 64, 121, 174, 203
Mons 18, 29, 30, 66, 78, 79, 86, 102,
117, 124, 129, 140, 141, 145, 151,
153, 159, 163, 166, 168, 178, 182,
183, 185, 188, 192, 206, 224, 227
Morris, Lieutenant Colonel George 19
Mountbellew 21, 28, 71, 84, 99, 100,
103, 125, 126, 132, 142, 167, 204,
209
Moycullen 21, 66, 81, 82, 85, 147, 156,
176, 179
Munster 22, 40, 57, 71, 85, 89, 93, 102,
110, 126, 136, 138, 139, 143, 146,
147, 156, 157, 158, 167, 172, 173,
176, 180, 181, 184, 186, 190, 192,
198, 214, 215, 217, 219, 224, 227

N

Neuve Chapelle 24, 41, 108, 185
Newtownsmith 22
New Zealand 22, 43, 53, 60, 92, 98, 99,
115, 148, 154, 189, 214
Nile Lodge 27
Northumberland Fusiliers 40, 57, 119,
130, 136, 154, 173, 177, 189, 192,
204, 207, 209

O

O'Sullivan, Margaret 13
Oughterard 21, 45, 66, 80, 115, 139,
154, 166, 169, 189, 208, 221, 222

P

Palestine 20, 25, 35, 41, 46, 54, 56, 104

Paris 19
Passchendaele 13, 26, 65, 220
Poyser, Fred 28
Prospect Hill 27, 40, 55, 141, 212

Q

Quay Street 36, 104, 128, 174, 222
Queen Mary 25

R

Raleigh Row 66, 105
Renmore 16, 20, 37, 38, 44, 45, 49, 50,
51, 56, 70, 202, 215, 216, 228, 229
Riga 20
Royal Army Medical Corps 89, 141,
158, 210
Royal Dublin Fusiliers 22, 73, 75, 76, 78,
79, 88, 90, 91, 100, 106, 109, 118,
121, 124, 127, 128, 130, 147, 148,
149, 152, 153, 163, 164, 170, 176,
182, 184, 186, 187, 188, 194, 195,
198, 199, 201, 202, 205, 209, 210,
214, 218, 219
Royal Field Artillery 38, 41, 48, 49, 50,
53, 55, 57, 63, 65, 67, 82, 90, 95,
105, 107, 108, 110, 114, 115, 122,
123, 134, 141, 149, 156, 158, 169,
178, 183, 195, 196, 197, 199, 203,
205, 211, 212, 214, 218, 220, 223
Royal Flying Corps 75, 76, 105, 132,
133, 227
Royal Irish Fusiliers 38, 71, 73, 74, 75,
76, 77, 81, 82, 85, 87, 88, 99, 102,
106, 110, 111, 133, 135, 148, 152,
153, 159, 163, 167, 178, 180, 181,
186, 187, 192, 211, 212, 225
Royal Irish Rifles 22, 29, 72, 88, 101,
102, 107, 108, 121, 127, 128, 144,
154, 165, 168, 171, 172, 173, 176,
200, 206, 213, 219, 226
Royal Munster Fusiliers 22, 71, 85, 89,

93, 102, 126, 136, 138, 139, 143,
146, 147, 156, 157, 158, 172, 176,
180, 181, 184, 186, 190, 192, 198,
214, 215, 217, 219, 224, 227
Russia 17

S

Salonika 25, 73, 80, 83, 95, 98, 99, 126,
134, 138, 142, 145, 146, 150, 154,
157, 158, 159, 160, 175, 184, 205,
215, 220
Scotland 51, 61, 80, 191, 199
Seaforth Highlanders 22, 135, 162, 213
Serbia 17
Soissons 19
Somme 25, 26, 33, 37, 40, 45, 48, 55, 57,
59, 66, 73, 74, 78, 80, 81, 82, 83,
85, 89, 90, 91, 92, 94, 97, 98, 99,
101, 102, 106, 107, 109, 110, 112,
114, 117, 119, 122, 125, 126, 127,
128, 129, 130, 131, 134, 135, 137,
138, 140, 142, 143, 146, 147, 148,
149, 151, 152, 153, 157, 158, 160,
161, 163, 164, 165, 167, 168, 171,
172, 173, 176, 177, 178, 179, 180,
182, 184, 185, 186, 187, 188, 189,
190, 192, 195, 196, 198, 199, 202,
205, 207, 208, 210, 211, 214, 216,
217, 218, 219, 221, 222, 224, 226,
227, 228
South Irish Horse 22, 37, 49, 80, 81, 91,
117, 166, 193, 197, 217, 227
Spanish Parade 37, 39, 152, 210
Spiddal 19, 42, 156, 165, 179, 180, 186
Suvla Bay 106
Switzerland 20

T

Tank Corps 121, 130
Taylor's Hill 119
Thiepval 26, 74, 78, 81, 83, 85, 94, 102,

107, 110, 112, 114, 117, 122, 125,
126, 129, 130, 134, 137, 138, 146,
149, 152, 153, 160, 163, 167, 171,
172, 173, 178, 179, 180, 184, 185,
186, 187, 192, 198, 202, 205, 211,
219, 221, 227, 228
Trieste 20
Tuam 14, 21, 27, 28, 29, 52, 53, 54, 58,
70, 75, 78, 81, 83, 86, 90, 100,
105, 107, 109, 112, 119, 124, 128,
130, 137, 138, 140, 141, 142, 144,
145, 151, 152, 160, 162, 164, 166,
167, 168, 169, 176, 177, 178, 184,
191, 192, 193, 194, 195, 199, 203,
204, 206, 207, 208, 209, 211, 216,
221, 222, 223, 224, 225
Turkey 18, 75, 79, 80, 86, 100, 106, 111,
113, 114, 117, 118, 123, 124, 138,
145, 148, 149, 154, 155, 160, 162,
164, 166, 170, 171, 175, 180, 183,
187, 188, 190, 198, 199, 203, 204,
209, 211, 215, 216, 227
Tyne Cot 23, 75, 84, 124, 133, 135, 136,
138, 150, 151, 153, 165, 167, 176,
177, 187, 192, 200, 205, 208, 214,
217, 220

U

Ulster 18, 75
United States 42, 44, 51, 52, 54, 88, 174

V

Villers Cotteret 19

W

Ward, Martin 31
Waterford 24, 67
Williamstown 21, 122, 152, 168, 190,
202, 216
Wood Quay 124, 181, 202, 220

Y

Ypres 13, 23, 24, 26, 29, 38, 43, 44, 45,
47, 65, 71, 73, 76, 78, 79, 81, 83,
88, 90, 91, 92, 95, 98, 99, 101,
104, 106, 111, 115, 116, 120, 122,
124, 125, 126, 128, 129, 131, 132,
133, 137, 139, 141, 142, 143, 144,
145, 148, 151, 154, 155, 156, 158,
159, 160, 161, 167, 168, 169, 170,
172, 173, 182, 183, 185, 186, 187,
188, 190, 192, 193, 195, 196, 200,
206, 208, 212, 214, 215, 216, 217,
219, 220

Galway and the Great War

William Henry

ISBN: 978 1 85635 524 7

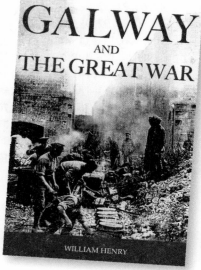

When the First World War was declared, a surge of euphoria swept across Great Britain and Ireland. In Britain, most men joined the army for 'king and country'. Many Galwaymen, convinced by conscription rallies of the imminent threat to their country, flocked to join the British Army.

Almost every family in Galway was affected by the Great War. However, with the dramatic change in the political climate after 1916, these men came home to a very different Ireland. Thousands left as heroes, but when they returned they were treated as traitors and were unable to tell anyone of the horrors and suffering they had witnessed.

This book examines the outbreak of the Great War, the impact it had on those left behind and, through contemporary letters and interviews with Galwaymen, the lives of the men at the Front.

> William Henry is an historian, archaeologist and author from Galway City. His other books include the highly acclaimed biography, *Supreme Sacrifice: The Story of Eamonn Ceannt*.

MERCIER PRESS
WHAT YOU NEED TO READ